Learning ClojureScript

Master the art of agile single page web application
development with ClojureScript

W. David Jarvis
Rafik Naccache
Allen Rohner

BIRMINGHAM - MUMBAI

Learning ClojureScript

Copyright © 2016 Packt Publishing

First published: June 2016

Production reference: 1290616

Published by Packt Publishing Ltd.

Livery Place

35 Livery Street

Birmingham B3 2PB, UK.

ISBN 978-1-78588-763-5

www.packtpub.com

Credits

Authors

W. David Jarvis
Rafik Naccache
Allen Rohner

Reviewer

Eduard Bondarenko

Commissioning Editor

Veena Pagare

Acquisition Editor

Kirk D'costa

Content Development Editor

Samantha Gonsalves

Technical Editor

Abhishek R. Kotian

Copy Editor

Pranjali Chury

Project Coordinator

Sanchita Mandal

Proofreader

Safis Editing

Indexer

Rekha Nair

Production Coordinator

Aparna Bhagat

Cover Work

Aparna Bhagat

Foreword

JavaScript is everywhere. The language was originally designed to permit non-programmers to add dynamic flairs to a new-fangled thing called a webpage. Two decades after its introduction, JavaScript has grown into a versatile, expressive, and complicated language—the most recent ECMAScript standard rivals the Java 1.8 language specification in terms of page count!

Yet in many ways, JavaScript still represents an older way of doing things. Nowadays, many industrial programmers are finding their way to functional programming. While JavaScript has some nice functional features, it lags far behind even the most recent decade of functional programming best practices.

Enter ClojureScript!

First released in 2011, ClojureScript has grown into an essential tool for the discerning programmer, who would love to tap into the reach offered by JavaScript, while leveraging some of best designed immutable datastructures and functional APIs in existence. Importantly, ClojureScript delivers these affordances without getting in the way of tight integration with the JavaScript host.

You can program webpages, iPhones, Androids, and Node.js, all using the same powerful Lisp programming model pioneered by John McCarthy so many years ago.

This book will show you how!

David Nolen,

ClojureScript Lead Developer

ClojureScript has long been reliable for producing high-quality, highly-performant web applications. At the same time, the ecosystem surrounding the language has grown, both in terms of developers embracing the language and in the availability of high-quality libraries and development tools.

Also, ClojureScript's fundamental promise of reach is being proven with new use cases outside web applications; it's being used for hybrid mobile apps and new, compelling self-hosted scenarios.

In short, ClojureScript has transitioned from being a novel language taken on by early adopters to being an important and relied-upon basis for a stack that is here to stay.

It's easy to find enthusiastic community support when developing with ClojureScript. And, of course, it is tremendous help that ClojureScript is itself extremely similar to Clojure. However, one area that it lacks in is comprehensive and polished documentation, especially with respect to the coverage of the slew of pragmatic issues that accompany the development of real-world applications.

This book fills this gap by providing practical information on how to get set up and running, how to use the constructs offered by the language—most importantly, how to effectively use the available tools in day-to-day development—and how to ultimately ship your app.

We can thank Rafik, David, and Allen for sharing their hard-earned experience with us, providing a one-stop guide with answers to the gamut of questions you are likely to face when using ClojureScript. This book is a much-needed and very welcome treatment of the subject; with it, you can confidently go out and build great ClojureScript apps!

Mike Fikes,

Author of the *Planck ClojureScript REPL*

About the Authors

W. David Jarvis is a software engineer living in San Francisco, California. In his spare time, he enjoys hiking, gardening, playing pool in dive bars, and overthinking everything. He is active in the open source Clojure and ClojureScript communities, and software authored by him has been downloaded over 10,000 times.

David has worked for a number of companies now living or dead, including Aggregate Knowledge, CircleCI, Standard Treasury, and Airbnb. He is currently responsible for the build, test, and deployment infrastructure at Airbnb.

The "W" is for "William" (now you know!).

While David has made the unfortunate mistake of exposing his previous scribblings to the world, this is his first actual book.

I would like to thank my companion, Kate, for her love and infinite patience in allowing this book to co-opt so many of my weekends. Without her initial support and enthusiasm, I would probably never have agreed to write the book that you are now reading.

Other debts of gratitude go to Ben Linsay (for inviting me into the technology industry), Allen Rohner (for introducing me to the joy that is Clojure), Daniel Kimerling (for being a friend in a time of need) and Keith Ballinger (for his constant wisdom and mentorship). I also owe thanks to my friends Heather Rivers and Margot Yopes, both of whom have made me a vastly better human being today than I would have been otherwise. Lastly, I would like to thank my parents and the rest of my family for providing me with a bottomless well of love and support. I am fortunate beyond words.

Rafik Naccache is a Tunisian experienced software architect and emergent technologies enthusiast. He earned his bachelors degree in computer science engineering from Tunis University of Science in 2001. Rafik fell in love with Clojure back in 2012, and he has been developing it professionally since 2013. He has occupied various positions in telecoms and banking, and he has launched some innovative internet startups in which he has been able to deploy Clojure apps. He also founded the Tunisian Clojure users community. He contributes to Open Source projects, such as Cryogen (`https://github.com/cryogen-project/cryogen/graphs/contributors`), Milestones (`https://github.com/automagictools/milestones`), and Scheje (`https://github.com/turbopape/scheje`). You can reach him as `@turbopape` on GitHub and Twitter.

First of all, I am grateful to my mom, Safia, and dad, Abdelaziz, for their love and the education that they generously gave me. It was certainly thanks to the Spectrum ZX that we had back in the eighties that I grew up as addicted to computers as I am right now, and this was the start of everything.

Warm thanks also go to my in-laws, Aunt Zohra and Uncle Hammadi, who always supported me and had blind and unconditional faith in whatever work I do, and who really wanted to see this book published.

I am very thankful to my editors, Samantha Gonsalves and Kirk D'Costa, and reviewers for their valuable advice and professional guidance towards the accomplishment of this book.

I have also special thoughts for my family, namely Tselma, Soussou, Dah, Hafedh, Zazza, Idriss and Ismael. I owe you all so much.

However, most of all, I am extremely thankful to my super wife, Khawla, who patiently had to suffer my moments away writing this book, while keeping her smile on and never complaining. I can say that this book would probably never have happened if hadn't she been there, along with our little Fatma Ezzahra and Elyes, casting their light to help brighten my hard journey towards achievement and success.

Allen Rohner is a software engineer and entrepreneur living in Austin, Texas. He is the founder of numerous startups. A few, including CircleCI, have even been successful.

Allen has been using Clojure and ClojureScript professionally since 2009, with commitments in Clojure core and dozens of other open source libraries. He has given multiple talks at Clojure/West and Clojure/conj.

Currently, Allen is working on a startup called Rasterize (`https://rasterize.io`), which helps companies improve conversion rate by optimizing website load times. While Allen has occasionally had blog posts go to #1 on Hacker News, this is the first 'real' book that he's collaborated on.

I'd like to thank my wife, Anna, for putting up with me on a daily basis.

About the Reviewer

Eduard Bondarenko is a software developer living in Kiev, Ukraine. He started programming using Basic on ZXSpectrum a long time ago. He works professionally in the web development domain. He has been using Ruby on Rails for many years. Sometime in 2009, he discovered Clojure, and he liked the language a lot. Except for Ruby and Clojure, he is interested in modern FP languages, machine learning, and logic programming.

www.PacktPub.com

For support files and downloads related to your book, please visit www.PacktPub.com.

eBooks, discount offers, and more

Did you know that Packt offers eBook versions of every book published, with PDF and ePub files available? You can upgrade to the eBook version at www.PacktPub.com and as a print book customer, you are entitled to a discount on the eBook copy. Get in touch with us at customercare@packtpub.com for more details.

At www.PacktPub.com, you can also read a collection of free technical articles, sign up for a range of free newsletters and receive exclusive discounts and offers on Packt books and eBooks.

https://www2.packtpub.com/books/subscription/packtlib

Do you need instant solutions to your IT questions? PacktLib is Packt's online digital book library. Here, you can search, access, and read Packt's entire library of books.

Why subscribe?

- Fully searchable across every book published by Packt
- Copy and paste, print, and bookmark content
- On demand and accessible via a web browser

Free access for Packt account holders

Get notified! Find out when new books are published by following @PacktEnterprise on Twitter or the Packt Enterprise Facebook page.

Table of Contents

Preface

Welcome to *Learning ClojureScript*!

ClojureScript is an exciting new language that leverages Clojure's familiar syntax for the JavaScript runtime. This means that ClojureScript, like JavaScript, is a tool to help you write software applications that can either run in a client-side (browser) or server-side environment. This also means that ClojureScript inherits all of the wonderful benefits of Clojure, including Lisp macros, immutable and high-performance data structures, and beautiful functional syntax.

This book aims to serve as an introduction to both the core and advanced concepts of ClojureScript development with the ultimate objective of teaching you how to build single-page web applications. Whatever your background and prior level of experience with either Clojure or ClojureScript, it is our hope that this book will prove to be an invaluable aid to you in learning how to develop ClojureScript programs for the modern web.

We've structured the book in such a way as to take you through on a soft progression. Beginning with the basics of getting your interactive environment set up, we'll take you all the way through advanced subjects such as logic programming and designing your applications to use Om, a ClojureScript wrapper for Facebook's React framework. By the end of this book, you should have a deep understanding of the complete process of developing modern single-page web apps with ClojureScript, and you should feel comfortable writing applications that you know how to configure and deploy in production environments.

What this book covers

Chapter 1, *Getting Ready for ClojureScript Development*, covers preparing an interactive development environment for the browser as well as some basic configuration options.

Chapter 2, *ClojureScript Language Fundamentals*, describes the basic syntax and building blocks of the ClojureScript language.

Chapter 3, *Advanced ClojureScript Concepts*, focuses on idiomatic functional programming, ClojureScript macros, and concurrent software design.

Chapter 4, *Web Applications Basics with ClojureScript*, covers working with the DOM, CSS, and HTML5 elements.

Chapter 5, *Building Single Page Applications*, teaches you how to make web applications that interact with third-party data providers, such as remote databases, OAuth providers, or embedded data stores.

Chapter 6, *Building Richer Web Applications*, covers more advanced topics, such as WebSockets, routing for single-page applications, and building applications using Om—a ClojureScript wrapper for React.

Chapter 7, *Going Further with ClojureScript*, showcases various core and third-party libraries that provide elegant and unique solutions to problems such as pattern matching, data validation, and logic solving.

Chapter 8, *Bundling ClojureScript for Production*, focuses on the tools that are necessary to properly package your ClojureScript libraries and applications for production usage. This chapter covers testing, compiler optimizations, and how to containerize your applications.

What you need for this book

In order to be able to run some of the example code in this book, you'll need a computer that is capable of running at least Java 6, and preferably Java 7 or 8. Oracle maintains a detailed list of hardware and software requirements for the latest versions of Java online at http://java.com/en/download/help/sysreq.xml. However, most modern laptop and desktop computers should be capable of running the latest version of Java without a problem. You'll also need a browser and an internet connection in order to download the relevant software and dependencies that are needed. For a browser, we recommend Google Chrome, but any modern web browser will do just fine.

Who this book is for

This book is for web application developers who want to benefit from the power of ClojureScript to get an agile and highly-productive development platform that targets mainly browser JavaScript.

You are not required to be fluent in Clojure, but it will be easier for you if you have a basic understanding of browser or server-side JavaScript.

Conventions

In this book, you will find a number of text styles that distinguish between different kinds of information. Here are some examples of these styles and an explanation of their meaning. Code words in text, database table names, folder names, filenames, file extensions, pathnames, dummy URLs, user input, and Twitter handles are shown as follows: "The def statement tells us that what follows will be a definition."

A block of code is set as follows:

```
(ns example-code)
cljs.user=> (+ 1 1)
;; => 2

cljs.user=> (* 2 3)
;; => 6
```

When we wish to draw your attention to a particular part of a code block, the relevant lines or items are set in bold:

```
(ns example-code)
cljs.user=> (+ 1 1)
;; => 2
cljs.user=> (* 2 3)
;; => 6
cljs.user=> (/ 9 3)
;; => 3
```

Any command-line input or output is written as follows:

```
cljs.user=> (map inc [1 2 3 4 5])
;; => (2 3 4 5 6)
```

New terms and important words are shown in bold. Words that you see on the screen, for example, in menus or dialog boxes, appear in the text like this: "If we check the page, we should see our **Page rendered!** alert logged to the console."

Warnings or important notes appear in a box like this.

Tips and tricks appear like this.

Reader feedback

Feedback from our readers is always welcome. Let us know what you think about this book—what you liked or disliked. Reader feedback is important for us as it helps us develop titles that you will really get the most out of.

To send us general feedback, simply e-mail `feedback@packtpub.com`, and mention the book's title in the subject of your message.

If there is a topic that you have expertise in and you are interested in either writing or contributing to a book, see our author guide at `www.packtpub.com/authors`.

Customer support

Now that you are the proud owner of a Packt book, we have a number of things to help you to get the most from your purchase.

Downloading the example code

You can download the example code files for this book from your account at `http://www.packtpub.com`. If you purchased this book elsewhere, you can visit `http://www.packtpub.com/support` and register to have the files e-mailed directly to you.

You can download the code files by following these steps:

1. Log in or register to our website using your e-mail address and password.
2. Hover the mouse pointer on the **SUPPORT** tab at the top.
3. Click on **Code Downloads & Errata**.
4. Enter the name of the book in the **Search** box.
5. Select the book for which you're looking to download the code files.
6. Choose from the drop-down menu where you purchased this book from.
7. Click on **Code Download**.

You can also download the code files by clicking on the **Code Files** button on the book's webpage at the Packt Publishing website. This page can be accessed by entering the book's name in the Search box. Please note that you need to be logged in to your Packt account.

Once the file is downloaded, please make sure that you unzip or extract the folder using the latest version of:

- WinRAR / 7-Zip for Windows

- Zipeg / iZip / UnRarX for Mac
- 7-Zip / PeaZip for Linux

The code bundle for the book is also hosted on GitHub at `https://github.com/learningclojurescript/code-examples`. We also have other code bundles from our rich catalog of books and videos available at `https://github.com/PacktPublishing/`. Check them out!

Errata

Although we have taken every care to ensure the accuracy of our content, mistakes do happen. If you find a mistake in one of our books—maybe a mistake in the text or the code—we would be grateful if you could report this to us. By doing so, you can save other readers from frustration and help us improve subsequent versions of this book. If you find any errata, please report them by visiting `http://www.packtpub.com/submit-errata`, selecting your book, clicking on the Errata Submission Form link, and entering the details of your errata. Once your errata are verified, your submission will be accepted and the errata will be uploaded to our website or added to any list of existing errata under the Errata section of that title.

To view the previously submitted errata, go to `https://www.packtpub.com/books/content/support` and enter the name of the book in the search field. The required information will appear under the Errata section.

Piracy

Piracy of copyrighted material on the Internet is an ongoing problem across all media. At Packt, we take the protection of our copyright and licenses very seriously. If you come across any illegal copies of our works in any form on the Internet, please provide us with the location address or website name immediately so that we can pursue a remedy.

Please contact us at `copyright@packtpub.com` with a link to the suspected pirated material.

We appreciate your help in protecting our authors and our ability to bring you valuable content.

Questions

If you have a problem with any aspect of this book, you can contact us at `questions@packtpub.com`, and we will do our best to address the problem.

1

Getting Ready for ClojureScript Development

ClojureScript's promise is to bring the expressiveness and agility of the Clojure programming language to JavaScript developers. Having such power at hands means that teams working on single page applications—and on Node.js services as well—more productivity and less frustration.

But to be able to take complete advantage of this platform, we must grasp its inner mechanisms and, sometimes patiently, work our way towards the perfect ClojureScript live-coding environment. In this chapter, we'll cover the material necessary to achieve this objective.

We'll begin by studying the ClojureScript ecosystem, focusing on its compiler internals and talking about the **Read-Eval-Print-Loop** (**REPL**) it offers. We'll then present some alternative building blocks that make it possible to expose interactive ClojureScript development work-flows through third-party tools. We'll finally leverage all of this knowledge in order to build full-fledged, integrated, and interactive ClojureScript development environments. To get started with adopting this approach, we'll discuss the following:

- Getting familiar with the ClojureScript ecosystem
- Live coding ClojureScript on top of **nREPL** with **PiggieBack** and **Weasel**
- Live coding ClojureScript with **Figwheel**
- Setting up **Emacs** for ClojureScript development

Getting familiar with the ClojureScript ecosystem

At the heart of the ClojureScript's ecosystem lies the compiler. In this section, we'll gain an insight into its internals: what is its underlying architecture, how does it work, and how can its functioning be tweaked in order to allow for leaner ClojureScript development?

Inside the ClojureScript compiler

The ClojureScript compiler is a piece of Clojure software packaged as a JAR along with Clojure itself, so the package is self-contained and can be manipulated easily. As such, the ClojureScript compiler requires the JVM for its operation. Currently, as ClojureScript developers have baked in the compiler, among many other things, an integration mode for **Nashorn**, the Java 8 embedded JavaScript engine, they recommend using the same version of the JVM. But, Java 7 is sufficient for the sole operation of the compiler.

 A bootstrapped version of ClojureScript, that is, one that uses pure ClojureScript for compilation, has recently been released. **Cljs-bootstrap** (`https://github.com/swannodette/cljs-bootstrap`), at the time of writing this, is still a work in progress, and offers worse performance than the JVM mainstream compiler. Besides, bootstrapped ClojureScript does not allow for the advanced compilation flags that its JVM counterpart offers.

At its most stripped down definition, the compiler accepts ClojureScript code, that is, mainly s-expressions obeying some Clojure subset semantics, and emits JavaScript artifacts that are passed on to the Google Closure Library (`https://developers.google.com/closure/`) in order to get it "polished".

The Google Closure Library is a set of JavaScript optimizing tools open sourced by Google, which it uses to support the development of its JavaScript-rich applications, such as Gmail or Maps. Using this library has the following benefits:

- It abstracts away the effort of managing inconsistencies across the many JavaScript engines of the market.
- It takes advantage of the Google Closure's complete program optimization with features such as JavaScript minification or dead code elimination.
- It exposes the namespace functionality, which is otherwise unavailable in Vanilla JavaScript. Actually, a ClojureScript namespace maps to a Google Closure namespace.

Now, let's see the ClojureScript compiler in action. To understand its fundamentals, we won't use any build-automation tooling such as **Leiningen** for the moment, though we'll for sure need it to construct our tooling later on. Let's begin by downloading the latest release of the compiler (1.7.48 as of the time of writing):

 Throughout this book, we assume that you are working on a POSIX compatible system, such as Linux or Mac OS X.

Create a new directory for your first project, label it `cljs_first_project`, and then download into it the compiler JAR:

```
mkdir cljs_first_project; cd cljs_first_project
wget \
https://github.com/clojure/clojurescript/releases/download/r1.7.48/cljs.jar
```

Once the compiler JAR is downloaded, you'll need to create a source directory and the path for your first namespace inside the project folder:

```
mkdir -p src/cljs_first_project; cd src/cljs_first_project
```

Now it's time to write your first ClojureScript namespace, which must conform to the path we're currently in (note that you should replace the underscores with dashes in the directory name). Type the following code in a file named `core.cljs`:

```
(ns cljs-first-project.core)
(js/alert "Hello world!")
```

This code just declares a namespace and the only operation that our program does is showing an alert popup with the familiar "Hello World!" greeting.

Now with the ClojureScript compiler being a Clojure library, we must write some Clojure code in order to trigger the building of the ClojureScript code we just wrote. Create a `Clojure` file at the root of our project (at the same level as the `/src` directory) and label it `build.clj` with the following Clojure code in it:

```
(require 'cljs.build.api)
(cljs.build.api/build "src" {:output-to "out/main.js"})
```

Building ClojureScript is a matter of requiring the `cljs.build.api` namespace and then launching the `build` function that takes two arguments. The first argument is where to look for the ClojureScript source code to build, that is the `src` directory in our case, and second one is where to output the result JavaScript; `out/main.js` as far as this example is concerned.

With this helper Clojure program under our belt, we can launch the ClojureScript compilation process. It is about launching the embedded Clojure from the JAR we downloaded and passing to it the build program we just wrote. When we run Clojure this way, we make sure that the ClojureScript facilities are loaded, especially the `cljs.build.api` namespace. To be able to achieve this, we'll have to add the JAR we downloaded as well as the `src` directory to the classpath when we invoke Clojure with the help of the `java` command:

```
java -cp cljs.jar:src clojure.main ./src/build.clj
```

After you've run this command, you'll notice that an `out` directory containing our target `main.js` file has just been created. In order to launch the output JavaScript artifact, we'll need an HTML page, which when loaded into our browser will greet us with a popup. On our HTML page, we must surely load the generated `main.js` file, but we must also bootstrap the Google Closure Library by loading the `out/goog/base.js` script.

Also, note that the `main.js` file only contains a description of the different namespaces' dependencies managed by the Google Closure Library and no logic of execution. So, we must explicitly set an entry point to our program by telling the Google Closure Library to require a namespace to start with, and that's our `cljs_first_project.core` namespace (note how the dashes got transformed to underscores in the HTML page). Here's what the HTML page, which we'll store under the `greet.html` file, at the root folder of your project, looks like:

```html
<html>
  <body>
    <script type="text/javascript" src="out/goog/base.js"></script>
    <script type="text/javascript" src="out/main.js"></script>
    <script type="text/javascript">
      goog.require("cljs_first_project.core");
    </script>
  </body>
</html>
```

Accessing this page from your browser greets you with a JavaScript `alert` popup. Congratulations! You've successfully written and compiled your first ClojureScript program!

There are more advanced ways to work with the architecture of the build process. For example, to get rid of all the `goog` requires in your HTML page, you can tell the compiler in your Clojure build program which namespace should be set as an entry point, as follows:

```
(require 'cljs.build.api)
(cljs.build.api/build "src"
```

```
{:main 'cljs-first-project.core
  :output-to "out/main.js"})
```

This lets you strip the necessary script declarations in your `greet.html` page down to the following:

```
<html>
  <body>
    <script type="text/javascript" src="out/main.js"></script>
  </body>
</html>
```

Another way to optimize the build process is to set the auto-build of your ClojureScript code on. The compiler can be triggered to be on the watch mode, thus recompiling the output JavaScript as soon as it observes any changes in the `src` directory. Set your Clojure build program to use the `watch` function instead of `build`, as shown here:

```
(require 'cljs.build.api)

(cljs.build.api/watch "src"
  {:main 'first-cljs-project.core
    :output-to "out/main.js"})
```

We've taken quite a deep dive inside the compiler. But, to be able to keep the promise of bringing agile development to JavaScript land, ClojureScript ought to offer a REPL to its users, as any decent lisp would do. Let's discover how ClojureScript addresses this matter in the next section.

Working with the ClojureScript REPL

ClojureScript comes bundled with REPL support for the browser, Node.js, Rhino, and Nashorn. The REPL functionality can be triggered through a call to the `repl` function from the `cljs.repl` namespace present in the ClojureScript JAR. Just as we did for the building process, we must create a REPL launching Clojure program. In this program, we begin by building our project and then launch the interactive REPL session. Create a `repl.clj` Clojure program containing the following listing:

```
(require 'cljs.repl)
(require 'cljs.build.api)
(require 'cljs.repl.browser)

(cljs.build.api/build "src"
  {:main 'cljs-first-project.core
    :output-to "out/main.js"
```

```
       :verbose true})

(cljs.repl/repl (cljs.repl.browser/repl-env)
  :watch "src"
  :output-dir "out")
```

Here, we'll build a REPL with evaluation on the browser, as we've used the
`cljs.repl.browser` namespace. Note how we set the `:watch` option, so our REPL
automatically gets fresh versions of the output JavaScript, providing for interactive
ClojureScript code evaluation. The `:output-dir` directive tells the REPL where to look for
generated artifacts so that they can be loaded into the relevant evaluation environment. As
the interactive evaluation session goes, output of the compilation goes into
`out/watch.log`, so we can follow along what's going on while the code interacts with the
REPL.

Now, you must set a connection to the REPL inside your ClojureScript program,
`core.cljs`. Once built, the resulting JavaScript program will stay in tune with the REPL
environment, by pushing to the browser any changes made to the ClojureScript source:

```
(ns cljs-first-project.core
  (:require [clojure.browser.repl :as repl]))

(defonce conn
  (repl/connect "http://localhost:9000/repl"))

(js/alert "Hello world!")
```

The connection has been defined with the `defonce` parameter to make sure that the same
connection is used across the many builds that will occur while the user interacts with the
REPL and triggers a new build per evaluation.

Now, launch the REPL, preferably using the `rlwrap` command, so the display on the
terminal is properly rendered:

```
rlwrap java -cp cljs.jar:src clojure.main repl.clj
```

Be patient while the first build, involving the construction of the connection to the REPL, is completed. When it completes, you'll see the **Waiting for browser to connect** message in your terminal. Once you see this message, point your browser to the HTML page we prepared before (greet.html) now through http://localhost:9000/greet.html. Accept the first greeting popup and go back to your terminal; you'll see the following output:

```
Watch compilation log available at: out/watch.log
To quit, type: :cljs/quit
cljs.user=>
```

Type another greeting to see if it gets automatically executed in your browser. Type in your REPL the following:

```
cljs.user=> (js/alert "Hello World From REPL!")
```

You'll see new greetings from the REPL interactively popping up without hitting refresh on your browser:

So far, were able to come up with a ClojureScript REPL that empowered us to interact with the browser. But, we are far from having a full-fledged development environment yet; the terminal through which we are coding is quite limited, and we lack several essential features such as code completion, syntax coloring, source code exploration, refactoring, or version control management to name a few. We need a much more complete and fluid coding experience and that's what we will strive to achieve in the next sections. We'll begin by exploring the two most promising facilities that permit text editors or integrated development environments to take advantage from the ClojureScript REPL. Then, we'll showcase two Emacs setups based on those facilities-one based on **CIDER** and another one backed byinf-clojure.

Live coding ClojureScript on top of nREPL with Piggieback and Weasel

Network REPL (nREPL) (`https://github.com/clojure/tools.nrepl`) is a Clojure library designed primarily to offer remote Clojure code evaluation. It follows a client-server architecture in which the server exposes the REPL functionality by responding to client code evaluation queries. nREPL has been created to offer a means to the makers of development tools to connect and explore running Clojure environments in a way that is agnostic to the platform these tools may be running on.

Many prominent Clojure development tools rely on nREPL to implement their functionality. In fact, CIDER on Emacs or Cursive on **Intellij IDEA**, the most used tools for developing Clojure at the time of writing this, both rely on nREPL (CIDER relying more on nREPL for code introspection than Cursive).

Naturally, ClojureScript also benefits from nREPL.

Piggieback (`https://github.com/cemerick/piggieback`) is an nREPL middleware that seizes this opportunity. Piggieback hooks into nREPL and changes its operation so it can evaluate and load ClojureScript code, while being understandable to the vast majority of existing Clojure tooling. In the next section, we'll take a closer look at Piggieback.

Working with Piggieback

Piggieback changes the nREPL behavior to turn it into a ClojureScript remote evaluation environment. It does this by functioning as a middleware layer on top of nREPL. Let's see how to do this using Leiningen.

 Leiningen, the Clojure build tool, can be downloaded from `http://leiningen.org/` or `https://github.com/technomancy/leiningen`. You can also find detailed instructions and documentation on how to install and get started with Leiningen on both the sites. We'll be using Leiningen a lot in this book, so you'll definitely want to install it.

We'll use this project management tool to create a new Clojure project:

```
lein new piggieback_project
```

Then, we'll have to modify the `project.clj` file (where project-specific configuration is kept) in order to turn our project into a ClojureScript one, adding ClojureScript as a dependency:

```
(defproject piggieback_project "0.1.0-SNAPSHOT"
  :description "FIXME: write description"
  :url "http://example.com/FIXME"
  :license {:name "Eclipse Public License"
            :url "http://www.eclipse.org/legal/epl-v10.html"}
  :dependencies [[org.clojure/clojure "1.8.0"]
                 [org.clojure/clojurescript "1.8.51"]])7.228"]])
```

Now, it is time to add Piggieback into the mix. Add its dependencies and its middleware to the `project.clj` file:

```
(defproject piggieback_project "0.1.0-SNAPSHOT"
  :description "FIXME: write description"
  :url "http://example.com/FIXME"
  :license {:name "Eclipse Public License"
            :url "http://www.eclipse.org/legal/epl-v10.html"}
  :dependencies [[org.clojure/clojure "1.8.0"]
                 [org.clojure/clojurescript "1.7.228"]]
  :profiles {:dev {:dependencies [[com.cemerick/piggieback"0.2.1"]
                                  [org.clojure/tools.nrepl"0.2.10"]]
  :repl-options {:nrepl-middleware
                 [cemerick.piggieback/wrap-cljs-repl]}}})
```

Piggieback is just an entry point to ClojureScript REPLs. Once we hook into our nREPL, we can operate in the same manner as we did when we were working with the REPL bundled with the compiler. Once again, we'll need to prepare a ClojureScript namespace that can define the connection to the REPL, and an HTML page that we can load into our browser. Create a `core.cljs` file under the `src/piggieback_project` folder:

```
(ns piggieback-project.core
  (:require [clojure.browser.repl :as repl]))
(defonce conn
  (repl/connect "http://localhost:9000/repl"))
```

Next, copy the `greet.html` file we wrote previously into the root of your new project.

We can now start an nREPL session. Type the following at the root of your project:

```
lein repl
```

In order to launch interactive code evaluation and loading in the browser, we must use some ClojureScript namespaces as to be able to hook Piggieback into our running nREPL session. We'll need to build the ClojureScript program we wrote at least once, so first we'll have to load the compiled JavaScript code to connect to the nREPL. Issue the following commands at the running REPL prompt:

```
user=> (require 'cljs.build.api)
user=> (cljs.build.api/build "src"
  #_=>    {:main 'piggieback-project.core
  #_=>     :output-to "out/main.js"
  #_=>     :verbose true})
user=> (require 'cljs.repl.browser)
```

We are now ready to hand over the code evaluation responsibility to Piggieback. Type the following:

```
user=>   (cemerick.piggieback/cljs-repl (cljs.repl.browser/repl-
  env))
```

You'll see that a JavaScript compilation process has been launched. It is our `core.cljs` file being compiled, and constructing a connection to the REPL. This will be our nREPL session—accessed through the JavaScript artifacts loaded via the `greet.html` page.

Once this operation has finished, you'll get the **Waiting for browser to connect** message that we previously encountered during our interaction with the REPL built by the ClojureScript compiler. As soon as you point your browser to `http://localhost:9000/greet.html`, you'll notice that the prompt has changed; it now shows the following:

```
cljs.user=>_
```

This means that the nREPL session has started accepting code to be compiled. The compiled JavaScript will automatically be evaluated on the connected browser. Try to generate a **Hello World!** popup from the browser from Piggieback this time:

```
cljs.user=> (js/alert "Hello World from Piggieback!")
```

And your browser says it with a popup, from your `nREPL/Piggieback` session.

We've now seen how we can change the nREPL's behavior so that it is turned into an entry point to the ClojureScript REPL. Code passed to the REPL executed on into the JavaScript environment-the browser in our context-via JavaScript files that are regenerated after each and every operation.

We can make this workflow even leaner by hot loading the JavaScript artifacts into the browser with websockets. This is what we will see in the next section, with the `Weasel` library.

Setting up Weasel with PiggieBack for browser live coding

`Weasel` (`https://github.com/tomjakubowski/weasel`) sets a up realtime communication channel using a websocket between a ClojureScript REPL and the JavaScript evaluation environment. The authors of this library say that choosing websockets as a means for delivering compiled JavaScript to runtime environments made it possible for them to profit from a simple and reliable transport. It also empowered them to reach a much wider range of JavaScript engines, especially those that don't properly support, the `<iframe>` tag (the main technology behind the vanilla ClojureScript browser REPL). Let's now add Weasel on top of the Piggieback-enabled nREPL environment that we've set up in the previous sections.

Let's first modify the `piggieback_project` file we worked on earlier to support `Weasel` by adding its dependency to the `project.clj` file:

```
(defproject piggieback_project "0.1.0-SNAPSHOT"
  :description "FIXME: write description"
  :url "http://example.com/FIXME"
  :license {:name "Eclipse Public License"
    :url "http://www.eclipse.org/legal/epl-v10.html"}
  :dependencies [[org.clojure/clojure "1.8.0"]
    [org.clojure/clojurescript "1.7.228"]
    [weasel "0.7.0" :exclusions
    [org.clojure/clojurescript]]]
  :profiles {:dev {:dependencies
    [[com.cemerick/piggieback"0.2.1"]
    [org.clojure/tools.nrepl "0.2.10"]]
    :repl-options {:nrepl-middleware
    [cemerick.piggieback/wrap-    cljs-repl]}}})
```

Let's modify our ClojureScript code so that it can connect to the websocket opened by `Weasel`:

```
(ns piggieback-project.core
  (:require [weasel.repl :as repl]))
(when-not (repl/alive?)
  (repl/connect "ws://localhost:9001"))
```

Just like we did in the previous section, we'll need to connect to our nREPL and plug Piggieback in on top of it, but this time, we'll run it with a Weasel browser. After making sure that you are at the root of the project folder, type in a terminal:

```
lein repl
```

First, let's compile our ClojureScript source so we have our JavaScript ready to connect to the format as code websocket. Run the following from your nREPL session:

```
user=> (require 'cljs.build.api)
user=> (cljs.build.api/build "src"
  #_=>     {:main 'piggieback-project.core
  #_=>      :output-to "out/main.js"
  #_=>      :verbose true})
```

Next, we require the Weasel REPL namespace:

```
user=> (require 'weasel.repl.websocket)
```

We hook Piggieback onto the current session and ask it to use the `Weasel` websocket as the REPL environment (we also set the IP address and the port we want our websocket to be listening to):

```
user=> (cemerick.piggieback/cljs-repl
  #_=> (weasel.repl.websocket/repl-env :ip "0.0.0.0" :port
  9001))
```

After Piggieback is launched, `Weasel` shows a message to inform us that it is awaiting incoming connections:

```
<< waiting for client to connect ...
```

Open the `greet.html` file in your browser (you need to open it from the files manager on your OS, as we are not serving it over HTTP this time!). As soon as the file opens, you see the following message in your nREPL session:

```
<< waiting for client to connect ...   connected! >>
```

The prompt in your nREPL session should change to the following:

```
cljs.user=> _
```

As usual, let's salute the world and see if our greeting pops up in the browser:

```
cljs.user=> (js/alert "Hello World from Weasel!")
```

Your browser should now emit an alert with a greeting message on it.

Until this point, we have been able to put together a powerful environment for developing ClojureScript. Thanks to Piggieback being hooked on nREPL, we can benefit from the integrated development tools that already exist for Clojure. Before we go too much further on this subject, let's see how we can write ClojureScript programs that target other JavaScript environments. In the following section, we'll focus on setting up a Piggieback powered nREPL that evaluates code on the Node.js platform.

ClojureScript REPLs on Node.js with Piggieback

Setting up Node.js REPLs is simpler than targeting the browser. You don't need to set up connections from the REPL process to the browser with the help of some vanilla JavaScript. All you have to do is make sure that the source is compiled, and set the REPL target to Node.js, so that the compiled output is handed over to that evaluation environment for running.

First, make sure that Node.js is installed. Under `piggieback_project`, change the `core.cljs` file so that it looks like the following:

```
(ns piggieback-project.core
  (:require [cljs.nodejs :as nodejs]))

(nodejs/enable-util-print!)

(defn -main [& args]
  (println "Hello world from Node.js!"))

(set! *main-cli-fn* -main)
```

Launch an nREPL session for your project by typing the following:

```
lein repl
```

We then require the namespaces necessary for the launch of our Node.js REPL:

```
user=>(require 'cljs.build.api)
user=> (require 'cljs.repl.node)
```

Now, launch the first build of our ClojureScript `core.cljs` source:

```
user=> (cljs.build.api/build "src"
 #_=>    {:main 'piggieback-project.core
 #_=>     :output-to "out/main.js"
 #_=>     :verbose true})
```

We can now hook a Piggieback REPL into this running nREPL session. Issue the following command:

```
(cemerick.piggieback/cljs-repl (cljs.repl.node/repl-env))
```

The nREPL session responds with a message saying that a Node.js REPL has been launched:

```
ClojureScript Node.js REPL server listening on 49449
```

And as usual, the prompt has been changed so as to notify us that we have successfully launched a ClojureScript REPL on top of our nREPL session:

```
cljs.user=> _
```

At this point, we can implement a program similar to the Node.js "Hello World," a little HTTP server that greets the browser that queries it. Type the following in your, now, ClojureScript-enabled nREPL session (we'll elaborate more on the syntax later on):

```
cljs.user=> (def http (js/require "http"))
cljs.user=> (.listen (.createServer http
       #_=>                    (fn [req res]
       #_=>                    (do
       #_=>                    (.writeHead res
       #_=>                    200
       #_=>                    (js-obj
       #_=>                    "Content-Type" "text/plain"))
       #_=>                    (.end res
       #_=>                    "Hello World from Node.js
                                  http server!"))))
       #_=>                    1337
       #_=>                    "127.0.0.1")
```

If you navigate your browser to `http://127.0.0.1:1337`, you should see the greeting from your Node.js server.

In the next section, we'll elaborate on a new contender in the realm of interactive ClojureScript coding environments: **Figwheel**, the new kid on the block that gets you to a ClojureScript browser REPL quickly.

Live coding ClojureScript with Figwheel

Figwheel (`https://github.com/bhauman/lein-figwheel`) is a Leiningen plugin that builds ClojureScript programs and delivers them to the browser for interactive evaluation. In contrast with nREPL-based work-flows, Figwheel does not rely on third-party REPLs. It is a self-contained library with its own ClojureScript REPL that relies on websockets to push your work to the browser as you edit your ClojureScript code. Figwheel also supports CSS live reloading in the browser, hence providing for a completely interactive web development experience. In this next section, we'll use Figwheel to get set up a ClojureScript live-coding experience on the browser.

Setting up Figwheel for browser live coding

Figwheel comes as a self-contained library that automatically builds and loads the generated JavaScript into the browser. This means we won't have to manually build the JavaScript that'll be pushed to the browser in order to establish the connection to the Figwheel REPL. Everything will be handled for us.

Let's begin by creating a new project that we will use to experiment with Figwheel:

```
lein new figwheel-project
```

We'll now need to change our `project.clj` file so that our project is aware of the `lein-figwheel` plugin:

```
(defproject figwheel-project "0.1.0-SNAPSHOT"
  :dependencies [[org.clojure/clojure "1.8.0"]
    [org.clojure/clojurescript "1.8.51"]]
  :plugins [[lein-figwheel "0.5.1"]]
  :clean-targets [:target-path "out"]
  :cljsbuild {
    :builds [{:id "dev"
      :source-paths ["src"]
      :figwheel true
      :compiler {:main "figwheel-project.core"}}]})
        :asset-path "js/out"
        :output-to "resources/public/js/main.js"
        :output-dir "resources/public/js/out"}}]})
```

Create a file named `core.cljs` under `src/figwheel_project/` so we can have a ClojureScript program that will be built and pushed to the browser. Code changes will be pushed to the browser automatically later on via this loaded file:

```
(ns figwheel-project.core)

(js/alert "Hello from Figwheel!")
```

As before, in order to load the compiled JavaScript that'll connect our browser to the running Figwheel process we need to have an HTML page. Since we're still compiling ClojureScript to the `main.js` file, we must load this file in order to get it evaluated in the browser. Create a `greet.html` file that you'll put in the root of your project. This page will contain the following:

```html
<html>
  <body>
    <script type="text/javascript" src="main.js"></script>
  </body>
</html>
```

Let's launch Figwheel. Note how this is done as a Leiningen plugin, and how we don't need to load a specific ClojureScript on top of an nREPL as we did with Piggieback:

```
lein figwheel
```

Your terminal should show a message that states that it is awaiting the client connection:

```
Prompt will show when figwheel connects to your application
```

For this, we are going to simply use the web server that comes embedded within Figwheel. Provided that we've put the previous `greet.html` in our browser. Open that HTML page as a regular file under the `public/resources` folder visit the following URL, `http://localhost:3449/greet.html`. As soon as the page loads, you'll see the greeting we programmed to show in the ClojureScript file, and once you've clicked on the **OK** button, you'll notice that the Figwheel invite is now showing a prompt accepting user requests for ClojureScript evaluation:

```
cljs.user=> _
```

Let's try to evaluate something in the browser. Type the following:

```
cljs.user=> (js/alert "Hi from Figwheel Again!")
```

Once again, this new greeting should pop up in your browser!

We've seen how it was easy to set up a browser live-coding session with Figwheel. In the next section, we'll experiment with Node.js evaluations.

Node.js interactive development workflows with Figwheel

Figwheel is mainly intended for the browser, and as such, configuring it to connect to Node.js is a bit trickier than what we just did. Since Figwheel does not rely on the core ClojureScript REPL or nREPL, and hence, there are some actions that need to be taken in order to add Node.js support to its default stack.

Getting Figwheel to provide a Node.js REPLs is a matter of preparing a special JavaScript artifact that, when run with Node.js, will implement a server that connects via websocket to a running Figwheel session. This server will evaluate the compiled JavaScript from the Figwheel REPL via the WebSocket connection. Let's implement this.

First create a new Clojure project and name it `figwheel_node`. Next, prepare the ClojureScript Node.js script that, once launched, will connect via a WebSocket to the REPL served by Figwheel:

```
(ns ^:figwheel-always figwheel-node-repl.core
  (:require [cljs.nodejs :as nodejs]))
(nodejs/enable-util-print!)
(def -main (fn [] nil))
(set! *main-cli-fn* -main)
```

Next, let's modify our `project.clj` file to target the Node.js runtime using the relevant bootstrapping library. We could configure the bootstrapping library ourselves, but instead we'll use a popular Leiningen plugin, Cljsbuild (`https://github.com/emezeske/lein-cljsbuild`), to automate this process for us. Let's add and configure it by editing your `project.clj` as follows:

```
(defproject figwheel-node "0.1.0-SNAPSHOT"
  :dependencies [[org.clojure/clojure "1.7.0"]
    [org.clojure/clojurescript "1.7.122"]]
  :plugins [[lein-cljsbuild "1.1.0"]
    [lein-figwheel "0.4.0"]]
  :clean-targets ^{:protect false} ["out"]
  :cljsbuild {
    :builds [{:id "server-dev"
      :source-paths ["src"]
```

```
            :figwheel true
            :compiler {:main figwheel-node-repl.core
                       :output-to "out/figwheel_node_repl.js"
                       :output-dir "out"
                       :target :nodejs
                       :optimizations :none
                       :source-map true}}]}
     :figwheel {})
```

Note that setting the `figwheel-node-repl.core` namespace as a main entry point will ensure that all the necessary imports are added to our compiled output before we execute any of the program logic via websockets. This way, the script can be painlessly run by Node.js.

Next, let's install the Node.js websockets client library, `ws`, so that our script can connect to the Figwheel session:

```
npm install ws
```

As we've done with the browser setup, launch the Figwheel REPL:

```
lein figwheel server-dev
```

As usual, you will see a prompt telling you that the Figwheel environment is awaiting a client connection. This time, the client will be the Node.js script we just developed. Launch it in a different terminal window from the one currently running our Figwheel server:

```
node out/figwheel_node_repl.js
```

At this point, you have two running environments: the Figwheel REPL, which now shows the `cljs.user=>` prompt and the Node.js process, which is actively evaluating the compiled JavaScript that is being pushed to it by Figwheel.

Let's evaluate, on the Figwheel REPL, the HTTP server we used in the previous sections:

```
cljs.user=> (def http (js/require "http"))
cljs.user=> (.listen (.createServer http
      #_=>                           (fn [req res]
      #_=>                             (do
      #_=>                               (.writeHead res
      #_=>                                 200
      #_=>                                 (js-obj
      #_=>                                   "Content-Type"
      #_=>                                     "text/plain"))
      #_=>                               (.end res
      #_=>                                 "Hello World from
                                            Node.js http server!")))))
```

```
#_=>                              1337
#_=>                              "127.0.0.1")
```

If you visit the URL exposed by this HTTP server, http://127.0.0.1:1337, you should see a greeting from Node.js, meaning that the ClojureScript you typed in the Figwheel REPL has been successfully compiled to JavaScript and evaluated by the running Node.js process.

We've studied two alternatives for exposing ClojureScript REPLs-one of them based on nREPL with Piggieback and the other using a standalone REPL environment based on Figwheel. In the next sections, we'll talk about how to set up development environments for ClojureScript on Emacs.

Setting integrated development environments for ClojureScript

Now that we've got the basic lay of the land, we can now focus on configuring a proper Integrated Development Environment. We'll also discuss how we can make it ClojureScript-aware using the REPLs we've covered so far.

In doing so, we strive to profit from the many ways IDEs can assist us. IDEs are powerful tools, exposing functionalities such as code completion, syntax highlighting, program structure introspection, and navigation.

We'll focus on Emacs, its Clojure development environment, CIDER, as well as another simpler package, inf-clojure. The reason why we chose these Emacs-based tools is that they are the most used IDEs for most Clojurists, and are actively maintained by a vibrant community of open source enthusiasts.

Working on Emacs with Piggieback and Weasel on CIDER

CIDER, or the **Clojure Interactive Development Environment that Rocks for Emacs** (https://github.com/clojure-emacs/cider), is an open source Emacs Library for working with Clojure on Emacs. Originally called **nrepl.el**, it is stable, feature-rich, and an active project that is highly beneficial to Clojure and ClojureScript developers.

If you're going to use CIDER, its authors have stated that they expect ClojureScript developers to use Piggieback and Weasel as their default toolkit.

Let's assume that you can launch a Piggieback/Weasel-enabled nREPL session for your ClojureScript project (refer to the *Live-coding ClojureScript on top of nREPL with PiggieBack and Weasel* section). We'll now focus on how CIDER empowers you to develop ClojureScript with Emacs.

Installing CIDER

Installing Cider is a matter of getting the relevant library from `package.el` (using **MELPA**, **MELPA Stable**, or **Marmalade** repositories) and issuing the following command (in Emacs):

```
M-x package-install [RET] cider [RET]
```

Alternatively, add the following lines to your Emacs configuration file:

```
(unless (package-installed-p 'cider)
  (package-install 'cider))
```

You'll also need to hook up the CIDER middleware into our nREPL. To do this, add the following to the `:user` section in your `~/.lein/profiles.clj` file:

```
:plugins [[cider/cider-nrepl "x.y.z"]]
```

We haven't spoken about Leiningen profiles too much prior to now. To learn more about how the `profiles.clj` file works, check out the Leiningen documentation at `https://github.com/technomancy/leiningen/blob/master/doc/PROFILES.md#declaring-profiles`. Take care, the `"x.y.z"` version number in `cider-nrepl` must match the CIDER version, otherwise you'll get a warning when trying to connect to a project's REPL.

Working with Clojure and ClojureScript REPLs on CIDER

At this point, you're free to tweak CIDER's configuration to add features like different autocompletion providers or syntax-highlighting behavior. Whether you choose to or not, you should have everything you need to get CIDER up and running at this point.

Once you have installed CIDER and its nREPL middleware, you can open a Clojure file (even an empty buffer to experiment in), launch an REPL on it and begin to work interactively. Most Clojure developers go back and forth between editing and sending code to the REPL for evaluation. To launch a Clojure nREPL session from Emacs use the following command:

M-x cider-jack-in

Now, how can we get this set up to work with ClojureScript? Let's go back to our `piggieback_project` from earlier in this chapter and get CIDER working for it.

First, we'll need to tell CIDER which ClojureScript evaluation environment we are going to use. CIDER defaults to **Rhino**, so for our case we'll need to tell CIDER to use Weasel. Customize the `cider-cljs-repl` file to set it to Weasel:

```
M-x customize-variable RET cider-cljs-repl RET Weasel RET
```

Make certain that your ClojureScript file contains the following connection code:

```
(ns piggieback-project.core
  (:require [weasel.repl :as repl]))
 (when-not (repl/alive?)
  (repl/connect "ws://localhost:9001"))
```

Make sure that this ClojureScript code has been successfully compiled at least once. Otherwise, we won't be able to load the websocket client.

Next, we'll use the `lein-cljsbuild` package. To activate this plugin make sure that your `project.clj` file looks as follows:

```
(defproject piggieback_project "0.1.0-SNAPSHOT"
  :description "FIXME: write description"
  :url "http://example.com/FIXME"
  :license {:name "Eclipse Public License"
    :url "http://www.eclipse.org/legal/epl-v10.html"}
  :plugins [[lein-cljsbuild "1.1.0"]]
  :cljsbuild {
    :builds [{:source-paths ["src"]
    :compiler {:main piggieback-project.core
    :output-to "out/main.js"
    :output-dir "out"
    :optimizations :none}}]}
  :dependencies [[org.clojure/clojure "1.7.0"]
    [org.clojure/clojurescript "1.7.122"]
```

```
    [weasel "0.7.0" :exclusions [org.clojure/clojurescript]]]
  :profiles {:dev {:dependencies [[com.cemerick/piggieback
    "0.2.1"]
    [org.clojure/tools.nrepl "0.2.10"]]
    :repl-options {:nrepl-middleware
      [cemerick.piggieback/wrap-cljs-repl]}}})
```

Now we'll build the code responsible for creating the connection. While in the project directory, type the following:

```
lein cljsbuild once
```

Now open any ClojureScript file in Emacs, and launch the nREPL session with:

```
M-x cider-jack-in-clojurescript
```

You'll see two REPLs, one for Clojure and the other for ClojureScript. The ClojureScript REPL should notify you that it is waiting for the client to connect.

Connect your browser to the Weasel session by opening `greet.html`. You should get the following screen in Emacs:

```
                          *cider-repl CLJS piggieback_project*
;; improvements) use <M-x cider-report-bug> to report it.
;;
;; Above all else - don't panic! In case of an emergency - procure
;; some (hard) cider and enjoy it responsibly!
;;
;; You can remove this message with the 'cider-repl-clear-help-banner' command.
;; You can disable it from appearing on start by setting
;; 'cider-repl-display-help-banner' to nil.
;; ===========================================================================
user> << started Weasel server on ws://127.0.0.1:9001 >>
<< waiting for client to connect ...   connected! >>
To quit, type: :cljs/quit
;;=> nil
cljs.user>
47:11 1x-*cider-repl CLJS piggieback_project*         Bot REPL , FlyC- +     Tue May 17 08:56 1.68
;; improvements) use <M-x cider-report-bug> to report it.
;;
;; Above all else - don't panic! In case of an emergency - procure
;; some (hard) cider and enjoy it responsibly!
;;
;; You can remove this message with the 'cider-repl-clear-help-banner' command.
;; You can disable it from appearing on start by setting
;; 'cider-repl-display-help-banner' to nil.
;; ===========================================================================
user>



43: 6 1x-*cider-repl piggieback_project*              Bot REPL , FlyC- +     Tue May 17 08:56 1.68
Starting a Weasel REPLm (see Readme for additional configuration)
```

Now, switch to the window containing the Clojure REPL and set it to show the buffer containing your `test.cljs` ClojureScript file.

Load the content of the file in your REPL using the following Emacs command:

    C-c C-k

Then, set the namespace of the REPL to be the one declared by the current source file:

    C-c M-n

Switch now to your ClojureScript REPL:

    C-c C-z

Start typing the name of the function. You'll notice that code completion should be working. In the minibuffer, Emacs should also help you with the signature of your function.

Now let's evaluate some ClojureScript in our REPL:

```
piggieback-project.test> (defn test-fn [your-name] (js/alert (+
  "hello " your-name)))
piggieback-project.test> (test-fn "Rafik")
```

And a popup should happily greet you from your connected browser.

Working on Emacs with Figwheel and inf-clojure

In order to use Figwheel with Emacs, we'll need to use `inf-clojure`, an Emacs package offering basic interaction with a running Clojure subprocess. In conjunction with clojure-mode, this setup will make sure that we benefit from static code analysis features. `inf-clojure` is not as feature rich as CIDER, which is worth keeping in mind. It is nevertheless, able to load files, switch namespaces, evaluate expressions, show documentation and source of symbols, and do macro-expansion.

Installing inf-clojure

Type the following in your Emacs:

```
M-x package-install [RET] inf-clojure [RET]
```

You may also want to add the following snippet to your Emacs configuration file:

```
(unless (package-installed-p 'inf-clojure)
  (package-install 'inf-clojure))
```

To enable `inf-clojure` whenever you visit a Clojure or ClojureScript file, add the following to your Emacs configuration file:

```
(add-hook 'clojure-mode-hook #'inf-clojure-minor-mode)
```

Configuring inf-clojure to run Figwheel as a Clojure subprocess

In order for Emacs to know that we want to use Figwheel as our REPL environment, we'll need to configure it explicitly. To do this, add the following to your Emacs configuration file (usually ~/.emacs):

```
(defun figwheel-repl ()
  (interactive)
  (run-clojure "lein figwheel"))
```

Restart Emacs or re-evaluate the the configuration file buffer for the modifications to take effect. Next, let's open a file in the source directory of the `figwheel_project` we've set up for the browser, say `core.cljs`, and launch the ClojureScript powered `inf-clojure` session by typing the following:

```
M-x figwheel-repl
```

You'll end up to a configuration like the one shown in the following screenshot, where Figwheel, run from `inf-clojure`, is awaiting connection from the browser:

As soon as you open the `greet.html` file within your browser, the user prompt should change to notify you that the evaluation environment is successfully connected to the Figwheel REPL:

```
*inf-clojure*
Figwheel: Configuration Valid. Starting Figwheel ...
Figwheel: Starting server at http://localhost:3449
Figwheel: Watching build - dev
Compiling "resources/public/js/main.js" from ["src"]...
Successfully compiled "resources/public/js/main.js" in 1.24 seconds.
Launching ClojureScript REPL for build: dev
Figwheel Controls:
          (stop-autobuild)              ;; stops Figwheel autobuilder
          (start-autobuild [id ...])    ;; starts autobuilder focused on optional ids
          (switch-to-build id ...)      ;; switches autobuilder to different build
          (reset-autobuild)             ;; stops, cleans, and starts autobuilder
          (reload-config)               ;; reloads build config and resets autobuild
          (build-once [id ...])         ;; builds source one time
          (clean-builds [id ..])        ;; deletes compiled cljs target files
          (print-config [id ...])       ;; prints out build configurations
          (fig-status)                  ;; displays current state of system
  Switch REPL build focus:
          :cljs/quit                    ;; allows you to switch REPL to another build
    Docs: (doc function-name-here)
    Exit: Control+C or :cljs/quit
 Results: Stored in vars *1, *2, *3, *e holds last exception object
Prompt will show when Figwheel connects to your application




To quit, type: :cljs/quit
cljs.user=>
 31:12 1 -*inf-clojure*                    Bot Inferior Clojure:run Projectile[figwheel_project]
```

Let's evaluate some ClojureScript. Split your window in two using the following:

    C-x 2

And load the buffer containing `core.cljs`:

    C-x b   core.cljs [RET]

You should end up with something like the following:

```
(ns figwheel-project.core)

(js/alert "Hello from Figwheel!")




4: 0 - -:DB:…/src/figwheel_project/core.cljs      All ClojureScript cljr yas +   Tue May 17 09:17 1.77
Prompt will show when Figwheel connects to your application



To quit, type: :cljs/quit
cljs.user=>



31:12 1x-*inf-clojure*                            Bot Inferior Clojure:run Projectile[figwheel_project]
```

Move the cursor to the (js-alert...) form and evaluate it by hitting the following:

    C-c C-c

You should see the greeting showing up in the browser.

We've now seen two different possible setups on Emacs: one based on Piggieback/Weasel, which is harder to set up but offers a fully-fledged Clojure development environment—CIDER, and another using Figwheel but offering less integrated development functionality. Which one you choose to use relies pretty much on personal taste, and how much effort you feel like putting in.

Summary

This concludes our section on getting started with ClojureScript development. We introduced you to the ClojureScript compiler, demonstrating how it runs on the JVM and leverages the Google Closure Library to optimize compiled JavaScript and provide namespace functionality.

We learned how the ClojureScript compiler can be used to build ClojureScript programs into JavaScript artifacts, how to access these artifacts and, finally, how to interact with them via a REPL targeting different JavaScript environments.

We covered how to use Piggieback in order to expose a JavaScript-enabled nREPL session, how to push the compiled JavaScript via websockets to the browser thanks to Weasel, and how to target Node.js using this setup.

After that, we saw how we could use Figwheel to get a single self-contained Leiningen plugin for developing with the browser. We also learned how to target Node.js using Figwheel.

Finally, we saw how one can use one of these setups with an integrated development environment based on CIDER or `inf-clojure`.

Now that you have your computer configured for ClojureScript development, lets tackle the language properly. In the next chapter, we'll dig into the core of the ClojureScript language.

2
ClojureScript Language Fundamentals

ClojureScript provides the developer with great expressive power, thanks to its elegant semantics and its bias toward functional programming-both artifacts of its heritage as a Lisp language.

It also encourages the use of a minimal set of pragmatic and efficient data structures that make it possible to productively write data-oriented programs that are bound by a set of unified operations, typically conforming to the powerful `seq` abstraction.

In this chapter, we are going to explore these semantics and data structures so that we can gain a deep knowledge of the ClojureScript language basics. We'll delve into its basic scalar types and collections, understand how expression evaluation and variable scoping work, study the `seq` abstraction along with the concept of laziness, and show how interoperability with JavaScript works. We'll be covering the following topics:

- Understanding ClojureScript functions
- ClojureScript data structures
- Advanced destructuring and namespaces
- Immutability
- JavaScript interoperability

Understanding ClojureScript functions

Before we dive too far into ClojureScript, we need to understand the syntax behind ClojureScript functions. Functions in ClojureScript work like functions in most computer languages.

Functions

Functions in ClojureScript are first-class entities, which means that we can store them as variables, or values in data structures, return them as values from other functions, and pass functions as arguments to other functions.

We'll be demonstrating quite a bit of code evaluation in this chapter. In order to follow along, start up an REPL following the instructions provided in the previous chapter.

Let's start by quickly seeing what a function call in ClojureScript looks like at the REPL:

```
cljs.user=> (+ 1 2)
;; => 3
```

ClojureScript, as a Lisp, looks unlike many other languages, including JavaScript. It is a language written in prefix notation, which means that the calling function is the first argument. The same operation, performed in JavaScript, would look like the following:

```
> 1 + 2
3
```

Let's start by just defining a simple function. Let's say we want to start by just taking a number and adding one. There is an existing function, inc, that does this for us already, but let's just reimplement it for now:

```
cljs.user=> (def inc2 (fn [x] (+ x 1)))
;; => #'cljs.user/inc2
cljs.user=> (inc2 8)
;; => 9
```

Let's break this apart: the def statement tells us that what follows will be a definition. The fn parameter is a ClojureScript macro that defines a function. Macros are like functions but somewhat more complicated; we'll cover them in greater detail in Chapter 3, *Advanced ClojureScript Concepts*. The x variable in brackets is the sole argument to our function; any additional arguments to the function, if they existed, would also go inside the brackets. What follows after that is the function body.

The `fn` parameter is a special macro in that it invokes `fn*`, which is a compiler special form. The most important part of function construction can't be built by a ClojureScript macro, which makes `fn` (or rather `fn*`) special indeed. We'll talk more about special forms later on in this chapter.

We can also define a function using the `defn` macro, which is a convenient shorthand for `(def (fn...))`. There's nothing special about the `defn` macro that we need to worry about for now; it's functionally the same as `(def (fn ...))`, although it makes it syntactically a little cleaner to attach metadata to the function:

```
cljs.user=> (defn inc2
  [x] (+ x 1))
;; => #'cljs.user/inc2
cljs.user=> (inc2 4)
;; => 5
```

The function we've defined previously is the same as the following JavaScript function:

```
function inc2(x) {
  return x + 1
}
```

If we're defining a function without arguments, we just use an empty vector:

```
cljs.user=> (defn yell [] (print "Aaaaagh!"))
;; => #'cljs.user/yell
cljs.user=> (yell)
Aaaaagh!
;; => nil
```

A documentation string (docstring) can be attached to a function by including it before the function's arguments:

```
cljs.user=> (defn inc2
  "Returns a number one greater than the number passed in."
  [x] (inc x))
;; => #'cljs.user/inc2
```

We can print out the docstring for our function by calling the `doc` parameter on it at the REPL. This is an incredibly useful tool when you want to quickly know what a function does. We recommend including docstrings for all of the functions you write in ClojureScript:

```
cljs.user=> (doc inc2)
-------------------------
cljs.user/inc2
([x])
```

```
    Returns a number one greater than the number passed in.
;; => nil
```

Multiarity and variadic functions

Sometimes you'll want to write a function that could take potentially different numbers of arguments. This function might behave differently with different argument lengths or it might just provide a convenient pointer to the same function but with a specified argument length (for instance, if you wanted to provide defaults). This is sometimes referred to as function overloading. Let's see how we can do this in ClojureScript:

```
cljs.user=> (defn inc2
  "Returns a number one greater than the number passed in. If
  two numbers are provided, sums them both and increments that
  sum by 1."
  ([x] (inc x))
  ([x y] (inc (+ x y))))
;; => 2
cljs.user=> (inc2 3)
;; => 4
cljs.user=> (inc2 3 4)
;; => 8
```

We can also write functions that take any number of arguments (also known as *variadic* functions). This is akin to writing *args in some other languages:

```
cljs.user=> (defn sum
  "Given any number of numbers, sum them together."
  [& args]
  (apply + args))
;; => #object[Function "function (seq37445) {
  return
  cljs.user.sum.cljs$core$IFn$_invoke$arity$variadic
  (cljs.core.seq.call(null,seq37445));
}"]
```

The apply parameter takes a function (in this case, +) and a collection (args) and applies the function to the argument list. Don't worry about the return value from the defn form for now-just know that it's saving the function body in the relevant var, sum. We'll leave off this REPL return value when we're defining functions for the rest of this chapter to save room, but don't be surprised to see it.

Vars in ClojureScript are functionally like variables in JavaScript, but they're actually much more powerful. For instance, you can attach arbitrary pieces of metadata to a var, which can, in turn, be used to enable some really incredible reflection programming at the macro level.

Let's test that our function works:

```
cljs.user=> (sum 5 4 3 2 1)
;; => 15
```

We can include arguments before the ampersand (&) here as well:

```
cljs.user=> (defn foo
  "A simple example function."
  [x y & args]
  (println "This is the first arg:" x)
  (println "This is the second arg:" y)
  (println "These are the remaining args:" args))
cljs.user=> (foo 1 2 3 4)
This is the first arg: 1
This is the second arg: 2
These are the remaining args: (3 4)
;; => nil
```

Anonymous functions

Note that we don't actually need to store our functions to be able to call them:

```
cljs.user=> ((fn [x] (println "The argument to this function
is:" x)) "Bonkers!")

The argument to this function is: Bonkers!
;; => nil
```

This gets back to what we were saying earlier about ClojureScript functions being first-class citizens. You'll find that you're using the so-called anonymous functions (functions that aren't stored as a specific variable) often. In other languages, these are sometimes called **lambda functions**.

ClojureScript, like Clojure, has a special syntactical shorthand that you can use when working with anonymous functions. You don't have to use it, but it's often more concise. Let's look at what the preceding example would look like in this shorthand:

```
cljs.user=> (#(println "The argument to this function is:" %1)
"Bonkers!")
```

```
The argument to this function is: Bonkers!
;; => nil
```

Here in the preceding syntactical shorthand, the function body is signaled by having a pound sign or hash before the opening parenthesis. The `%1` variable tells us to use the first argument (if the function only takes one argument, you can also drop the `1` and just use `%`). If we wanted to make a variadic function, we can use `%&` where we would normally use `&` args:

```
cljs.user=> (#(println "The arguments are:" %&) "Bonkers!"
"a2")

The arguments are: (Bonkers! a2)
;; => nil
```

This sort of syntactic shorthand is great for defining simple and quick functions on a single line, but doesn't make for very clear reading when working with more complicated logic. If you can't easily fit a function on a single line, you're better off sticking to the default function declaration syntax.

Side effects

Any code inside of parentheses, as well as any data literal, that can be evaluated is known as a form. Each form is evaluated in isolation and the value of that form is passed on to the upstream code containing it.

When we execute forms at the REPL, the values are immediately returned. Sometimes, however, whether at the REPL or as part of a program, we want to execute code for its side effects. Side effects might include things like updating state, saving a value to a database, popping up an alert, or printing a value out to the JavaScript console.

Most of the time, evaluating a form that only performs side effects returns `nil`. For instance, if we have a Figwheel REPL open, executing the command to log a value to the JavaScript console returns `nil`:

```
cljs.user=> (js/console.log "I am a side effect")
nil
```

Note that in our browser's JavaScript console, the following value was printed:

```
> I am a side effect
```

Sometimes, we might want to evaluate multiple side effects as part of a function or evaluate one or more side effects and also return a different value. For that, we use the do special form, which lets us evaluate multiple forms, only returning the last one. Let's see an example:

```
cljs.user=> (do
  (println "I am a side effect")
  (+ 1 2)
"This is the returned string"))

I am a side effect
;; => "This is the returned string"
```

Special forms work like regular forms and functions, but they work directly with the ClojureScript compiler. Special forms are so called because without them, the language wouldn't have the core functionality needed to Bootstrap itself.

Let's take a closer look at what happened here. First, note that each of the contained forms was evaluated; we can tell this because the println function was called and printed I am a side effect to our REPL's standard output. We also see that the (+ 1 2) form has not been returned (though it has, in fact, been evaluated). Lastly, the string This is the returned string was returned.

The use of the do special form gives our programs considerably more flexibility; we'll be using it frequently, either directly or indirectly, in many of our programs.

Local variables

We've defined some local variables within our function bodies, but this will not be enough for us in the long run-we'll want to have the ability to define other local variables as we need them. We can use the let macro to do this:

```
cljs.user=> (let [x 10] (println x))
10
;; => nil
```

As you can see from the preceding example, we've bound the value 10 to the local variable x the let macro always takes an even number of arguments within its binding vector since. The arguments are paired-the first the name of the binding variable, the second the values or references being bound. Let's see an example where we bind multiple values:

```
cljs.user=> (let [a 1
                  b 2]
                  {a b})
```

```
;; => {1 2}
```

Within the context of a function, we can redefine a previously defined local variable:

```
cljs.user=> (defn bar [x] (let [x true] x))
;; => #'cljs.user/bar
```

Here, the function already has an argument x, but we've redefined x to be true within the body of let. This function is equivalent to the following JavaScript:

```
var bar = function(x) {
  x = true;
  return x;
}
```

Let's verify that the locally redefined variable is returned:

```
cljs.user=> (bar 5)
;; => true
```

The let macro also functions as an implicit do block:

```
cljs.user=> (let [a 5]
  (println a)
(+ a 3))

5
;; => 8
```

The ClojureScript data structures

ClojureScript shares all of Clojure's basic scalar types, but due to the difference in runtime platform, it relies on different underlying mechanics for implementation. Let's begin by quickly reviewing the basic language types first.

Scalar types

As with Clojure, scalars in ClojureScript are directly linked to the host platform. In this case, this means that ClojureScript scalars are just basic JavaScript types.

Numbers

ClojureScript numbers are nothing but JavaScript numbers. Type at your REPL the following:

```
cljs.user> (type 3)
;; => #object[Number "function Number() {
  [native code]
}"]
```

Unlike Clojure, this is true for all numeric types, whereas Java breaks numeric types into different types like Bigint, Integer, Float and Double, and all numeric types in ClojureScript are just JavaScript numbers:

```
cljs.user> (type 1.1)
;; => #object[Number "function Number() {
  [native code]
}"]
cljs.user> (type
  572934872093847902387492837498273498273598237492873492873592
  374982759238749328759238472938579287598243759287592837492387
  9238749812379582735982374928374982375923874928374982374)
;; => #object[Number "function Number() {
  [native code]
}"]
cljs.user=> (type 0.0000000000057829734923)
;; => #object[Number "function Number() {
  [native code]
}"]
```

Working with numbers in ClojureScript is similar to working with numbers in other languages:

```
cljs.user=> (+ 1 2)
;; => 3
cljs.user=> (- 5 1)
;; => 4
cljs.user=> (* 3 4)
;; => 12
cljs.user=> (/ 8 2)
;; => 4
```

 Note that ClojureScript, like Clojure, doesn't have a % function (modulo division) as it is a reserved character for use in anonymous functions (which we'll cover in Chapter 3, *Advanced ClojureScript Concepts*). Instead, we have the rem function:

```
cljs.user=> (rem 10 3)
;; => 1
```

In addition to the preceding code, ClojureScript also has the `inc` and `dec` functions, which just add or subtract 1 from the argument being passed in. In this regard, they are exactly the same as calling `(+ x 1)` or `(- x 1)`. We can even verify this at the REPL with the `source` macro, which prints out a function's source code:

```
cljs.user=> (source inc)

(defn inc
  "Returns a number one greater than num."
[x] (cljs.core/+ x 1))

;; => nil
```

Strings and characters

Strings in ClojureScript are just JavaScript strings under the hood:

```
cljs.user> (type "A String")
;; => #object[String "function String() {
  [native code]
}"]
```

Unlike Java, JavaScript does not have a `char` type, so characters in ClojureScript are just one-character strings:

```
cljs.user> (type \a)
;; => #object[String "function String() {
  [native code]
}"]
```

We can create strings just by surrounding them with double-quote marks. We can also coerce various other data types to their string forms by calling either `str` or `name`:

```
cljs.user=> (str {})
;; => "{}"
cljs.user=> (str 1)
;; => "1"
```

Notice that the user of `str` on keywords preserves the colon in the string, while `name` gets rid of it:

```
cljs.user=> (str :hamburger)
;; => ":hamburger"
```

```
cljs.user=> (name :sandwich)
;; => "sandwich"
```

The `str` type is typically used to create a new string that is the concatenation of individual strings:

```
cljs.user=> (str "this" "is" "all" "one" "word" "now")
;; => "thisisallonewordnow"
```

You can get the length of a string with `count`:

```
cljs.user=> (count "my-string")
;; => 9
```

Slice a string into a substring with `subs`:

```
cljs.user=> (subs "parents just don't understand" 8 18)
;; => "just don't"
```

And there is much more! The `clojure.string` namespace has a host of handy functions for working with strings, including functions for capitalization, substitution, and splitting. You can expect to see these functions getting used throughout this book.

Nil

The concept of `nil` in Clojure and ClojureScript has many analogies in other languages. If you're coming from a scripting language background, you might be familiar with Python's `None` or Ruby's `nil`. JavaScript has the concept of `null`, and ClojureScript's implementation of `nil` is built on this.

The `nil` type is a special type in ClojureScript, which means asking its type at the REPL returns a somewhat confusing `nil` as an answer:

```
cljs.user=> (type nil)
;; nil
```

Does this mean that `nil` doesn't actually have a type? No. It's just a special type whose type is not accessible at runtime.

The `nil` type is very important in ClojureScript, and we'll be relying on it frequently, particularly when we want to check for the presence of something or do any sort of logical gating with Boolean values.

Boolean values and truthiness

Like most programming languages, ClojureScript retains the basic concept of `true` and `false` as the two possible values for its Boolean type. ClojureScript Booleans are just JavaScript Booleans:

```
cljs.user=> (type true)
;; => #object[Boolean "function Boolean() {
  [native code]
}"]
cljs.user=> (type false)
;; => #object[Boolean "function Boolean() {
  [native code]
}"]
```

In ClojureScript, truth of an expression is decided according to a very simple rule, which is sometimes described as checking for whether or not a value is truthy. Put simply, everything which is neither `false` nor `nil` evaluates to `true` when placed in a conditional expression. Truthiness is a language design pattern that can be found in a number of other languages such as Clojure, Python, and Ruby. Unlike other Lisp languages, this manner of evaluation means that empty lists are not considered to be "falsey", as they are neither explicitly `false`, nor are they `nil`. Let's look at some examples:

```
cljs.user> (if (js-obj "field" "value") "js object is true" "js
object is false")

;; => "js object is true"
cljs.user> (if 5 "a number is true" "a number is false")

;; => "a number is true"
```

As we noted earlier, empty lists are not considered `false`. This holds `true` for all empty collections as well; we'll learn more about them shortly:

```
cljs.user> (if [] "an empty vector is true" "an empty vector is
false")

;; => "an empty vector is true"
cljs.user> (if {} "an empty map is true" "an empty map is
false")

;; => "an empty map is true"
```

Only `false` and `nil` are considered `false`:

```
cljs.user> (if nil "nil is true" "nil is false")
;; => "nil is false"
cljs.user> (if false "false is true?!" "false is false.")
;; => "false is false."
```

ClojureScript has a special predicate (that is, a function that returns `true` or `false`), `nil?`, which tests if some given quantity is `nil` or not. For instance, empty collections are not `nil`:

```
cljs.user> (nil? '())
;; => false
```

The inverse function of `nil?` is called `some?` and explicitly checks that the thing in question is *not* `nil`:

```
cljs.user> (some? '())
;; => true
cljs.user> (some? nil)
;; => false
```

One final note on Booleans: ClojureScript also has two helper functions for working with Booleans: `true?` and `false?`. These are *not* "truthy"; they're literally checking to see if the value in question is `true` or `false`. Observe the following:

```
cljs.user=> (true? 5)
;; => false
cljs.user=> (true? true)
;; => true
cljs.user=> (false? false)
;; => true
cljs.user=> (false? nil)
;; => false
```

A truthy expression does not mean that the expression is literally `true`.

Keywords

Keywords are a particular type that don't have a direct analogy in many languages. They denote quantities that evaluate to themselves:

```
cljs.user> :some-keyword
;; => :some-keyword
```

Keywords' literals are written using a colon (:) like you can see in the previous example. If you want a fully qualified keyword, that is, a keyword represented as a name appended to the namespace it belongs to (we'll see namespaces in depth shortly), you could use a double colon (::) in its literal representation:

```
cljs.user> ::some-ns-keyword
;; => :cljs.user/some-ns-keyword
```

Keywords are conceptually used to represent tags, like key values in HashMaps (though you don't necessarily have to), or different values that a given quantity could take.

Since keywords can be evaluated, they're frequently used as functions on maps. When called, they return the value for that same key in the map. If this sounds confusing, don't worry-we'll expand more on this when we cover maps later on in this chapter.

Symbols

Symbols function sort of like pointers or references in other languages-they resolve to other values. Since ClojureScript is a Lisp, not only are we able to manipulate the underlying values of these symbols, but we can also write code that points to and manipulates the symbols themselves via macros, which we'll cover in detail in Chapter 3, *Advanced ClojureScript Concepts*. For now, let's define a var object:

```
cljs.user> (def a 4)
```

Now let's check the type of a. To be clear, we want to check the type of the symbol a, not the 4 that a resolves to. In order to do this, we must work with a as a symbol, else it will simply give us the type of what a evaluates to. We do this by calling quote on a, which tells ClojureScript to pass the code itself to the outer form, rather than evaluating it and then passing the evaluated result:

```
cljs.user> (type (quote a))
;; => cljs.core/Symbol
```

When we look at macros, we'll see more advanced constructs involving symbols.

Whew! Now we've discussed the basic ClojureScript types and the concepts of true, false, and nil, let's take a deep breath and delve into one of ClojureScript's great strengths: its immutable collection types.

ClojureScript collections

At the heart of ClojureScript's collections are a series of interfaces, which dictate what functions you can use with a given data type as well as how those functions work.

If you're not familiar with the notion of interfaces, an interface is simply a set of functions that a given data type must have an implementation for. The implementation does not have to be the same-it just has to have the same name-and typically has to take and return the same types as its arguments and return values. In ClojureScript, interfaces are defined using ClojureScript protocols, which we'll talk more about later in this chapter. We'll be using the term **protocol** henceforth whenever we want to talk about either the abstract idea or the specific implementation of an interface.

In this section, we're going to introduce you to the core collection data types, after which we'll dive deeper into some specific collection protocols that you'll want to know about. Before we do that, however, we'll talk about the one protocol that all collections satisfy: the collection protocol, **ICollection**.

As an example, having this protocol means that the function to add something to a collection has the same name, `conj`, regardless of whether you're adding to a list, a vector, a map, or a set. The collection protocol includes the following three functions:

- `conj`: This function adds a new element to a collection
- `count`: This function returns the number of items in a collection
- `seq`: This function converts a collection to a sequence

As we go through each of these data structures, we'll show an example of the usage of `conj` and `seq`, but since `count` is fairly straightforward, it doesn't really warrant repeated demonstrations.

Lists

At the heart of all Lisp languages is the list, and ClojureScript is no exception. If you haven't worked with a Lisp language previously, this might be confusing-you might be thinking "lists? I haven't seen any lists so far!" If that's true, you're in for a surprise.

You've probably noticed by now that all of the code you've written in ClojureScript is wrapped in parentheses—in some cases many, many parentheses. What you may not have realized is that these expressions you've been writing so far are not only code, they're also data: lists.

Let's look at an extremely simple example:

```
cljs.user=> (+ 1 2)
;; => 3
```

In this example, the expression (+ 1 2) is actually a ClojureScript list with three items in it: the function +, and the integers 1 and 2. Let's prove it by checking its type:

```
cljs.user=> (type (+ 1 2))
;; => #object[Number "function Number() {
  [native code]
}"]
```

Wait, what's going on here? We just said it was going to be a list-were we lying? Well, no. What's happening is that the ClojureScript compiler is first evaluating the contents of the list and then passing the result to our type call. In effect, we've just done the same thing as follows:

```
cljs.user=> (type 3)
;; => #object[Number "function Number() {
  [native code]
}"]
```

Lists are unique among ClojureScript collections in that when they are passed to the ClojureScript compiler, they're automatically evaluated as function calls. If we want to keep them in list form and not evaluate the function in the calling position, we'll need to rely on the quote function we used earlier:

```
cljs.user=> (quote (+ 1 2))
;; => (+ 1 2)
cljs.user=> (type (quote (+ 1 2)))
;; => cljs.core/List
```

The quote function isn't really a function; it's another special form, which means it works directly with the ClojureScript compiler. If we want to create lists without having to call quote on them, we can also use the list function to create them directly. Let's give that a shot:

```
cljs.user=> (list + 1 2)
;; => (#object[cljs$core$_PLUS_ "function
cljs$core$_PLUS_(var_args) {
  var args6798 = [];
  var len__5243__auto___6804 = arguments.length;
  var i__5244__auto___6805 = (0);
  while(true) {
    if((i__5244__auto___6805 < len__5243__auto___6804)) {
      args6798.push((arguments[i__5244__auto___6805]));
```

```
      var G__6806 = (i__5244__auto___6805 + (1));
      i__5244__auto___6805 = G__6806;
      continue;
    }
    else {
    }
    break;
  }
  var G__6803 = args6798.length;
  switch (G__6803) {
    case 0:
    return cljs.core._PLUS_.cljs$core$IFn$_invoke$arity$0();
    break;
    case 1:
    return
    cljs.core._PLUS_.cljs$core$IFn$_invoke$arity$1
      ((arguments[(0)]));
    break;
    case 2:
    return cljs.core._PLUS_.cljs$core$IFn$_invoke$arity$2
      ((arguments[(0)]),(arguments[(1)]));
    break;
    default:
    var argseq__5262__auto__ = (new
    cljs.core.IndexedSeq(args6798.slice((2)),(0)));
    return
    cljs.core._PLUS_.cljs$core$IFn$_invoke$arity$variadic
      ((arguments[(0)]),(arguments[(1)]),argseq__5262__auto__);
  }
}"] 1 2)
```

Whoa, what happened there!? It looks like the + operator was replaced with a whole lot of obfuscated JavaScript code.

 This sort of JavaScript code generation often involves the creation of variables with unique names like `argseq__5262__auto__`. It's likely that the JavaScript code generated on your computer will look different from the preceding code and could be significantly different if you're using an REPL that targets a different JavaScript runtime.

When we were talking about symbols, we tried calling `quote` on a and got the name of the variable back, that is, we got a back, not 4, even though we had defined the var a as 4. Something similar is happening here because we're using `quote` on a list that includes + and everything inside the list is quoted, meaning that the + we get back is a *symbol*, not the underlying function. By contrast, when we create the list directly, we get the value that has been defined for +, which in this case is the underlying JavaScript code for + in string form.

Let's test this hypothesis out at the REPL. Let's grab the first element from the list:

```
cljs.user=> (first (quote (+ 1 2)))
;; => +
```

Now let's see what type it is:

```
cljs.user=> (type (first (quote (+ 1 2))))
;; => cljs.core/Symbol
```

We'll avoid reprinting that obfuscated JavaScript function here in this book to save space, but we can confirm that the the value of + really is that function by just entering + by itself into the REPL:

```
cljs.user=> +
;; => <long JavaScript function here>
```

Let's look at some simpler list examples. Although lists are usually used for code, there's no reason we can't use them as simple data carriers as well:

```
cljs.user=> (def l (list 1 2 3))
;; => #'cljs.user/l
```

If we `conj` a new element onto the list, note that it gets prepended to the front:

```
cljs.user=> (conj l 4)
;; => (4 1 2 3)
```

Because lists satisfy the Sequence protocol, calling `seq` on a list just returns the list:

```
cljs.user=> (seq l)
;; => (1 2 3)
```

Vectors

In principle, ClojureScript vectors can be thought of as sort of like immutable JavaScript arrays. Since immutable arrays don't exist natively in JavaScript, ClojureScript vectors are custom implementations of the idea. The important thing to understand here is that the two are not the same, and although you can trivially convert from one to the other, they're not interchangeable. We'll be covering immutability at greater length later on in this chapter, but, for now, the key thing to realize is that the items in a ClojureScript vector can't be changed but the items in a JavaScript array can.

Vectors can be instantiated directly using either brackets or the vector constructor function:

```
cljs.user=> ["a" "vector" "of" "awesome" "things"]
;; => ["a" "vector" "of" "awesome" "things"]
cljs.user=> (vector "another" "cool" "vector")
;; => ["another" "cool" "vector"]
```

You can also create them by casting a different collection type to a vector:

```
cljs.user=> (vec (list "I" "once" "was" "a" "list"))
;; => ["I" "once" "was" "a" "list"]
```

Vectors are great for whenever you might want to keep an ordered list of things that you want to index into.

Adding a new element to a vector is straightforward and gets added to the end. Note that because vectors are immutable, this is technically creating an entirely new vector and returning it with the new values:

```
cljs.user=> (conj [1 2 3] 4)
;; => [1 2 3 4]
```

You can retrieve a value from the vector by calling the get function with the item's index:

```
cljs.user=> (get ["peanut" "butter" "sandwiches"] 2)
;; => "sandwiches"
```

Trying to retrieve a value from an index outside of the bounds of the vector will return nil unless a default value is provided as an argument to get:

```
cljs.user=> (get ["peanut" "butter" "sandwiches"] 3)
;; => nil
cljs.user=> (get ["peanut" "butter" "sandwiches"] 3 "nub")
;; => "nub"
```

You can also call the vector directly, which behaves the same as calling get:

```
cljs.user=> (["peanut" "butter" "sandwiches"] 1)
;; => "butter"
```

Calling seq gives us a sequence:

```
cljs.user=> (seq [1 2 3])
;; => (1 2 3)
```

Converting between JavaScript arrays and ClojureScript vectors is easy. Let's start by creating a JavaScript array at the REPL. There are a few different ways we can do this. One way is by invoking the js interop namespace:

```
cljs.user=> (js/Array. 1 2 3)
;; => #js [1 2 3]
```

Another way involves using the #js reader macro. If this sounds confusing, don't worry-we'll cover JavaScript interoperability in more detail later on in this chapter.

```
cljs.user=> #js [4 5 6]
;; => #js [4 5 6]
```

Let's just check to make sure it's the right type:

```
cljs.user=> (type #js [])
;; => #object[Array "function Array() {
    [native code]
}"]
```

Great, that's what we were expecting. Let's store an array as a var and compare it to a ClojureScript vector with the same values:

```
cljs.user=> (def arr (js/Array. 1 2 3))
;; => #'cljs.user/arr
cljs.user=> (def v [1 2 3])
;; => #'cljs.user/v
```

Note that even though they have the same values, they're not the same:

```
cljs.user=> (= arr v)
;; => false
```

We can easily convert from one type to the other by relying on two of ClojureScript's handy interoperability functions: clj->js and js->clj:

```
cljs.user=> (clj->js v)
;; => #js [1 2 3]
```

Great, so they should be equal now, right?

```
cljs.user=> (= (clj->js v) arr)
;; => false
```

Wait, what? Two arrays with the same values aren't equal? Maybe we're converting them wrong. What about if we just compare two JavaScript arrays with the same values:

```
cljs.user=> (= #js [1 2 3] #js [1 2 3])
;; => false
```

That's just how JavaScript works! Let's test this out in our browser's JavaScript console (press Cmd +Option +J to open a console on chrome on Mac):

```
> a = []
[]
> b = []
[]
> a == b
false
> a === b
false
> a == a
true
> a === a
true
```

In JavaScript, testing array equality checks to see if the objects themselves are the same, not whether their values are the same. The equality check of JavaScript arrays exhibits the same behavior when executed from ClojureScript as it does in JavaScript.

We've already proven that two JavaScript arrays with the same values aren't equal, but what about the same array? That should be equal to itself:

```
cljs.user=> (= arr arr)
;; => true
```

Since casting from ClojureScript to JavaScript will create a new JavaScript array each time, this means unfortunately we can't check equality for the same ClojureScript vector if we cast it to an array multiple times:

```
cljs.user=> (= (clj->js v) (clj->js v))
;; => false
```

Fortunately, the same behavior isn't true in the other direction! If we cast both objects to ClojureScript, where vectors are immutable, we have no problem comparing them on the basis of their values:

```
cljs.user=> (= (js->clj arr) v)
;; => true
```

When should I use lists versus vectors?

Although it can be confusing to understand what makes lists and vectors distinct, the two data structures have very different algorithmic properties. New elements are appended to the front of a list in constant time, while new elements are added to the end of a vector in constant time. Specific elements can be retrieved and updated from a vector in constant time (assuming you know which index the element is at), whereas accessing the *n*th element of a list requires linear time and cannot be changed without instantiating and allocating memory for a new list.

Under the hood, vectors are similar to arrays as as algorithmic data structures, while lists can be thought of as linked lists.

In practice, since ClojureScript lists are used primarily as data to be to be passed to the compiler, and due to prepend efficiency being useful only in specific use cases, lists are usually used when you're writing or manipulating code, while vectors tend to be used when you're writing and manipulating data (which will be most of the time).

Maps

Like vectors, ClojureScript's maps can be considered as akin to immutable versions of JavaScript objects. They are key-value data structures ideal for storing and passing around data and you should expect to use them frequently:

You can instantiate them directly as follows:

```
cljs.user=> {:name "David" :age 28}
;; => {:name "David", :age 28}
cljs.user=> (hash-map :type :book :title "Learning ClojureScript")
;; => {:type :book, :title "Learning ClojureScript"}
```

 Note that because maps are key-value data structures, you should take care to make sure every key has a value defined, otherwise the compiler will throw an exception.

You can store maps within maps, as both keys and values. For instance:

```
cljs.user=>{:address {:city "San Francisco"} {:family "siblings"}
{:brother "paul"}}
    ;; => {:address {:city "San Francisco"}, {:family "siblings"} {:brother
"paul"}}
```

Similarly, and unlike JavaScript objects, ClojureScript maps can use fairly arbitrary types as keys. It's rarer for something to not be a valid map key than the other way around.

For maps, due to the need for an addition to have both a key and a value, `conj` requires that the item being added be able to use `seq` (and to be include at least two elements, though everything after the first two will be dropped). This means that this throws an exception:

```
cljs.user=> (conj {} :a)
;; => #object[Error Error: :a is not ISeqable]
```

But both of the following will work (among other possibilities):

```
cljs.user=> (conj {} [:a 1])
;; => {:a 1}
cljs.user=> (conj {} {:a 1})
;; => {:a 1}
```

You can remove keys from a map by calling `dissoc`:

```
cljs.user=> (dissoc {:a 1 :b 2} :b)
;; => {:a 1}
```

There are several ways you can retrieve a value from a map. If the key is a keyword, you can call it as the accessor function:

```
cljs.user=> (:a {:a :b})
;; => :b
```

As with vectors, the `get` function also works on maps and takes two arguments: the first is the key you're trying to retrieve and the second is an optional default value if that key isn't found:

```
cljs.user=> (get {1 :a} 1)
;; => :a
cljs.user=> (get {2 :b} 3)
;; => nil
cljs.user=> (get {3 :c} 1 "other-value")
;; => "other-value"
```

Again, as with vectors, you can call the map directly as if it were any other function; this is another shorthand for calling the `get` function and behaves the same way:

```
cljs.user=> ({1 :a} 1)
;; => :a
```

Calling `seq` on a map will return a sequence where each element is a vector pair of a single key and its associated value:

```
cljs.user=> (seq {:b 1 :c 2})
;; => ([:b 1] [:c 2])
```

Like vectors, you can also easily cast a ClojureScript map to a JavaScript object:

```
cljs.user=> (def m {:name "David"})
;; => #'cljs.user/m
cljs.user=> (clj->js m)
;; => #js {:name "David"}
```

As with arrays, JavaScript doesn't support direct equality comparisons on the basis of JavaScript object values. Two objects are only equal if they are the same object:

```
cljs.user=> (= #js {"name" "Rafik"} #js {"name" "Rafik"})
;; => false
cljs.user=> (def obj #js {"name" "Rafik"})
#'cljs.user/obj
cljs.user=> (= obj obj)
;; => true
```

And again, ClojureScript's data structures support equality on the basis of data equality since the underlying structure is immutable:

```
cljs.user=> (= {:name "David"} {:name "David"})
;; => true
```

Different types of maps

Most of the time in ClojureScript, you'll be working with either ArrayMaps or HashMaps. ArrayMaps happen to be very efficient at small sizes (typically when there are less than eight keys), but HashMaps are more efficient at larger sizes. ClojureScript will automatically convert ArrayMaps to HashMaps for you as your map grows. Observe the following:

```
cljs.user=> (def y {:a 1 :b 2 :c 3})
;; => #'cljs.user/y
cljs.user=> (type y)
;; => cljs.core/PersistentArrayMap
cljs.user=> (type (assoc y :d 4 :e 5 :f 6 :g 7 :h 8 :i 9))
;; => cljs.core/PersistentHashMap
```

When you use the generic map syntax { }, ClojureScript will automatically figure out which type is more appropriate for you. You can also deliberately create a new map of a specific type by calling the constructor function for that map type (that is, either HashMap or ArrayMap).

In addition to array-maps and hash-maps, ClojureScript also has support for sorted-maps, which, as the name suggests, preserve the keys in sorted order. These can be created simply as follows:

```
cljs.user=> (sorted-map :c 3 :b 2 :a 1)
;; => {:a 1, :b 2, :c 3}
```

Sets

Last, but certainly not the least, are ClojureScript's set data structures. These are simply instantiated as follows:

```
cljs.user=> (def s #{1 2 3})
;; => #'cljs.user/s
```

You can also create a set with the hash-set function:

```
cljs.user=> (hash-set 1 1 2 3)
;; => #{1 2 3}
```

Note that while duplicate items will be automatically removed when you use hash-set, if you try to include them as part of the default set syntax, an exception will be thrown:

```
cljs.user=> #{1 1}
;; => clojure.lang.ExceptionInfo: Duplicate key: 1 {:type :reader-
exception, :line 1, :column 7, :file "NO_SOURCE_FILE"}
```

New items can be easily added with conj:

```
cljs.user=> (conj s 4)
;; => #{1 3 2 4}
cljs.user=> (conj s 1)
;; => #{1 3 2}
```

And they can be removed with disj:

```
cljs.user=> (disj s 2)
;; => #{1 3}
```

You can check for `set` membership with `get`, like with vectors and maps:

```
cljs.user=> (get #{1 2 3} 1)
;; => 1
cljs.user=> (get #{1 2 3} "other")
;; => nil
cljs.user=> (get #{1 2 3} "other" :default)
;; => :default
```

You can also use `contains?` to check `set` membership:

```
cljs.user=> (contains? #{1 2 3} 1)
;; => true
```

And as with vectors and maps, you can also call sets as functions:

```
cljs.user=> (#{1 2 3} 2)
;; => 2
```

This introduces a very handy way of using the `filter` function to filter for specific values:

```
cljs.user=> (filter #{1 2 3} [1 3 5])
;; => (1 3)
```

Like strings, ClojureScript supports a host of other operations via an external namespace-in this case, `clojure.set`. Let's take a look at some of these core operations:

```
cljs.user=> (clojure.set/union #{1 3} #{1 2})
;; => #{1 3 2}
cljs.user=> (clojure.set/difference #{1 3} #{1 2})
;; => #{3}
cljs.user=> (clojure.set/intersection #{1 3} #{1 2})
;; => #{1}
```

Although ES6 introduced support for sets, at the current moment, browser support for them is not universal. As a result, calling `clj->js` creates a JavaScript array instead:

```
cljs.user=> (clj->js s)
;; => #js [1 3 2]
```

Sequences

Lastly, we have sequences. Sequences are an abstraction rather than a specific data type, though their semantics are so consistent that the abstraction feels very much like a single data structure. In this regard, it can be helpful to think of sequences as a "view" on top of a concrete underlying data structure. Sequences are one of the most important abstractions in both Clojure and ClojureScript, and as their analog doesn't exist in many languages, it can take a while for those new to the language to understand what makes sequences so special.

A sequence is a logical list with a head (the first item of the sequence) and a remainder (the remaining elements of the list). Sequences are commonly referred to as `seq`s; these terms can be used interchangeably but we'll refer to them as sequences in this book.

Attempting to construct a sequence with no elements returns `nil`. Since `nil` is falsey, this is the idiomatic method for testing if a collection has no elements:

```
cljs.user=> (seq {})
;; => nil
cljs.user=> (if (seq {}) true false)
;; => false
```

Sequences are associated with the concrete protocol `ISeq`, which requires three functions: `first`, `rest` and `cons`:

- `first`: This function returns the first element in the sequence.
- `rest`: This function returns the remaining elements in the sequence. If there are no elements remaining, it returns an empty sequence.
- `cons`: This function creates a new sequence, with the new element appended to the head of the sequence.

You may be wondering about the difference between the `conj` and `cons` functions since both functions add new elements to the front of the underlying list:

```
cljs.user=> (conj (seq [1 2 3]) 3)
;; => (3 1 2 3)
cljs.user=> (cons 3 (seq [1 2 3]))
;; => (3 1 2 3)
```

The difference is that `cons` always returns a lazy sequence and doesn't require realizing the collection that is passed in, while `conj` returns a realized collection of the same type that is passed into it.

It's worth noting that all sequences are collections, but not all collections are sequences (though they can all be explicitly cast to sequences by means of the seq function). For instance, vectors aren't sequences, though they can be cast as such.

Sequences and most of their related functions are akin to iterators like for or foreach, but function differently. Since sequences are immutable, they aren't stateful cursors into a collection, but rather are persistent and immutable views.

It is possible to write new data structures that are not immutable and that satisfy the sequence protocol, but this is a bad idea. Because a sequence can be evaluated lazily, building one on top of a mutable data structure might mean that the underlying data structure sees changes happen after seq has been called. It is, in general, an especially bad idea to attempt to mutate a data structure that a sequence has been built on top of.

Laziness

Due to the nature of sequences, most sequences are *lazy*. This means that functions that return sequences do so incrementally as they are consumed. New functions that return sequences can be written to return lazy sequences by wrapping the body in the lazy-seq macro.

We can see what laziness looks like in practice:

```
cljs.user=> (defn lazy-func [x] (println "Printed" x))
;; => #'cljs.user/lazy-func
cljs.user=> (take 2 (map lazy-func (seq [1 2 3 4 5])))
Printed 1
Printed 2
;; => (nil nil)
```

Here, even though we passed in a sequence with five elements, lazy-func was only evaluated twice because both seq and map are lazy functions.

One really cool consequence of lazy sequences is that we can actually have sequences that are infinitely long! The range function, for instance, when invoked with no arguments, returns an infinite sequence. Don't try to call it at the REPL; it'll generate an infinite sequence of numbers and eventually your REPL will run out of memory and crash (and potentially your whole computer, while you're at it!).

You can bypass this sort of infinite consumption by setting the global dynamic variable `*print-length*` to something finite as follows:

```
cljs.user=> (set! *print-length* 5)
;; => 5

cljs.user=> (range)
;; => (0 1 2 3 4 ...)
```

If you want to call an infinitely long sequence, make sure you're very careful to only reference a specific number of its elements, like so:

```
cljs.user=> (take 5 (range))
;; => (0 1 2 3 4)
```

Or, alternatively:

```
cljs.user=> (range 5)
;; => (0 1 2 3 4)
```

Collection protocols

We've already covered the general collection protocol earlier in this chapter, but there are a few other collection protocols that are worth talking about.

Sequential

The sequential protocol (not to be confused with sequences that we've been talking a lot about) requires that the core functions of sequences are supported (`first`, `rest`, `cons`), but also that the collection retains a linear ordering under insertion and deletion.

Let's take a look at these in the context of vectors:

```
cljs.user=> (first [1 2 3])
;; => 1
cljs.user=> (rest [1 2 3])
;; => (2 3)
cljs.user=> (cons 4 [1 2 3])
;; => (4 1 2 3)
```

You can check to see if a given value is sequential with sequential?

```
cljs.user=> (sequential? [])
;; => true
cljs.user=> (sequential? {})
;; => false
cljs.user=> (sequential? #{})
;; => false
cljs.user=> (sequential? (list 1 2 3))
;; => true
```

Associative

Associative collections support key-value lookups. Under the hood, associative data structures implement the following methods:

- -lookup: This returns the value at the given key
- -assoc: This store a new value at the given key

In practice, you should use more idiomatic ClojureScript functions like get, contains?, and assoc when working with associative data structures. We've covered the usage of the get request earlier in this chapter, but we haven't talked about the others yet, so let's cover those.

The contains? function is like get, only it just checks to see if a value exists at that key and returns Boolean true or false:

```
cljs.user=> (contains? {:a 1 :b 2} :a)
;; => true
cljs.user=> (contains? {:a 1 :b 2} :c)
;; => false
```

Maps are the canonical associative collections as key-value data structures, but what may not be obvious is that vectors are also associative due to the fact that their indexes operate like keys. Let's give that a try:

```
cljs.user=> (contains? ["apple" "pear" "banana"] 1)
;; => true
cljs.user=> (contains? ["apple" "pear" "banana"] 3)
;; => false
```

Note that this isn't a search for the contents of the vector:

```
cljs.user=> (contains? ["apple" "pear" "banana"] "apple")
;; => false
```

Lastly, we have `assoc` as a way of setting new values at a given key:

```
cljs.user=> (assoc {:a 3} :b 2)
;; => {:a 3, :b 2}
cljs.user=> (assoc {:a 3} :a 2)
;; => {:a 2}
```

This also works with vectors in the same way as `get`, where the key is the vector's index:

```
cljs.user=> (assoc ["apple" "pear" "banana"] 0 "peach")
;; => ["peach" "pear" "banana"]
```

Although you can add new keys to a map with `assoc`, if you're going to add a *new* key to a vector that way, you'll need to be precise about adding to the index one further than the length of the vector, as attempting to set a value at an index more than one beyond the range of the vector will throw an exception:

```
cljs.user=> (assoc ["apple" "pear" "banana"] 3 "peach")
;; => ["apple" "pear" "banana" "peach"]
cljs.user=> (assoc ["apple" "pear" "banana"] 4 "peach")
#object[Error Error: Index 4 out of bounds   [0,3]]
Error: Index 4 out of bounds   [0,3]
```

You can check to see if a given value is associative by calling `associative?`:

```
cljs.user=> (associative? [])
;; => true
cljs.user=> (associative? {})
;; => true
cljs.user=> (associative? #{})
;; => false
```

Sorted

As the name suggests, a sorted collection is able to support fast insertion and retrieval operations while maintaining a sorted order. Both `sorted-maps` and `sorted-sets` functions satisfy the sorted protocol. You can check whether a collection satisfies the sorted protocol by asking `sorted?`:

```
cljs.user=> (sorted? (sorted-map :a 1 :b 2))
;; => true
cljs.user=> (sorted? (hash-map :a 1 :b 2))
;; => false
```

Calling `seq` on a sorted collection will return a sequence that has the elements in sorted order, but be aware that the generated sequence no longer satisfies the sorted protocol. This means that once you cast `seq` on a sorted collection, any inserts to the returned sequence will not retain a sorted order.

Counted

Collections that satisfy the counted protocol execute `count` in constant time. Lists, maps, sets, sequences, and vectors all satisfy counted, but lazy sequences do not. Lazy sequences not satisfying count should be obvious reasons in order to obtain the count the sequence would have to be evaluated, which by definition would not be lazy! Let's take a look again at that example of laziness from earlier, but this time let's try getting the `count`:

```
cljs.user=> cljs.user=> (count (map lazy-func (seq [1 2 3 4 5])))
Printed 1
Printed 2
Printed 3
Printed 4
Printed 5
;; => 5
```

In order to get the count of the original data structure, we needed to realize the entire sequence, which means we ended up calling `lazy-func` on each item in the sequence? This is an aspect of laziness that one needs to be aware of-if side effects (like printing to the console's standard output) are an aspect of the lazy sequence, then calling `count` on them will cause those side effects to be evaluated!

There's another gotcha to remember when calling `count`-remember how we talked about infinite lazy sequences earlier on in this chapter? Don't call `count` on an infinite sequence-it'll attempt to realize the entire sequence, which will cause you to run out of memory!

You can check whether a collection satisfies counted protocol with `counted?`:

```
cljs.user=> (counted? (seq [1 2 3]))
;; => true
cljs.user=> (counted? (seq {:a 1 :b 2}))
;; => true
```

Although strings are not collections, and therefore cannot satisfy the `counted?` interface, calling `count` on a string does return in constant time:

```
cljs.user=> (count "banana")
;; => 6
```

Reversible

The reversible protocol has a single method, `rseq`, and in general means that the sequence in question can be accessed from the opposite end in constant time. Vectors, sorted-maps, and sorted-sets are all reversible. The `rseq` method functions just like `seq`, only it returns a sequence in reverse sequential order:

```
cljs.user=> (rseq (sorted-map :c 3 :b 2 :a 1))
;; => ([:c 3] [:b 2] [:a 1])
cljs.user=> (rseq [1 2 3])
;; => (3 2 1)
```

Object-oriented programming

Even though ClojureScript is a functional language, it has support for object-oriented style programming. In particular, ClojureScript, like Clojure, has the notion of protocols, types, and records. We've already encountered *protocols*, and now we're going to take a closer look at how the dynamics of these concepts work in practice.

Protocols

As we should now know from our exploration of ClojureScript's collections, a protocol in ClojureScript specifies a function interface that an object must support. For instance, let's define a new protocol, `IMonster`:

```
cljs.user=> (defprotocol IMonster
  (roar [this])
  (scare [this other]))
;; => nil
```

Here we've defined a new "monster" protocol. In order for any subsequently defined object to satisfy the monster protocol, it must have implementations of the two methods, `roar` and `scare`, we've enumerated here. The `roar` method only takes the monster itself as an argument, but the `scare` method requires an `other` argument to be passed in as well. Although ClojureScript doesn't strictly enforce this, you'll probably want to make sure your implementations all take and return the same types.

Types

A type in ClojureScript is analogous to a class in many other languages-we're declaring an object that supports certain methods and we're also defining the specific implementation of those methods:

```
cljs.user=> (deftype Human [name age]
  Object
  (getName [this] name)
  (getAge [this] age)
  (panic [this] (println "Aaaaaaagh!")))
;; => nil
```

Here we've defined a new type, Human, which inherits from the base type, Object. A human must have an age and a name. Let's define a new Human, which we'll name after my mom:

```
cljs.user=> (new Human "Hazel" 50)
;; => #object[cljs.user.Human]
```

Let's store hazel as a var and make sure she's really a Human:

```
cljs.user=> (def hazel (new Human "Hazel" 50))
;; => #'cljs.user/hazel
cljs.user=> (.getName hazel)
;; => "Hazel"
cljs.user=> (.getAge hazel)
;; => 50
cljs.user=> (.panic hazel)
;; => Aaaaaaagh!
nil
```

Whew! Okay. Now, let's define a monster as well:

```
cljs.user=> (deftype Troll [name]
  IMonster
  (roar [this] (println "ROAAAAR!!!")))
;; => cljs.user/Troll
```

Let's make sure Troll satisfies IMonster:

```
cljs.user=> (satisfies? IMonster (new Troll "Bork"))
true
```

Hmmm. That's weird. `Troll` doesn't actually satisfy `IMonster` since it's missing an implementation for scare. Unfortunately, the compiler takes its cue from the fact that we told it that `Troll` was an `IMonster` and doesn't throw an error when not all of the functions have implementations-the responsibility for making sure our Trolls are really monsters is on us. Let's try that again:

```
cljs.user=> (deftype Troll [name]
IMonster
(roar [this] (println "ROAAAAR!!!"))
(scare [this other] (.panic other)))
;; => cljs.user/Troll
```

Great. Now, just for laughs, let's have `Wilhelm` scare `hazel`:

```
cljs.user=> (def wilhelm (new Troll "Wilhelm"))
;; => #'cljs.user/wilhelm
cljs.user=> (scare wilhelm hazel)
Aaaaaaagh!
;; => nil
```

One difference you might notice, if you're playing around with this code at your own REPL, is that we can call `scare` directly without a period in front of it, that is, without using special JavaScript interoperability syntax sugar. This is because the `defprotocol` defines new ClojureScript functions over defined data types, whereas specifying the function within the context of the `deftype` without an associated protocol means that the function is only defined as a JavaScript method on that type.

Records

Lastly, we have records. Records are similar to types, only instead of being extremely bare-bones objects, they are extensions of a base class that provides built-in `hash-map` like features for fast and easy accessing of attributes. It can be helpful to think of records as being basically maps that happen to support additional functions and that can also satisfy protocols.

Like protocols and types, records are defined simply with `defrecord`. Let's define a basic record for ourselves:

```
cljs.user=> (defrecord Lair [place])
;; => cljs.user/Lair
cljs.user=> (def hideout (new Lair "cave"))
;; => #'cljs.user/hideout
cljs.user=> (:place hideout)
;; => "cave"
```

Records satisfy the `map` protocol and as such can be treated like maps:

```
cljs.user=> (map? hideout)
;; => true
cljs.user=> (assoc hideout :atmosphere "dark and wet")
;; => #cljs.user.Lair{:place "cave", :atmosphere "dark and wet"}
```

Note, however, that if you `dissoc` a required key from a record, you'll get back a plain map, not an instance of the given record type:

```
cljs.user=> (dissoc (assoc hideout :atmosphere "dark and wet") :place)
;; => {:atmosphere "dark and wet"}
```

Like types, records can also satisfy protocols:

```
cljs.user=> (defrecord Vampire [name]
IMonster
  (roar [this] (println "Actually, we vampires are rather quiet. "))
  (scare [this other] (.panic other)))
;; => cljs.user/Vampire
cljs.user=> (def drac (new Vampire "Dracula"))
;; => #'cljs.user/drac
cljs.user=> (roar drac)
Actually, we vampires are rather quiet.
;; => nil
cljs.user=> (:name drac)
;; => "Dracula"
```

Extending types and protocols

So far we've seen how to define types and protocols in a single block, but ClojureScript also gives us tools with which to extend existing types and protocols. Let's define a new record:

```
cljs.user=> (defrecord WereWolf [name])
;; => cljs.user/WereWolf
```

Now, our `WereWolf` record doesn't satisfy `IMonster` yet. But we can extend it so that it does:

```
cljs.user=> (extend-type WereWolf
IMonster
(roar [this] (println "Growl!"))
(scare [this other] (println "*silent panic*")))
;; => #object[Function "function (this$,other){
var this$__$1 = this;
return cljs.core.println.call(null,"*silent panic*");
}"]
```

```
cljs.user=> (roar (WereWolf. "james"))
Growl!
;; => nil
```

We can also go about this by another way-adding a protocol and associated implementations to an existing type:

```
cljs.user=> (defprotocol ISecretive
  (hide [this]))
;; => nil
cljs.user=> (extend-protocol ISecretive
  Vampire
  (hide [this] (println "..."))
  WereWolf
  (hide [this] (println "rustle rustle")))
#object[Function "function (this$){
var this$__$1 = this;
return cljs.core.println.call(null,"rustle rustle");
}"]
```

Note that this will also extend any existing instances of the relevant type:

```
cljs.user=> (hide drac)
...
nil
```

Reify

Lastly, if you know that you're not going to need a full record or type definition, you can declare a single instance of an anonymous type with `reify`. Unlike `deftype` and `defprotocol`, `reify` doesn't create factories for new instances of its provided type:

```
cljs.user=> (def mouse
                (reify ISecretive
                (hide [this] (println "Squeak!"))))
;; => #'cljs.user/mouse
cljs.user=> (hide mouse)
Squeak!
;; => nil
```

Other ClojureScript types

We're almost at the end of our tour of ClojureScript types, but there are two important types remaining: regular expressions and atoms. Both are extremely important and are likely to come up at some point as you work in ClojureScript, so it's worth talking about them.

Regular expressions

ClojureScript regular expressions are simple JavaScript `RegExp` instances. You can create them using ClojureScript's regular expression literal syntax:

```
cljs.user=> (type #"^Clojure")
;; => #object[RegExp "function RegExp() { [native code] }"]
```

You can also create them directly as JavaScript `RegExp` instances:

```
cljs.user=> (js/RegExp. "^Clojure$")
;; => #"^Clojure$"
```

In addition to supporting basic JavaScript `RegExp` functions via ClojureScript's direct interoperability, there are a number of core regular expression methods including:

- `re-find`: This returns the first match of a regular expression in a string. If there are multiple matches or groups, it returns a vector.
- `re-matches`: This returns the match of a regular expression in a string if it fully matches.
- `re-pattern`: This compiles a regular expression from a string.

Regular expressions are a deep area of study and fully explaining how regular expressions work in JavaScript is beyond the scope of this book. However, there are many resources online that will help. A good place to start is Mozilla's developer reference available at https://developer.mozilla.org/en-US/docs/Web/JavaScript/Guide/Regular_Expressions.

Atoms

Atoms in ClojureScript are mutable data structures that are useful to manage changing states in your application. Atoms are metastructures that can hold any of the data structure we've talked about in this chapter. Atoms are created with the `atom` function:

```
cljs.user=> (def an-atom (atom 5))
;; => #'cljs.user/an-atom
cljs.user=> an-atom
;; => #object [cljs.core.Atom {:val 5}]
cljs.user=> (def another-atom (atom {:a "value"}))
;; => #'cljs.user/another-atom
cljs.user=> another-atom
;; => #object [cljs.core.Atom {:val {:a "value"}}]
```

To extract the specific value in an atom, you can dereference it with `deref` or with the syntactical shorthand @:

```
cljs.user=> @an-atom
;; => 5
cljs.user=> @another-atom
;; => {:a "value"}
```

To update the value within an atom, you have two options: you can use `swap!` to atomically apply a function to the existing contents of the atom or you can use `reset!` to directly store a new value in an existing atom. Both `swap!` and `reset!` return the updated value being stored in the atom.

Since `reset!` is simpler, let's look at that first:

```
cljs.user=> (reset! an-atom 3)
;; => 3
```

Now, let's look at some examples of using `swap!`. First, let's try just increasing the value in `an-atom` by 1:

```
cljs.user=> (swap! an-atom inc)
;; => 4
cljs.user=> (swap! another-atom assoc :b "Other")
;; => {:a "value", :b "Other"}
```

We can also add a `watch` function to the atom, which will be called whenever the state of the atom changes:

```
cljs.user=> (def new-atom (atom {}))
;; => #'cljs.user/new-atom
cljs.user=> (defn watcher-fn [key the-atom old-value new-value]
  (println key the-atom old-value new-value))
;; => #'cljs.user/watcher-fn
cljs.user=> (add-watch new-atom :watcher-key watcher-fn)
;; => #object [cljs.core.Atom {:val {}}]
cljs.user=> (reset! new-atom {:a 2})
:watcher-key #object [cljs.core.Atom {:val {:a 2}}] {} {:a 2}
;; => {:a 2}
```

The `add-watch` parameter requires three functions: the atom to watch, a key, and the `watcher` function. The key value here in this case is so that you can remove a watcher later, if you want:

```
cljs.user=> (remove-watch new-atom :watcher-key)
;; => #object [cljs.core.Atom {:val {:a 2}}]
cljs.user=> (reset! new-atom {:b 4})
```

```
;; => {:b 4}
```

The `watcher` function itself takes four arguments: the key of the `watcher` function, the atom itself, its value prior to the change, and its value after the change.

Immutability

Now that you've had a basic introduction to ClojureScript's data structures, let's talk a bit about *immutability*. Almost all of ClojureScript's data types are immutable, which means that once they're defined, including them in an expression won't change their underlying value. This concept can take a bit of getting used to, so let's take a look at a few examples. As a point of contrast, we'll use JavaScript as an example of a language where data types are *mutable*.

Let's start with an example using a vector. First, we'll define a vector with one element in it, the integer 1:

```
cljs.user=> (def x [1])
;; => #'cljs.user/x
```

Now, we'll call `conj` on x. We've already talked a bit about how `conj` works earlier in this chapter, but just to review, the `conj` function returns a new vector that consists of the original vector with any of the following arguments added to the original vector:

```
cljs.user=> (conj x 2)
;; => [1 2]
```

Notice that the value of x itself hasn't changed-it's still the original, single-element vector:

```
cljs.user=> x
;; => [1]
```

If we actually wanted x to reflect the larger vector, we'd have to re-define x:

```
cljs.user=> (def x (conj x 2))
;; => #'cljs.user/x
```

x should now contain both values:

```
cljs.user=> x
;; => [1 2]
```

Let's contrast this with a JavaScript array and the `push` method at the console:

```
> x = [1]
[1]
> x.push(2)
2
> x
[1, 2]
```

Here, the array x hasn't been redefined; rather, the original object itself has been changed. If we wanted to redefine x in the same way we did with ClojureScript earlier, we could use JavaScript's `concat` method instead, which doesn't mutate the underlying object:

```
> x = [1]
[1]
> x.concat(2)
[1, 2]
> x
[1]
> x = x.concat(2)
[1, 2]
> x
[1, 2]
```

So, JavaScript does have the ability to enable you to write programs without mutating the underlying objects, but it requires you to know which functions to use. The vast majority of ClojureScript data structures, by contrast, never mutate the underlying object; so you don't have to worry about doing so by accident. Let's look at another example of immutability, this time with ClojureScript maps and JavaScript objects.

We start by defining a ClojureScript map:

```
cljs.user=> (def m {:key :lock})
#'cljs.user/m
```

Now let's `assoc` a key and value into our map. Again, we've covered `assoc` in more detail earlier in this chapter, but for now let's just remember that it returns a new map with a key-value pair added to the original map:

```
cljs.user=> (assoc m :color "gold")
{:key :lock, :color "gold"}
```

Note that, as with `conj`, the underlying var, m, hasn't been changed:

```
cljs.user=> m
{:key :lock}
```

As previously, if we want to change the value of m itself, we'll need to re-define it:

```
cljs.user=> (def m (assoc m :shape "round"))
#'cljs.user/m
cljs.user=> m
{:key :lock, :shape "round"}
```

 Note that redefining variables in this way is discouraged. A better pattern, if you know a variable is going to need to point to a different value at some point in the future, is to use an atom.

Let's compare this with a JavaScript object:

```
> o = {}
Object {}
> o.key = "value"
"value"
> o
Object {key: "value"}
```

As with JavaScript arrays, we haven't redefined o, but by setting the key attribute, we've mutated the underlying object.

You may be wondering why immutability is a desirable characteristic. The answer is that mutability makes it possible for underlying data to be changed at times and in ways that aren't intended or obvious.

For instance, what would happen if you wrote a program that expected the value of o.key to be value but a callback somewhere had set o.key to a different value? Your program would probably throw an error with a stack trace that pointed to the part of your program where you were expecting o.key to be value, but you'd have no easy way of figuring out what line of code was actually responsible for changing the value of o.

This might sound like a contrived example, but in practice, in large production applications, this sort of thing happens all the time and is extremely difficult to debug (particularly if o is being mutated by some sort of asynchronous callback triggered by an event that your application does not directly control or invoke). By contrast, when you encounter a bug in ClojureScript where a map has a value you don't expect, it is easy to walk up the call stack and figure out what part of the program was responsible for adding or using the assoc function for the new value in question.

Another way in which immutability is incredibly valuable, which we've already talked about in this chapter, is that you no longer have to worry about whether or not two objects are "identical" in the JavaScript sense (meaning that they are literally the same object and occupy the same memory address). Instead, you need only to care about whether or not the two objects are functionally equal (as can be calculated by a comparison of their values or any other comparison implementation you might use).

Advanced destructuring and namespaces

In this section, we'll dig further into ClojureScript's destructuring syntax. We'll also learn about ClojureScript namespaces. If you're familiar with JavaScript ES6 modules, namespaces are sort of akin to that-they're essentially modules within which variable and function definitions are located and a collection of imported libraries can be defined, often with local bindings for convenience.

Destructuring

Destructuring in ClojureScript provides a way of binding values to local variables. We've already seen a few simple examples of how this works with the code in previous sections, but destructuring in ClojureScript is extremely powerful and so comprehensive that it's worth looking at some more advanced patterns of it.

First, let's try destructuring the vector [1 2]:

```
cljs.user=> (let [[a b] [1 2]] (+ a b))
;; => 3
```

The same destructuring logic works in a nested fashion:

```
cljs.user=> (let [[[a b] c] [[1 2] 3]] (+ a b c))
;; => 6
```

Alternatively, we could first bind the original vector and then attempt to grab a specific element from it and bind that as well:

```
cljs.user=> (let [[a b] [[1 2] 3]
                  c (first a)]
              (println a)
              c)
[1 2]
;; => 1
```

You'll quickly find that one of the advantages of vector destructuring is that it enables you to bind many values in a small amount of code, without having to individually bind each element as you might in the following case:

```
(let [a (first [1 2 3])
      b (second [1 2 3])
      c (nth [1 2 3] 2)] [a b c])
;; => [1 2 3]
```

Note again that the `let` functions just like `do`, but with a binding section at the beginning. We don't need to bind everything, and similarly we can attempt to bind more than exists in the original vector:

```
cljs.user=> (let [[a] [1 2 3]] [a])
;; => [1]
cljs.user=> (let [[a b c] [1]] [a b c])
;; => [1 nil nil]
```

As we've seen with variadic functions earlier in this chapter, we can use & to bind a variable number of remaining values in a sequence or collection. If we use that first example again but with a variable binding, it might look like the following:

```
cljs.user=> (let [[a & b] [1 2 3]] [a b])
;; => [1 (2 3)]
```

We can also bind the value of the original data structure as follows:

```
cljs.user=> (let [[a & b :as one-two-three] [1 2 3]] one-two-three)
;; => [1 2 3]
```

You might be wondering why we would do this when we already have the original data structure at hand. One obvious example is that we use the same destructuring syntax for function argument declarations, for instance:

```
cljs.user=> (defn my-func [[a :as original]] original)
;; => #'cljs.user/my-func
cljs.user=> (my-func [1 2 3])
;; => [1 2 3]
```

Here, when we declare the function and its arguments, we have no idea what might be passed into it later. We might well want to be able to grab the original contents, and so having the option to bind the original data structure is particularly valuable.

Although the examples we've been using so far have all involved vectors, this sort of destructuring syntax actually works for any indexed data structures as well as sequences:

```
cljs.user=> (let [[zero one two & more] (range 5)]
               (list zero one two more))
;; => (0 1 2 (3 4))
```

We can also destructure associative structures like maps:

```
cljs.user=> (let [{name :name} {:name "David" :age "28"}] name)
;; => "David"
```

Here, we're binding the name variable to be the value of the `:name` key in the data structure passed in. We could also name it something else to make it clearer:

```
cljs.user=> (let [{n :name} {:name "David" :age "28"}] n)
;; => "David"
```

As with indexed structures, attempting to bind a key that isn't in the relevant data structure just binds `nil` to it. This is what we would expect from how we know accessor functions like `get` work with associative structures:

```
cljs.user=> (let [{c :city} {:name "David" :age "28"}] c)
;; => nil
```

As with `get`, we can pass in a default value in case the key we're trying to access can't be found. We can do this by using the `:or` keyword:

```
cljs.user=> (let [{c :city :or {c "San Francisco"}} {:name "David" :age
"28"}] c)
;; => "San Francisco"
```

We can destructure multiple values and include multiple defaults. A default will only be used when that key doesn't exist in the original structure:

```
cljs.user=> (let [{c :city n :name a :age :or {c "San Francisco" age
"30"}} {:name "David" :age "28"}] [c n a])
;; => ["San Francisco" "David" "28"]
```

As with indexed structures, we can also bind the original data structure with `:as`:

```
cljs.user=> (let [{c :city :as original} {:name "David" :age "28"}]
original)
;; => {:name "David", :age "28"}
```

Although we've used keywords as examples of the keys we're accessing, we can destructure anything that is a key in the map. For instance, if we were destructuring a map with integers as keys, we could destructure those as well:

```
cljs.user=> (let [{one 1} {1 "One" 10 "Ten"}] one)
;; => "One"
```

The usual idiom for binding keys that have keyword accessors is to bind them to a variable with the same name as the key. ClojureScript has a convenient shorthand, `:keys`, that lets us do this without having to repeat ourselves:

```
cljs.user=> (let [{:keys [a b c]} {:a "one" :b "two" :c "three"}] (list a b c))
;; => ("one" "two" "three")
```

Similar shorthand functions also exist for string and symbol keys `:strs` and `:syms`:

```
cljs.user=> (let [{:strs [a b c]} {"a" "one" "b" "two" "c" "three"}] (list a b c))
("one" "two" "three")
cljs.user=> (let [{:syms [a b c]} {'a "one" 'b "two" 'c "three"}] (list a b c))
;; => ("one" "two" "three")
```

Lastly, it's important to know that we can destructure things in a nested fashion. Let's try to destructure a map with a vector as its stored value:

```
cljs.user=> (let [{[a b] :name} {:name ["David" "Jarvis"]}] (str a " " b))
;; => "David Jarvis"
```

Namespaces

Namespaces in ClojureScript are akin to Python or Ruby modules, or Java classes. They're containers for `vars` and are often used to group related functionality in modular and reusable ways. Namespace are declared with the `ns` macro, which you can usually expect to find at the top of every ClojureScript file. A simple namespace declaration might look like the following:

```
(ns app.core"Main app logic goes here")

(def app "I'm actually just a string, whoops!")
```

The default namespace at our REPL is `cljs.user`, which is why we see that at our REPL prompt. If we wanted to, though, we could easily create a new namespace. Let's try that now, but first let's quickly store a var in our current namespace:

```
;; if you entered the previous code sample at the REPL, you can
;; get back to the `cljs.user` ns by just entering (ns cljs.user)
;; at the REPL
cljs.user => (def x 5)
;; => cljs.user/x
cljs.user=> (ns repl.experiment)
;; =>
repl.experiment=>
```

Notice how our REPL prompt now shows the new namespace we're in? Now, we could have just done (ns repl), but it's considered poor style to have a top-level namespace since it suggests that there isn't more logical grouping available (this is, at least in part, an area where ClojureScript shows its roots, since Java, and therefore Clojure, doesn't like single-segment namespaces). In cases where you really only do need one namespace, the idiomatic convention in ClojureScript is to append .core to the namespace-in this case, we might do (ns experiment.core) or (ns repl.core).

The ns macro is idempotent with regard to the namespace's state. This means that the first time you call ns, it'll create a new namespace for you, but if you call the same ns a second time it won't recreate or overwrite the existing namespace. It will, however, set the current namespace to be the namespace you've just called.

Remember how we defined x previously? Let's see if we can access it from our new repl.experiment namespace:

```
repl.experiment=> x
WARNING: Use of undeclared Var repl.experiment/x at line 1
<cljs repl>
;; => nil
```

The ClojureScript compiler doesn't know what we're referring to because no variable called x has been declared within the repl.experiment namespace, only in cljs.user. We can access x explicitly by referencing it with the namespace prepended to the variable:

```
repl.experiment=> cljs.user/x
;; => 5
```

This only works because we've already loaded the `cljs.user` namespace in the course of this REPL session. If for some reason `x` was stored in a namespace that we hadn't loaded, referring to it this way would cause the REPL to tell us that no such namespace yet existed. Let's say we had a file in a project called `located` at `src/repl/other.cljs`. Its namespace declaration might look like the following:

```
(ns repl.other)
(def y 10)
```

Now, from the REPL, if we try to access this directly, we'll get the following error:

```
repl.experiment=> repl.other/y
WARNING: No such namespace: repl.other, could not locate
repl/other.cljs, repl/other.cljc, or Closure namespace "" at line 1 <cljs
repl>
WARNING: Use of undeclared Var repl.other/y at line 1 <cljs repl>
#object[TypeError TypeError: Cannot read property 'y' of undefined]
...
```

All of this is great so far but doesn't give us a real example of how namespaces work together in the context of a larger application, so let's take a look at how you can load namespaces.

Let's create a new ClojureScript project to test this out. Type `lein new figwheel experiment` into your terminal to create a new ClojureScript project named `experiment` with Figwheel support. Right now, there's only one file in our `src` directory: `src/experiment/core.cljs`. Let's create a new one, `utils.cljs`, also in `src/experiment`.

We'll want to start a new Figwheel REPL running within this project at some point, which we can do by calling `lein figwheel` from within any folder inside our project. Let's fill in the contents of `utils.cljs` now-we'll just give it a simple function for the moment:

```
(ns experiment.utils)
(defn adder
  [x y]
  (+ x y))
```

You'll notice that the namespace name lines up with its location on the directory path. This isn't a coincidence; the ClojureScript namespace loader expects to find namespaces at specific file locations. When we invoke the `ns` macro at the REPL, we avoid that necessity, but when you're including `ns` declarations in files, the filename and the namespace name need to line up.

One other thing to be aware of is that a hyphen in a namespace should correspond to an underscore for the filename. This isn't strictly enforced (the way it is in Clojure), but is a widely used convention (and one that comes in handy when writing portable code for both Clojure and ClojureScript), so we'll stick with it in this book.

Now, let's replace the original content of `core.cljs` with the following:

```
(ns experiment.core
  (:require [experiment.utils]))
(defn adder-multiplier
  [x y z]
  (* z (experiment.utils/adder x y)))
;; we could replace this, but it's more convenient in the short
   term to leave it here.

(defn on-js-reload []
  ;; optionally touch your app-state to force rerendering
     depending on
  ;; your application
  ;; (swap! app-state update-in [:__figwheel_counter] inc)
)
```

Here, we've used the :require syntax within the `ns` macro to specify that we'd like to make the `experiment.utils` namespace accessible from within `experiment.core`. This is what enables us to reference the adder function in adder-multiplier. This syntax is actually shorthand for the `require` function, which we could call directly outside of an `ns` declaration if we wanted, like so:

```
(require 'experiment.utils)
```

We can test out that this function works the way we expect at the REPL. Our project's default configuration should automatically load `experiment.core` due to the fact that the project's `project.clj` configuration file specifies a Figwheel configuration flag for :on-jsload that loads `experiment.core`:

```
cljs.user=> (experiment.core/adder-multiplier 1 2 3)
;; => 9
```

Implicitly, this means that `experiment.utils` has also been loaded for use at the REPL. Any time you load a namespace that loads other namespaces, you can then access secondary vars that have been loaded downstream:

```
cljs.user=> (experiment.utils/adder 1 3)
;; => 4
```

All of this is fine, but it's a little verbose. We can create aliases for loaded namespaces to keep things concise using `:as`. Let's change the first part of `experiment.core` to reflect that:

```
(ns experiment.core
  (:require [experiment.utils :as utils]))
(defn adder-multiplier
  [x y z]
  (* z (utils/adder x y)))
```

This is widely done as a best practice and it makes your programs more readable.

If we only want to import a specific `var` from a `namespace`, we can use `:refer` to import specific things. If we only wanted to import the `adder` function, for instance, we could rewrite the first part of `experiment.core` to look as follows:

```
(ns experiment.core
  (:require [experiment.utils :refer [adder]]))
(defn adder-multiplier
  [x y z]
  (* z (adder x y)))
```

You can refer any number of vars in that vector and you can require as many namespaces as you like.

By default, everything in `cljs.core` is imported and directly available (for example, you don't need to reference `conj` with `cljs.core/conj`; you can just reference it directly). If for some reason you want to store a `var` with the same name as something in `cljs.core` (which is generally inadvisable, but there are times when it'll make sense), you can use `:refer-clojure` `:exclude` to explicitly not import that `var` from `cljs.core`:

```
(ns experiment.core
  (:refer-clojure :exclude [conj])
  (:require [experiment.utils :refer [adder]]))
```

The `ns` macro has other capabilities as well, including :import for JavaScript interoperability and `:refer-macros` for importing macros, but we'll cover those in greater detail when we need them.

JavaScript interoperability

One of the most powerful things about ClojureScript is the ease with which one can access and interact with the JavaScript runtime. In this section, we'll take a closer look at how you can work with native JavaScript code from ClojureScript.

JavaScript collections

Odds are good that you won't want to work too much with JavaScript collections directly now that you've gotten an understanding of how powerful ClojureScript's collection objects are, but it's still important to know how to access these from ClojureScript as well as to make sure you're comfortable converting JavaScript data types to ClojureScript and vice versa. Learning about this syntax will also prove useful when calling JS libraries from ClojureScript.

Arrays

Following is an example of defining and then accessing a JavaScript array from the ClojureScript REPL:

```
cljs.user> (def a (array 1 2 3))
;; => #'cljs.user/a
cljs.user=> a
;; => #js [1 2 3]
cljs.user> (type a)
;; => #object[Array "function Array() {
    [native code]
}"]
cljs.user> (get a 0)
;; => 1
```

You can also create an array using the #js reader macro:

```
cljs.user=> #js [4 5 6]
;; => #js [4 5 6]
```

Throughout this chapter, we've seen how ClojureScript objects can be cast to JavaScript objects using the clj->js conversion function. The reverse also works and casts arrays into vectors:

```
cljs.user=> (js->clj a)
;; => [1 2 3]
```

We can retrieve specific values from JavaScript arrays using `aget`, which works much like `get` for ClojureScript vectors (only without allowing the specification of a default argument). Under the hood, this is the same as indexing into the JavaScript array like `a[0]`:

```
cljs.user=> (aget a 0)
;; => 1
cljs.user=> (aget a 2)
;; => 3
```

Lastly, because JavaScript arrays are mutable, we can actually update the value at a specific index. Let's set the second value to `banana`:

```
cljs.user=> (aset a 1 "banana")
;; => "banana"
cljs.user=> a
;; => #js [1 "banana" 3]
```

JavaScript objects

To create a JavaScript object, we use the `js-obj` function and pass in the associated field/value pairs:

```
cljs.user=> (def obj (js-obj "name" "rafik" "age" 39))
;; => cljs.user/obj
cljs.user=> obj
;; => #js {:name "rafik", :age 39}
```

We can retrieve values by calling the key as a property on the object:

```
cljs.user=> (.-name obj)
;; => "rafik"
```

We can also use `aget` to retrieve values:

```
cljs.user=> (aget obj "name")
;; => "rafik"
```

Like with arrays, we can use `aset` to set a particular value:

```
cljs.user=> (aset obj "job" "programmer")
;; => "programmer"
cljs.user=> obj
;; => #js {:name "rafik", :age 39, :job "programmer"}
```

Note how ClojureScript represents JSON objects as maps with a `#js` annotation. Let's get the type of such a JavaScript object:

```
cljs.user> (type obj)
;; => #object[Object "function Object() {
  [native code]
}"]
```

Note that, like arrays, you can also create a JSON object using the `#js` reader macro:

```
cljs.user=> #js {"Key" "Value"}
;; => #js {:Key "Value"}
```

It may not surprise you at this point to learn that converting a JSON object to ClojureScript will return a map:

```
cljs.user=> (js->clj obj)
;; => {"name" "rafik", "age" 39, "job" "programmer"}
```

The `js->clj` parameter takes an optional argument to specify whether you want to keywordize any strings:

```
cljs.user=> (js->clj obj :keywordize-keys true)
;; => {:name "rafik", :age 39, :job "programmer"}
```

JS interop syntax

We've seen a few examples of how to work with JavaScript already in this chapter, but let's take a closer look at the specific syntax for working with JavaScript.

New instances of a particular object can be instantiated with (`new Type ...`) or (`Type ...`), with the latter syntax being preferred:

```
cljs.user=> (new js/String "Ta-da!")
;; => #object[String Ta-da!]
cljs.user=> (js/String. "Magic!")
;; => #object[String Magic!]
```

When invoking either instance methods or accessing attributes, we can simply include the full method chain, much as we would in JavaScript:

```
cljs.user=> (js/console.log "Show me your moves!")
;; => nil
cljs.user=> js/Math.PI
;; => 3.141592653589793
```

Although this style is common, it doesn't give us an implication at the code level as to whether something is a property or a method on an object. ClojureScript allows us to be explicit about this by using slightly different notations. For methods, we use simple dot notation:

```
cljs.user=> (.log js/console "Show me your moves!")
;; => nil
```

And for attributes, we use the `.-` notation:

```
cljs.user=> (.-PI js/Math)
;; => 3.141592653589793
cljs.user=> (def v #js {})
;; => #'cljs.user/v
cljs.user=> (set! (.-foo v) "bar")
;; => "bar"
cljs.user=> v
;; => #js {:foo "bar"}
```

The Google Closure Compiler and using external JavaScript libraries

Eventually, you're likely to want to use external JavaScript libraries as dependencies. You can go about doing this either by referencing external libraries that are loaded as scripts or by bundling them with your ClojureScript application.

One thing to understand before going down this road is the extremely close relationship between the Google Closure Compiler and ClojureScript itself. The two are so closely related that the Google Closure Library is bundled with ClojureScript by default and can be easily imported and referenced, much as one would normal ClojureScript code, for instance:

```
(ns experiment.goog
  (:import goog.history.Html5History))
(defonce hist (Html5History.))
```

You'll notice a new `ns` syntax here, `:import`, which is used only when we want to load a particular Google Closure Library.

Most ClojureScript applications will be built with the Google Closure Compiler when comes the time to deploy them in a production environment due to the Closure Compiler's advanced optimization features. These features include dead code elimination, general minification and optimization of code, and error notifications in the compilation process. The `cljsbuild` macro allows us to specifically configure the degree of compiler optimization we'd like to use; in general, we'll be using :optimizations `:none` when we're developing. We'll discuss deploying code to production more in `Chapter  8`, *Bundling ClojureScript for Production*.

Generating optimized production code via the Closure Compiler renames almost every symbol in your application to a shorter version of itself to save space. This is fine when our entire application is written in ClojureScript, but when we're dependent on an external JavaScript library, renaming that symbol will cause the reference to the library to change, which will make our code stop working. Again, this behavior won't happen when you're using `:optimizations  :none`, but will happen once you start using `:optimizations :advanced`.

The consequence of this behavior is that most external JavaScript libraries aren't usable by default when you compile your code for production. If that were the end of the story, ClojureScript wouldn't be all that useful, so fortunately there are ways to work with JavaScript libraries that account for the nature of the Closure Compiler.

Referencing external libraries with externs

The most basic way of using an external JavaScript library with your ClojureScript application is not to bundle it with the application at all but just to reference it directly. For instance, as the relevant external library is loaded (either via your application or via the HTML page that loads your application), you can simply reference the JavaScript as you would any other JavaScript code.

Let's say we'd like to reference the following library, which we'll call `treeact`. It may sound similar to another library you've heard of by a company with a name like **TreeBook**, but don't think too hard about that. Let's add this to the `index.html` file in our experiment project's `resources/public` directory, just before our application is loaded:

```
<script type="text/javascript">
  treeact = function() {
    var tree = {};
    tree.render = function() {
      console.log("Page rendered!");
    }
    return tree;
```

```
  };
</script>
```

To use this library from ClojureScript, we can just reference it directly as long as we're using `:optimizations :none`. Now, let's add the following function to our `experiment.core` namespace:

```
(defn render
  []
  (.render (js/treeact)))

(render)
```

Figwheel should automatically reload this file when we save it, which will call the `render` function. If we check the page, we should see our **Page rendered!** alert logged to the console. If you don't see it, make sure you've refreshed the page so that the application can pick up the external script.

Unfortunately, the preceding code will stop working once we start using advanced compilation. We can make this continue to function as desired by adding an externs file. The externs file tells the Google Closure compiler what names not to rename when it's compiling our application. For our simple `treeact` library, our externs file would look like the following:

```
var treeact = function() {}
treeact.render = function() {}
```

Assuming this function is named `treeact-externs.js`, we can then add it to our Cljsbuild's `:compiler` options for our `min` configuration in our `project.clj`. This means the entire `:compiler` value should look like the following:

```
:compiler {:output-to "resources/public/js/compiled/experiment.js"
           :main experiment.core
           :externs ["treeact-externs.js"]
           :optimizations :advanced
           :pretty-print false}}
```

Let's stop our Figwheel REPL and build this with `lein clean; lein cljsbuild once min`. We won't have a Figwheel server running any more, but we can manually load our page by opening the HTML file located at `resources/public/index.html`. You should see the **Page rendered!** alert in the console-it worked!

We can also get away without using an externs file by using strings instead of symbols. The Google Closure Compiler doesn't rename strings, but writing code this way is generally only recommended if you have a very small number of external variables you're trying to keep track of, for instance:

```
(let [tree ((goog.object.get js/window "treeact"))]
  ((goog.object.get tree "render")))
```

Bundling external libraries

In addition to referencing external libraries, you can also bundle them as part of your application. This has the advantage of pushing everything into a single file and allowing the Google Closure Compiler to optimize all source code and dependencies for production simultaneously.

Google Closure Compiler compatible code

Libraries that are written to be compatible with the Google Closure Compiler (meaning they expose their namespaces using `goog.provide`) are easy to add as dependencies and require almost no additional configuration. All you have to do is add the library in question to your `project.clj` `cljsbuild` configuration with the `:libs` key. For instance, if we had a version of the popular library jQuery on hand that had been modified to be compatible with the Google Closure Compiler, we could just add the following section to our `project.clj` and then we'd be able to reference it directly:

```
{:cljsbuild {:compiler {:libs ["jQuery.js"]}...}}
```

This is an extremely convenient way of bundling external JavaScript libraries. Unfortunately, at the time of this book's publications, relatively few libraries are currently written to be compatible with the Google Closure Compiler.

Foreign JavaScript

Libraries that aren't yet written to be compatible with the Google Closure Compiler can still be used in ClojureScript applications. You'll need to use an externs file like the one we wrote earlier in this chapter, but you'll also need to add a `:foreign-libs` map to your `cljsbuild` `:compiler` options in your `project.clj` for the `min` profile. Let's remove our script section in our application's `index.html` and move it into an external file in the root of our project, which we'll call `treeact.js`. We can now add the following section to our `project.clj` `:compiler` map to bundle it under advanced compilation:

```
:foreign-libs [{:file "treeact.js"
```

```
        :provides ["t"]}]
```

We'll also have to modify our application-specifically, we'll modify the namespace declaration to import Treeact explicitly. We don't actually need to modify the function definition-the reason we import it is to inform our application of the namespace and its contents:

```
(ns experiment.core
  (:require [experiment.utils :refer [adder]]
            [t]))
```

Now, let's rebuild our application with `lein clean`; `lein cljsbuild once min` and reload the `index.html` page that we were just looking at. We should, once again, see an alert printed on the console. Woohoo!

CLJSJS

We've now examined a number of different ways in which you can include external JavaScript libraries in your code, from referencing to bundling. However, you've probably noticed that adding external libraries can often require some work, especially if you have to build an externs file. Fortunately, for most common JavaScript libraries, there's a better way. The CLJSJS project (located online at cljsjs.github.io) is a community-driven effort to package up the most common and popular JavaScript libraries in a way that's easily consumable by ClojureScript applications and is compatible with the Google Closure Compiler.

To use a CLJSJS project, for example, Facebook's React, all you need to do is to add the following to your `project.clj` `:dependencies` key:

```
[cljsjs/react "0.14.3-0"]
```

You can then reference React directly in your application as `js/React`. In general, CLJSJS dependencies are far and away the easiest way to bundle external JavaScript code in your ClojureScript applications.

Summary

You now have all the basic tools to write simple ClojureScript programs. You've learned about ClojureScript's data types as well as the language's core syntax. You've seen how immutability enables us to write programs that are easier to reason about and how to write programs with smooth interoperability with other JavaScript libraries.

In the next chapter, you'll learn more about how to write idiomatic ClojureScript as well as some of the differences in design patterns between JavaScript and ClojureScript. We'll also dig into more advanced ClojureScript concepts such as macros, functional programming patterns, and concurrent design.

3
Advanced ClojureScript Concepts

In this chapter, we'll introduce some more advanced concepts of ClojureScript as a language. At this point, you should already have all the tools you need to write basic ClojureScript programs, and this chapter will help take you from that level of expertise to one at which you feel comfortable tackling more complicated and extensive engineering tasks. This chapter will cover the following topics:

- Functional programming concepts
- Control flow
- Writing macro for ClojureScript
- Concurrent design patterns using `core.async`

Functional programming concepts

We've already talked a little bit about how ClojureScript is a functional language in `Chapter 2`, *ClojureScript Language Fundamentals*, when we introduced the function syntax and talked about how functions in ClojureScript can be stored, passed, and referenced like any other variable. We've even seen a few examples of passing functions as arguments to other functions, as we did when we looked at laziness in `Chapter 2`, *ClojureScript Language Fundamentals*, and passed `println` as an argument to `map`. In this section, we'll take a closer look at these concepts and flesh them out with some helpful examples.

Loops and iteration

Sooner or later, almost every software program has to iterate through some sort of collection and perform a transformation on it. In mutable languages, this typically takes the form of iterating through each object in the collection and mutating the underlying collection, or perhaps calling a function with a known side effect. In this section, we'll take a look at various design patterns for iterating through collections.

When used from ClojureScript, these programming patterns are overwhelmingly used for the execution of side effects. Some, like loop and recur, for, and doall do have a specific return value that you can control, but others including doseq and dotimes explicitly return nil. Be careful when using these that you understand what return value you'll be getting!

Loop and recur functions

Let's consider a sample JavaScript program that does this:

```
x = [1, 2, 3, 4, 5]

for (var i = 0; i < x.length; i++) {
  console.log(x[i]);
}
```

The preceding function, when executed, prints out the numbers 1 through 5 to the console, with each number on its own line. In ClojureScript, the most direct translation of the aforementioned program would look like the following:

```
(def x [1 2 3 4 5])
(loop [i 0] ;; set our starting point
  (println (nth x i))
  (when (< (inc i) (count x))
    (recur (inc i)))) ;; let's do the time warp again!
```

Although this program does work (and especially well for fans of *The Rocky Horror Picture Show*), it's not regarded as an idiomatic way of programming in ClojureScript. For one, it's quite verbose, and secondly, it's extremely imperative. If we had wanted to actually return modified versions of the values in question, we would have had to have included quite a bit of extra code to accommodate for the immutability of vectors. This second issue will be an ongoing theme in this section until we get around to learning about higher-order functions.

Note that `recur` also works to design recursive functions. In a recursive function, you don't need to specify `loop` independently of the function definition `recur` will automatically go to the top of the function definition.

Let's give this a shot with our previous example:

```
(defn looper
  "Don't get me confused with the popular 2012 film"
  [i]
  (println (nth x i))
  (when (< (inc i) (count x))
    (recur (inc i)))) ;; without loop head, go to fn start
```

Invoking `(looper 0)` should have the same effect as our original `loop` code.

for

Let's consider the example from the previous section, but let's make both the JavaScript and ClojureScript versions slightly more idiomatic by assuming we won't actually need to mutate the values in question:

```
x = [1, 2, 3, 4, 5]
for (var i in x) {
  console.log(x[i]);
}
```

And the corresponding ClojureScript:

```
(def x [1 2 3 4 5])
(for [i x]
  (println i))
```

This aligns more closely with a slightly cleaner version of the original JavaScript program, although ClojureScript's `for` is lazy and returns a sequence, while the JavaScript loop runs immediately.

The `for` loop accepts up to three different modifiers: `:when`, `:let`, and `:while`. The `:let` modifier allows you to bind additional local variables within the `for` block, `:when` only executes the body when the predicate matches (though it continues to iterate), and `:while` terminates iteration when the provided predicate function returns `false`:

```
(for [i x
  :let [y (* i 2)]
  :when (odd? i)
```

```
    :while (< i 4)]
    (println i y))
1 2
3 6
;;=> (nil nil)
```

dotimes

We could also do away with the original array using `dotimes`, which executes a body of code n times (presumably for side effects):

```
(dotimes [n 5] (println (inc n)))
```

 Note that we're careful to increment n by 1 before printing since `dotimes` starts at . Also, be aware that `dotimes` only allows you to bind one variable: the number of times the body will be executed. The variable n also doesn't have to be called n —we could have called it `rubber-chickens` if we had wanted to.

doseq

Like `dotimes` and `for`, `doseq` allows for the binding of individual elements of a sequence and then repeated execution of the following body, presumably for side effects. However, `doseq` is different from `dotimes` and `for` in a few notable ways. First, it operates on a provided sequence, rather than on an integer. A quick example might look like the following:

```
(doseq [a (range 5)]
   (println a))
```

Remember in Chapter 2, *ClojureScript Language Fundamentals*, when we talked about lazy sequences and realizing infinite sequences? `doseq` is one tool for working with lazy (and potentially infinite) sequences. It only realizes a single value at a time, and once it's done working with it, it discards it and moves on to the next value in the sequence. `doseq` also has special logic for dealing with chunked sequences, which is not true of all functions that take a lazy sequence.

`doseq` accepts binding multiple sequences at once and operates over a Cartesian cross of their values. In simpler terms, this means it executes once for each possible sequence value combination. Let's take a look at the following commands:

```
(doseq [a ["a" "b" "c"]
  b (range 3)]
  (println a b))
a 0
a 1
a 2
b 0
b 1
b 2
c 0
c 1
c 2
;; => nil
```

`doseq` returns `nil`, and like `for` accepts the `:let`, `:while`, and `when` modifiers.

doall

In addition to `doseq`, we have `doall`. While the purpose of `doseq` is to hold in memory (and invoke side effects) for one element in a sequence at a time, the purpose of `doall` is the opposite. `doall` seeks to realize every element (and, consequently, invoke every side effect), load it into memory, and return it.

> Closely related to `doall` is `dorun`, which avoids holding the entire sequence in memory and also returns `nil`.

Developers new to lazy evaluation often find themselves confused by circumstances where their code hasn't evaluated. If you think you might be in one of these situations (and know that the sequence or collection that should have been evaluated isn't too large to fit into memory), try calling `doall` on it to see if it evaluates. Let's look at an example using the lazy `map` function, which we'll be taking a closer look at in the next section:

```
cljs.user=> (def x [1 2 3 4 5])
#'cljs.user/x
cljs.user=> (do
  (map println x)
  true)
;; => true
```

Here, because `map` is evaluated lazily, the `do` block returns `true` but never calls `println` on the individual elements of `x`. If we wanted to force the `map println` to evaluate, we could call `doall` on it:

```
cljs.user=> (do
  (doall (map println x))
  true)
1
2
3
4
5
;; => true
```

Higher-order functions

Up until now, we've been looking at very imperative design patterns—patterns that often require explicitly creating local bindings of variables in order to iterate through a sequence or collection. From this point on, we'll be looking at higher-order functions as a way of both invoking side effects on a collection and returning new versions of the sequence being passed in.

The use of higher-order functions in ClojureScript is more idiomatic than more imperative software patterns due to the immutability of the language's core data structures (an issue we discuss in `Chapter 2, ClojureScript Language Fundamentals`). We can't mutate a data structure as we iterate over it and we can't easily build a new data structure up while we're iterating. Instead, we use higher-order functions that perform transformations on the input sequence and return new, transformed sequences for us to use.

There are many higher-order functions in ClojureScript, and as you become more familiar with the language, it's very likely you'll end up writing your own. For now, we'll begin with an introduction to the three most common and critical higher-order functions: `map`, `filter`, and `reduce`. Each of these functions takes any sequence or collection as an input and returns a lazy sequence. There are also alternative versions of the `map` and `filter` functions that explicitly return a vector: `mapv` and `filterv`.

These core higher-order functions are valuable not only for their simplicity and elegance, but also because they do a much better job than `for` of expressing intent.

map

map takes at least one collection and returns a single new, transformed collection. This transformed collection is created by calling the provided function on each element in the provided collections in turn. You can also pass in zero collections, in which case map returns what's known as a transducer; we'll talk more about transducers later on in this chapter.

If map is passed one or more collections, it returns a lazy sequence consisting of the result of applying the input function to the first items in each provided collection, followed by the result of applying the input function to the second items in each collection, and so on, until any one of the collections has been exhausted. Any remaining items in the other collections are ignored. The input function should accept as many arguments as there are collections being passed to map.

This explanation is a bit of a mouthful, so let's start with a simple example. We'll use map to write up a more functional implementation of our previous examples of printing the numbers 1 through 5:

```
cljs.user=> (map println [1 2 3 4 5])
1
2
3
4
5
;; => (nil nil nil nil nil)
```

 A quick note here: you may be wondering why, if map is lazy, it's still evaluating println on each item in the sequence. The reason is that since we're calling it directly at the REPL, the REPL knows that it has to print out the return value for us to read and so it realizes the entire sequence.

println as a function returns nil, so this isn't a great example of how we could transform an input sequence (it does explain the return value as a sequence of 5 nil values, though). Let's try to write a more idiomatic version in which we increment each item in the sequence by 1 and return that. JavaScript has its own implementation of map, so such a program might look like the following in JavaScript:

```
[1, 2, 3, 4, 5].map(function(x) { return x + 1 })
```

The return value of this statement is a new array with the contents [2, 3, 4, 5, 6].
ClojureScript functions similarly, but is slightly cleaner since it has a built-in `inc` function to
increment the values by 1:

```
cljs.user=> (map inc [1 2 3 4 5])
;; => (2 3 4 5 6)
```

We could use anonymous function syntax here as well, just to show off how easily you can
write ClojureScript functions with little boilerplate:

```
cljs.user=> (map #(+ % 1) [1 2 3 4 5])
;; => (2 3 4 5 6)
```

Now that we've seen some examples where we've passed in a single collection, let's see
what happens when we pass in multiple collections simultaneously:

```
cljs.user=> (map * [1 2 3 4] [2 5 8])
;; => (2 10 24)
```

Here, `map` returns a sequence where `*` is applied first to the first element in each collection,
then the next, and so on. We get 2 from `(* 1 2)`, 10 from `(* 2 5)`, and so on. When we
get to 8, the second sequence is empty and so `map` stops evaluating, even though there's a
remaining element in our first collection.

Using `map` with a HashMap will map over key-value pairs as vectors:

```
cljs.user=> (map identity {:a 1 :b 2 :c 3})
;; => ([:a 1] [:b 2] [:c 3])
```

Although they have the same name, be careful not to confuse `map` with the map data type.

The filter and remove functions

`filter` takes a predicate function (a function that returns a "truthy" value) and either zero
or one collections. If called without a collection, it returns a transducer. If called with a
collection, it will return a new sequence comprising only the items for which the predicate
function returned a truthy value. Let's take a look at a quick example:

```
cljs.user=> (filter even? [1 2 3 4 5])
;; => (2 4)
cljs.user=> (filter #(<= % 2) [1 2 3 4 5])
;; => (1 2)
```

Note that as both `map` and `filter` are lazy, the functions you provide to them should be free of side effects.

`filter` has a twin function, `remove`, which does the inverse: it removes any items in the input collection for which the predicate evaluates as truthy:

```
cljs.user=> (remove even? [1 2 3 4 5])
;; => (1 3 5)
cljs.user=> (remove #(<= % 2) [1 2 3 4 5])
;; => (3 4 5)
```

reduce

Lastly, we have `reduce`. `reduce` incrementally builds a new value up from a collection. One good way of thinking about it is as a way of "rolling up" a collection. We begin with an initial state that is then updated with each additional item to be reduced.

`reduce` takes as its arguments a reducer function, an optional initial value, and a collection. The supplied reducing function must be able to accept two arguments: the first, the value being reduced into, and the second, the current value to reduce. `reduce` behaves quite differently depending on whether or not the optional initial value is provided, so we'll dig into how the function works both with and without an initial value.

If the initial value is not supplied, `reduce` returns the result of applying the input function to the first two arguments in the collection, then applying the function to that result and the third item, and so forth. Let's look at a simple example using the + operator:

```
cljs.user=> (reduce + [1 2 3 4 5])
;; => 15
```

If the collection is empty, the supplied function must also be capable of accepting no arguments; `reduce` will return the result of calling the supplied function with no arguments:

```
cljs.user=> (reduce + [])
;; => 0
cljs.user=> (+)
;; => 0
```

If the collection has only one item, it is returned and the supplied function is not called:

```
cljs.user=> (reduce js/Math.abs [-5])
;; => -5
```

If an initial value is supplied, `reduce` returns the result of applying the supplied function to the initial value and the first item in the collection, then applying the supplied function to that result and the second item, and so on:

```
cljs.user=> (reduce + 10 [1 2 3 4 5])
;; => 25
```

If the collection contains no items and an initial value is supplied, `reduce` just returns the initial value without calling the supplied function:

```
cljs.user=> (reduce str 10 [])
;; => 10
```

Transducers

Transducers are a relatively new member of the ClojureScript family and are a fairly advanced functional programming concept. In essence, a transducer is a function that takes one reducing function and returns another. In this context, a **reducing function** is a function that can be passed to `reduce`-a two-argument function where the arguments are the cumulatively reduced data thus far and the data to be reduced in the current step.

Okay, so that tells us what transducers are, but not much about how we'd actually use them. Transducers in general are not an intuitive thing to reason about, and so perhaps the best place to begin is with examples.

Note that by convention, transducers are referred to as `xform`. So if you're looking at the function documentation generated by doing, say, `doc into`:

```
--------------------------
cljs.core/into
([to from] [to xform from])
  Returns a new coll consisting of to-coll with all of
the items of
    from-coll conjoined. A transducer may be supplied.
```

The `xform` in the preceding function means that `into` is expecting a transducer to be passed in as an argument.

Let's take a look at the `sequence` function, which coerces a collection to a (possibly empty) sequence. A basic use of `sequence` might look like the following:

```
cljs.user=> (sequence [1 2 3 4 5 6])
;; => (1 2 3 4 5 6)
```

While one can call `sequence` with just a collection, you can also provide a transducer to it, and it'll lazily generate the sequence with the transformation applied. Let's take a fairly simple transducer, `(map inc)`, and use that as a function argument to `sequence`:

```
cljs.user=> (sequence (map inc) [1 2 3 4 5])
;; => (2 3 4 5 6)
```

If you've had a chance to familiarize yourself with the `->>` macro (we'll cover it later in this chapter when we talk about macros), the preceding command is very similar to the following:

```
cljs.user=> (->> [1 2 3 4 5] (map inc))
;; => (2 3 4 5 6)
```

This latter case is slightly different in that the type that is being returned is a `LazySeq`, whereas the use of a transducer causes the return type to be a `LazyTransformer`.

 Transducers represent transformations on data. However, they have some critical differences from other higher-order functions in ClojureScript that transform data. Principally, transducers don't care about what the function does, the context of what's being built up, or the source of inputs.

The most critical differentiating characteristics of transducers is that they don't care about the source of inputs. Other higher-order functions (`map`, `filter`, `reduce`, and so on) are critically tied to the collection (and hence sequence) abstractions. For instance, one really awesome use of transducers is to apply a transformation to everything that goes through a `core.async` channel. We'll learn a little bit more about `core.async` later on in this chapter, but a quick code snippet should provide an idea of how these transformations work:

```
(ns experiment.async
  (:require [cljs.core.async :as async])
  (:require-macros [cljs.core.async.macros :as async-macros]))

(defn sample-transducer-channel
  "A simple example of a transduced channel. Increment by one
   all values that pass through this channel. For demonstration
   purposes we'll just hard-code the number 5 for now."
  []
```

```
      (let [c (async/chan 1 (map inc))]
        (async-macros/go (async/>! c 5))
        (async-macros/go (js/console.log (async/<! c)))))
```

Now, if we call our new function at the REPL, we should see the number 6 in our browser's JavaScript console.

Transducers can be used for reducing with a transformation:

```
      (def inc-xform (map inc))
```

We can test this transducer at the REPL as follows:

```
      cljs.user=> (transduce inc-xform + 0 [1 3 5])
      ;; => 12
      ;; For clarity, the order here is equivalent to the following,
      ;; only evaluated non-lazily:
      ;; (reduce + 0 (apply inc (1 3 5)))
```

They can also be used for building a new collection from a transformation of another (again, non-lazily—basically the non-lazy version of sequence with a specific collection as the output):

```
      cljs.user=> (into [] inc-xform '(1 1 2 3 5 8))
      ;; => [2 2 3 4 6 9]
```

Transducers are a powerful tool for transforming data and creating reusable and composable functions for doing so.

Control flow

At this point, we've already seen many examples of ClojureScript functions and their associated control flows, but we haven't really covered them in explicit detail. In this section, we'll look at various branching control flow special forms and macros, and we'll cover how to handle exceptions.

if and when

Like almost every programming language, ClojureScript uses if for basic conditional logic. if in ClojureScript is a special form rather than a function or a macro. Syntactically, if takes a predicate, a form that is evaluated and yielded if the predicate returns true, and an optional form that is evaluated and yielded if the predicate returns false. If the optional form for the `false` case is not supplied, it defaults to `nil`:

```
cljs.user=> (if (= 1 1)
  "One equals one!"
  "One does not equal one :(")
;; => "One equals one!"
cljs.user=> (if (= 1 2)
  "One equals two!") ;; implicit nil return value when false
;; => nil
```

`when` like a combination of `if` and an implicit `do` block when its predicate returns `true`:

```
cljs.user=> (when true
  (println "I'm a side effect!")
  ["apples" "bananas"])
"I'm a side effect!"
;; => ["apples", "bananas"]
```

if-let and when-let

Often, when working with predicates, you'll want to bind the return value to a local variable and continue to evaluate a code block with that local variable. ClojureScript provides two convenient macros to make doing so concise: `if-let` and `when-let`.

Since you're already aware of the syntax for `if`, `when`, and `let`, the syntax for `when-let` should seem fairly straightforward:

```
cljs.user=> (if-let [x false]
  "I'm true!"
  "I'm false!")
;; => "I'm false!"
cljs.user=> (when-let [x "true"]
  (println "Oh hi!")
  x)
Oh hi!
;; => "true"
```

 Note that both `if-let` and `when-let` can only bind a single variable—the form that will be used as the dispatch value to determine truthiness.

cond and condp

cond and condp are both used to run through many possible predicates and to return the body associated with the first to evaluate as truthy. Let's look at cond first:

```
cljs.user=> (cond
  false "Nope."
  nil "Not happening."
  (empty? [1]) "Still not happening."
  true "Finally!")
;; => "Finally!"
```

By convention, it's common when using cond to include an :else clause that includes a default value like the following:

```
cljs.user=> (cond
  false "Nope."
  nil "Not happening."
  :else "I'm a default value!")
;; => "I'm a default value!"
```

Note that there's nothing special about :else here—it just happens to be truthy since it's a keyword. The choice of :else is, however, a common convention that you'll find in most open-source code that has a default value.

If none of the predicates evaluate to true, cond returns nil. Calling cond by itself (for example, (cond)) therefore returns nil.

condp functions similar to cond, but instead of evaluating a different predicate at each tier, it takes a predicate and an initial value and compares the result against various possible values. Finally, it takes a single optional default value (which, unlike cond, does not need an accompanying :else or similar truthy value preceding it):

```
cljs.user=> (condp = [1 2 3 4 5]
  "a string?" false
  'another-value false
  :keyword false
  [1 2 3 4 5] true
  "finally, a single default value")
;; => true
```

Evaluating the preceding code block returns true because that's the return value associated with the possible value of [1 2 3 4 5]. Note that both cond and condp are sequentially evaluated, meaning that as soon as they've met a satisfactory value or predicate, they'll return the corresponding value (without continuing to evaluate any remaining predicates or values). Only the matched value, if any, is ever evaluated.

case

case functions like a special case of condp where the predicate is =.

Note that unlike Clojure, case in ClojureScript does evaluate the test constants; they don't have to be compile-time literals.
In general, you should prefer cond or condp over case; case is a lower-level construct in JVM Clojure, and while this distinction matters less for ClojureScript, it's worth keeping that convention.

A simple example might look like the following:

```
cljs.user=> (case [1 2]
  [] "empty vec"
  (vec '(1 2)) "my vec"
  "default")
;; => "my vec"
```

You can also include any number of test constants that evaluate to the same result, for instance:

```
cljs.user=> (case [1 2]
  [] "empty vec"
  ([1 2] [3 4]) "my vec"
  "default")
;; => "my vec"
```

Again, we get the same result.

Exception handling

So far, we've talked a lot about how to write programs, but we haven't talked at all about what happens when things go wrong. Let's take a look how exception handling works in ClojureScript. Let's take a look at how exception handling works in ClojureScript now, starting with how we can deliberately throw an exception:

```
(throw (js/Error. "You weren't supposed to do this!"))
```

Simple enough. ClojureScript also has the same sort of exception handling facilities you would expect from a high-level language-critically, tools for trying a code block, catching any exceptions, and finally executing a recovery block.

```
cljs.user=> (try
  (throw (js/Error. "I'm an error!"))
  (catch js/Error e
    (println "Error message: " e))
  (finally
    (println "A successful result!")))
Error message:  #object[Error Error: I'm an error!]
A successful result!
;; => nil
```

Here we've explicitly captured the error of type js/Error, but almost anything can be thrown as an error in JavaScript. This isn't recommended, but does sometimes come up with third-party libraries. Consequently, if you're trying to catch any exception that might be thrown, you can use :default instead of js/Error to catch anything that might be thrown. More general exception handling usually looks something like the following:

```
cljs.user=> (try
  (throw "Exception")
  (catch js/Error err
    ;; whatever error handling you might want
    (println "error was of type js/Error"))
  (catch :default err
    ;; perhaps more general error handling here
    (println "Some non-error type was thrown."))
  (finally
    (println "Done!")))
Some non-error type was thrown.
Done!
;; => nil
```

Be aware that anything within a finally block will only be executed for side effects and not for their return value. The return value of a try block is: first, if no exceptions are thrown, the last value of the try block is returned. If any exceptions are thrown, the last value of the appropriate catch block is returned.

Writing macros for ClojureScript

If you're new to Lisp languages, you may not be familiar with macros. In essence, Lisp macros differ from macros in other languages in that they are a mechanism by which code itself can be transformed and rewritten. We've already used a number of macros so far in the examples in this book, and, indeed, macros are a core part of ClojureScript and you can and should expect to find yourself using them frequently. They enable us to do things that would not otherwise be possible and to optimize and refactor code in powerful ways.

read and eval

In order for all of what we're about to say to make sense, it'll probably be helpful to first understand a little bit about how programming languages work. With most languages, there exists a `reader` function in the compiler that takes a series of strings and transforms the text you provided into an abstract syntax tree. That abstract syntax tree is then passed on to an evaluator, which knows how to take the contents of the abstract syntax tree and turn it into, for instance, machine code or byte code, or whatever low-level code is appropriate for the language you're working in.

The key thing to understand about this is that in general, for most computer languages, the abstract syntax tree that is generated by the reader is not accessible to the program that is actually being executed. You know the old saying, *"Physician, heal thyself!"*? Most programs, if they were physicians, couldn't heal themselves.

The special thing about Lisp languages is that the abstract syntax tree of the program is no different from the data that the language operates on (remember how we showed that the form for calling functions was just a normal `list` in Chapter 2, *ClojureScript Language Fundamentals*?). And since we know that the data the language operates on is definitely accessible at the program's runtime, it follows that we can also access and operate on the abstract syntax tree of the program itself!

This is very cool in that it means that we can have macros that transform and manipulate both data and code. Let's see a quick example of what the process we've just described looks like. Passing a string of source code to the reader looks like the following:

```
cljs.user=> (cljs.reader/read-string "(+ 1 3)")
;; => (+ 1 3)
```

Now, let's try treating this piece of source code as we might any data structure:

```
cljs.user=> (conj (cljs.reader/read-string "(+ 1 3)") "apples")
;; => ("apples" + 1 3)
```

Cool. Next, let's try passing a string through the reader to the evaluator:

```
cljs.user=> (eval (cljs.reader/read-string "(+ 1 3)") "apples")
WARNING: Use of undeclared Var cljs.user/eval at line 1 <cljs repl>
#object[TypeError TypeError: Cannot read property 'call' of undefined]
```

Hmm. What happened there? Well, it turns out that with the ClojureScript project in its current state, `eval` is not available during the ClojureScript runtime (including at REPL evaluation time). Rather, `eval` of ClojureScript forms is handled by a JVM Clojure process, which is how the REPL we've been using actually works (it's calling the relevant vanilla Clojure code that corresponds to `eval`).

You may be wondering, if `eval` of ClojureScript code is only available to the JVM Clojure process, how is that we're able to evaluate code in the browser? The answer lies in what's actually being evaluated. When we're in the browser environment, the code being evaluated is JavaScript that we've compiled from ClojureScript. Actually trying to evaluate ClojureScript code within the browser, won't work.

It's possible that the future may bring the ability for us to use `eval` within ClojureScript; in 2015, David Nolen (the primary developer and maintainer of ClojureScript) announced that ClojureScript had reached the point where it was able to compile itself. Self-compiling ClojureScript means that it becomes possible to evaluate ClojureScript code at runtime (we no longer need distinct compilation-time and run-time behavior). At the moment, however, even though some of the larger technical problems have been addressed, the functionality hasn't been made a core part of the ClojureScript language and build system because using JVM Clojure for compilation is still considerably faster.

If you're interested in experimenting with a self-hosted version of ClojureScript, the ClojureScript wiki has a page on the current state of the project (`https://github.com/clojure/clojurescript/wiki/Bootstrapping-the-Compiler`) as well as a list of some projects that are currently relying upon self-hosted ClojureScript. At the time of this writing, self-hosted ClojureScript is still in an experimental/proof of concept phase, so we can't recommend it yet for production applications.

The fact that `eval` isn't available to the current ClojureScript runtime has direct implications for how macros work in ClojureScript as well. Since `eval` is only available to the JVM Clojure process, ClojureScript macros are also only able to be evaluated at compile time, rather than at run time, and they must be written in either a `.clj` (normal Clojure) file or a `.cljc` (reader conditional Clojure) file. Either way, code that is generated by a macro must target the runtime capabilities of ClojureScript, even if the macro itself is written in Clojure.

In practice, this also means that ClojureScript macros need to be evaluated before we get around to actually calling them anywhere. The most common way of achieving this is to define them in another namespace than the one in which they are going to be called. They are then imported into the calling namespace using the special :require-macros keyword in namespace declarations, for instance:

```
(ns my.namespace
  (:require-macros [my.macros :as my]))
```

A ClojureScript namespace can require macros from a namespace with the same name (that is, a my/namespace.cljs file could require macros from a my/namespace.clj file). There's one gotcha to be aware of with this—an imported macro and a function can share the same name. If that happens, ClojureScript will resolve the symbol to a macro if it's in a calling position, and to a function if it's not. For instance, if + were both a macro and a function, it would be a macro in (+ 1 1) and a function in (reduce + [1 1]). We recommend avoiding this situation in your programs.

Your first macro

Whew, that was a lot of precursor text! Enough chatter; let's get our hands dirty. Let's start by writing an incredibly simple macro—so simple, it'll look just like a function. For the exercises we'll be doing in this section, let's go back to our experiment project that we were using in Chapter 2, *ClojureScript Language Fundamentals*, and we'll create two new files: one at src/experiment/macros.clj and one at src/experiment/consumers.cljs.

We'll create macros.clj first and put in a simple namespace declaration:

```
(ns experiment.macros)
```

In consumers.cljs, we'll also add a namespace declaration, and we'll make sure to import any macros in our macros file:

```
(ns experiment.consumers
  (:require-macros [experiment.macros :as m]))
```

We'll also want to make sure we can access anything we do here in a browser setting, so let's add a :require section to our main namespace, experiment.core:

```
(ns experiment.core
  (:require [experiment.consumers :as consumers]))
```

Let's start with an incredibly simple macro that does the same thing as the built-in `inc` function:

```
(defmacro increment
  "Given a form, increment it by 1 and return"
  [x]
  (+ x 1))
```

Now, since we have a ClojureScript file that imports these macros, we should immediately be able to access and test this macro out in our ClojureScript REPL. Let's give it a shot:

```
cljs.user=> (experiment.macros/increment 2)
;; => 3
```

So far, so good. Let's see what happens when we try to pass in a larger form, say `(+ 1 2)`:

```
cljs.user=> (experiment.macros/increment (+ 1 2))
;; => clojure.lang.ExceptionInfo: clojure.lang.PersistentList cannot be
cast to java.lang.Number at line 1 <cljs repl> {:file "<cljs repl>", :line
1, :column 1, :tag :cljs/analysis-error}
```

Hmm, that's different! What could be going on? Let's see what's different about a function versus a macro. Let's try a very simple comparison where we see what actually ends up being passed in as an argument. In our `macros` namespace, let's define the following simple macro:

```
(defmacro printer-macro
  "Given a form, increment it by 1 and return"
  [x]
  (println x))
```

And in `consumers.clj`, let's define the following function:

```
(defn printer-func
  [x]
  (println x))
```

Now, let's try calling both of them at the REPL and see what the result is using the same argument we were just using to our `increment` macro:

```
cljs.user=> (experiment.macros/printer-macro (+ 1 2))
(+ 1 2)
(+ 1 2)
;; => nil
cljs.user=> (experiment.consumers/printer-func (+ 1 2))
3
;; => nil
```

Two things stand out here: first, our macro printer printed a different input (the actual form (+ 1 2) rather than what it evaluates to, 3), and second, the macro printer printed it twice!

The reason the macro printer prints out the full form is that that's how macros work: they receive the full form that's passed in before the evaluator has had a chance to turn that form into its underlying value. Macros are ultimately normal functions that run at compile time, and the compiler doesn't evaluate their arguments before calling.

The reason it prints out the value twice is that when we call println in ClojureScript, it actually does print out the value twice—once to our REPL and once in our browser's JavaScript console. When we evaluate the same logic from within a macro, however, it only has access to the JVM printing environment, and so the value is printed out twice there.

Now, this is all interesting so far, but it doesn't actually let us write very powerful macros. That's where the power of syntax-quoting comes into play. Let's rewrite our original increment macro so that it won't choke when passed a form that needs to be evaluated:

```
(defmacro increment
  "Given a form, increment it by 1 and return"
  [x]
  `(+ 1 ~x))
```

Here, we've made two changes: we've added a backtick (`` ` ``) before our form and we've added a tilde (~) for consistency in front of the x. These are examples of Clojure **macro characters**, and they have special significance to the Clojure reader. The backtick character is known as the syntax-quote character, the tilde is known as the unquote character, and a combination of a tilde and an @ sign, ~@, is the unquote-splicing marker.

For all forms in Clojure that aren't a symbol, a list, a vector, a set, or a map, syntax-quoting a form is the same as quoting it. Syntax-quoting a symbol resolves the symbol within its current context. If the symbol isn't namespace qualified and ends in a pound or hash sign, it will resolve to a generated symbol with a unique ID (this resolution is consistent) so that all references to that symbol within a larger syntax-quoted expression will resolve to the same generated symbol.

Most importantly, syntax-quoting a list, vector, set, or map creates a template of the corresponding data structure (let's not forget that lists are the canonical data structure for Clojure as well as ClojureScript code). Within the template, ordinary forms act as if they, too, have been syntax-quoted, but forms can be exempted from this by unquoting or unquote-splicing them. Forms exempted will be treated as expressions and will be replaced in their template by their value (or sequence of values).

What does all of this mean? In the case of our *increment* macro, we've syntax-quoted the form `(+ 1 ~x)` and we've unquoted x. This means that the macro will try to evaluate whatever is passed in as x and then replace that result with x in the template. In this particular case, the net effect of all of this magic is just to get us back to having our increment macro behave like a function. Let's try writing another function in our `experiment.consumers` namespace:

```
(defn increment-func
  "Increment y by 1"
  [y]
  (m/increment y))
```

And now let's try calling it from the REPL:

```
cljs.user=> (experiment.consumers/increment-func (+ 1 2))
;; => 4
```

Nifty!

Writing more advanced macros

Let's try a slightly more advanced macro. We'll write a macro that takes a normal function body-let's say something like `(+ 1 2 3 4)`-and replaces the function in the calling position with a provided function. What we want to do here is to construct a new form with the provided function at the front and then to have the rest of the original body, without its original function. Such a macro might look like the following:

```
(defmacro fnswap
  "Replace the form in the calling position of body with the function
   f, evaluate and return."
  [f body]
  `(~f ~@(rest body)))
```

Most of this new macro should look pretty familiar to us: we're syntax-quoting the form and we're returning a new form with our new function, unquoted, at the front. We're also using the `rest` function to extract the remaining elements of the form that's passed in. The new syntactical element here that we haven't used previously is the unquote-splicing marker, `~@`. Unquote-splicing takes the contents of the form being provided and un-nests them from the form they're in (typically a list) into the form outside of it.

Let's test out calling our function:

```
cljs.user=> (experiment.macros/fnswap - (+ 1 2))
;; => -1
```

Here, we've swapped out the + in the calling position with its mathematical counterpart, −. Let's quickly verify that it worked:

```
cljs.user=> (- 1 2)
;; => -1
```

Cool. Let's try stepping through what's actually happening. First, the fully non-macroexpanded form looks the following:

```
`(~f ~@(rest (+ 1 2)))
```

The `rest` function removes the + operator:

```
`(~f ~@(1 2))
```

The unquote-splice drops the contents of the (1 2) list into the outer form:

```
`(~f 1 2)
```

Finally, the function is replaced by the function we've passed in:

```
`(- 1 2)
```

This body is then returned to the caller and evaluated, where it returns −1.

Gensyms and local binding in macros

We touched on this a little bit earlier in this section, but creating local bindings within a syntax-quoted block doesn't work the way you might expect. Let's give it a shot anyways and see what happens. Try adding the following macro to experiment.macros:

```
(defmacro bad-binding
  "An example of how local binding in macros does not work"
  []
  `(let [x 5]
     x))
```

Seems fairly straightforward, right? Sadly, it won't work—the macro reader won't let us bind to a plain symbol, and attempting to call this macro from the REPL will throw an exception:

```
cljs.user=> (experiment.macros/bad-binding)
;; => clojure.lang.ExceptionInfo: Invalid local name:
experiment.macros/x at line 1 <cljs repl> {:file "<cljs repl>", :line 1,
:column 1, :tag :cljs/analysis-error}
```

Instead, we have to bind local variables to **gensyms** (**generated symbols**). These are syntactically different from ordinary symbols in that the symbol name is followed by a hash, or pound sign, as follows:

```
(defmacro good-binding
  "An example of how local binding in macros does work"
  []
  `(let [x# 5]
    x#))
```

Now let's try this out at the REPL:

```
cljs.user=> (experiment.macros/good-binding)
;; => 5
```

Under the hood, all that gensyms do is generate new symbols with unique names that the macro reader knows how to look up.

Don't repeat yourself!

Often, when writing macros, you'll find that you're passing as an argument to the macro an entire body of code that you want to be evaluated. Maybe your macro rewrites the body before evaluating it, or maybe it sets some additional local bindings before the body is evaluated, or maybe it does any number of things. The key thing to realize is that it is entirely possible for you to inadvertently end up evaluating the body that is passed in multiple times.

This sounds like it might not be that big of a deal, and for the sort of examples we've been working with so far, it's not. But let's imagine you're working on some hypothetical application where you need a macro that does some analytics and logging for database queries or API calls. If you were to write such a macro as follows:

```
(defmacro db-metrics
  "Analyze and log the query."
  [body]
  `(do
    (analyze ~body)
    (log ~body)))
```

With the intent of calling it as follows:

```
(defn store-data
  "Write data to our data store."
  [data]
  (db-metrics
    (db/store data)))
```

Then you'd be calling your data storage function twice since the macro calls ~body twice! This sort of mistake is surprisingly easy to make, so it's critical when developing to keep an eye out for it.

A personal favorite – Threading macros

So far in this chapter, we've talked a lot about writing macros, but have said little about using them. In practice, you'll usually find yourself using macros all the time, and often you won't even know that you're doing it! For instance, did you know that even really basic logical forms like when and and are macros in ClojureScript rather than functions?

One set of macros that we use all the time are known as the **threading macros**. These macros can be used to take the evaluated value of one form and immediately hand it over to the next form for evaluation. For instance, the -> macro takes the first form, evaluates it, and inserts it as the second item in the next form, and takes that result and does the same with the next form, and so on. Let me show you an example:

```
cljs.user=> (-> 3
              inc
              (+ 4)
              (str "...is the final result"))
;; => "8...is the final result"
```

This piece of code is exactly the same as writing the following:

```
(str (+ (inc 3) 4) "...is the final result")
```

The ->> macro works similarly, but instead of inserting each stage's result as the second argument, it inserts it as the last argument, for instance:

```
cljs.user=> (->> 3
              inc
              (* 4)
              (- 15)
              (str "The final result is: "))
;; => "The final result is: -1"
```

This may not seem like a big deal, and, in truth, it's more of a style choice than anything. However, you'll often find yourself composing *pipelines* of data transformations where you're passing the return value of one small pure function to another small pure function. Using the threading macro makes it easy to compose these pipelines without using so many parentheses, while also making it clear how the different functions work together.

Our favorite threading macros, however, are some-> and some->>. These macros work just like -> and ->>, but stop evaluating as soon as any function returns nil. For instance, let's add the following functions to our experiment.consumers namespace:

```
(defn always-nil
  "Just return nil."
  [& args]
  nil)
(defn example
  "An example of early form termination."
  []
  (some->> 3
      inc
      always-nil
      (println "I should never be evaluated.")
      true))
```

Since we know that the always-nil function should always return nil, we should never see that println statement evaluated. Let's make sure that's the case at the REPL:

```
cljs.user=> (experiment.consumers/example)
;; => nil
```

Bellissimo. The some-> and some->> macros are great to use in cases where the final function they're supposed to be passed to can't take a nil value (maybe because it's an external library that'll throw an exception when passed a nil value, or because they're computationally expensive functions that are just doing busywork with nil). Think of these macros as lazy evaluation for sequences, but applied to program logic. Only use what you need.

A closing note on macros

Before ending this section on macros, it's worth considering what their ultimate place is in the context of your ClojureScript libraries and applications. Unquestionably, macros are an incredibly powerful tool. You can use them to essentially rewrite, on the fly, any code that's passed into them, and they can be used to generate domain-specific languages, complete powerful refactoring efforts, and establish different local bindings. You can use macros to do almost anything.

And yet, you probably shouldn't. Most of the time, you can accomplish what you're trying to do using a plain function, not a macro. Functions are easier to write, easier to read, and, perhaps most importantly, easier to understand and reason about. Macros, by contrast, can easily become complicated and difficult to read. It can be difficult to understand the runtime implications of macros, and how they compose together.

 You can reduce macros' complexity by writing functions that do some of the heavier lifting and then calling those functions from the macros.

That's not to say that you shouldn't use them. There are definitely times when, for the domain you're working in, it's totally appropriate for the vast majority of your library or application to be comprised of macros. But if you can accomplish the same goals using a simpler tool, you should do so. The version of yourself that'll return to your code two years later will thank you.

Concurrent design patterns using core.async

Like its host language, JavaScript, and its parent language, Clojure, ClojureScript has a rich set of concurrency-oriented design patterns that are available to developers by default. In ClojureScript's case, these design patterns are heavily event-driven as an asynchronous event/message queue is the default concurrency model of JavaScript. However, it also has access to CSP-style concurrency software design primitives and options through the use of the powerful `core.async` library, which has been available for both Clojure and ClojureScript since mid-2013.

In this section, we'll review what these different concurrency models look like and learn how we can use `core.async` to author programs that are easier to reason about at scale.

Before getting started with the examples in this section, you'll want to make sure you have two dependencies in your `project.clj` file (at the root directory of our `experiment` project).

The first, `core.async`, should already be listed in your dependencies since a new Figwheel project will include it by default `[org.clojure/core.async "0.2.374"]` (the specific version you use likely won't matter, but it'd be a good idea to make sure you're using at least that version).

Second, we'll want to include `cljs-ajax`, a simple Ajax client for ClojureScript and Clojure. To add that, just add the following to your `:dependencies` key: `[cljs-ajax "0.5.3"]`. You'll need to restart your Figwheel REPL in order for these changes to take effect and you should delete the previously compiled files in `/resources/public/js/compiled` in order for Figwheel to properly pick up the new dependencies.

JavaScript is event-driven by default

If you're familiar with the JavaScript runtime, you're aware of the fact that one of the more unique features of JavaScript is its *event loop*. The event loop is, essentially, a message queue in which messages are associated with functions and are evaluated as they are received. JavaScript's event loop makes for a very unique concurrency model that strongly emphasizes asynchronous behavior; instead of blocking while waiting on an I/O operation, it handles those through callbacks and promises.

A callback is a function that is passed to another function that is usually triggered at some point during that function's execution. In JavaScript, this often takes the form of success and failure callbacks based on the result of some sort of asynchronous operation, such as I/O operations.

A promise is a more abstract pattern of working with asynchronous code, and it represents the eventual result of an asynchronous operation. Typically, promises are used in combination with callbacks; a JavaScript promise is an object or function with three states: pending, fulfilled, or rejected. The promise takes a function, `then`, which takes two arguments, `onFulfilled` and `onRejected`, which are typically both callback functions.

This means that in comparison to more synchronous languages like Java or C, JavaScript is able to process other inbound messages and functions while waiting for an I/O operation to complete.

A concrete example of this might be making a database query or an API call and then receiving a mouse click event. When making such a query or call in a language like Java or C, unless the program explicitly released the current thread, the program would block (wait) for the query or call to return before being able to handle the click event. By contrast, JavaScript immediately goes on to process the click event and doesn't attempt to do anything with the response of the database query or API call until it has actually returned.

Event-driven programming in ClojureScript

ClojureScript is even more of a functional language than JavaScript, and the use of design patterns that orient around callbacks and promises are both common and frequently seen. One could even say that since ClojureScript compiles to JavaScript, they represent the default option for concurrent program design.

As a simple example, if you decide to use the popular `cljs-ajax` library for making asynchronous HTTP requests, you'll often make requests in which you specify a success handler and an error handler. The following code is taken from the `cljs-ajax` README and shows an example of how we might use callbacks:

```
(ns foo
  (:require [ajax.core :refer [GET]]))

(defn handler [response]
  (.log js/console (str response)))

(defn error-handler [{:keys [status status-text]}]
  (.log js/console (str "something bad happened: " status " " status-
text)))

(GET "http://www.your-server.com/hello-world"
    {:hander handler
     :error-handler error-handler})
```

Here we've passed two possible callback functions, `handler` and `error-handler`, in an options map to the `GET` function, which will call one of the two functions based on what ultimate response code it receives from the target server when making the HTTP request.

The Communicating Sequential Processes concurrency model

ClojureScript's `core.async` library differs considerably from JavaScript's default concurrency model in that it is modeled heavily on a formal language for describing patterns of interaction in concurrent systems known as communicating sequential processes. **Communicating sequential processes**, or **CSP**, is a member of a family of different concurrency theories that are oriented around the notion of message passing via channels.

In the context of ClojureScript, a CSP concurrency model means that rather than designing programs off of a single message queue (the JavaScript runtime event loop), the creation and maintenance of an arbitrary number of message queues is used instead. These message queues, typically referred to as channels, can have messages enqueued by any part of a program and dequeued anywhere else, and allow for programs and systems to be designed with a stronger separation of concerns between the producers of data and their consumers and processors.

In JVM Clojure, `core.async` provides a handy API for managing message passing between threads. Since ClojureScript shares JavaScript's single-threaded runtime, in practice the experience of writing programs with `core.async` gives the feel of writing a multithreaded program, without either the headache or the actual implementation concerns. For those of you coming from a JavaScript background, there's also no callback hell!

Another advantage of `core.async` is that it's fast, especially when compared to JavaScript's promises. David Nolen, the primary author and maintainer of ClojureScript, published a blog post, "Make No Promises", not too long after the initial release of `core.async` comparing the speed of vanilla JavaScript promises to messages passed over a `core.async`. While individual tests vary widely, on average, the messages passed using `core.async` were evaluated two to three times as quickly, and, in some cases, five times faster. The post itself is available at `http://swannodette.github.io/2013/08/23/make-no-promises/`.

If all of this doesn't make sense just yet, don't worry—concurrency models can seem very complicated when discussed in the abstract. What's important to know is the following.

First, CSP represents a very different model from the default model of callbacks and promises that you may be used to in JavaScript. Second, this model is highly flexible and allows you to write code that separates the behavior of data consumers and processors from their producers. Finally, this new model is optional-that's why it's in a library rather than a part of the core language.

We believe that `core.async` is incredibly powerful, and so does the ClojureScript community at large. You'll find that many open source libraries are built upon its concurrency model because it's easier to reason about and more elegant to work with.

Getting started with core.async

Let's get our hands dirty. Let's create a new file at `src/experiment/async.cljs`. We'll populate that file with the following code:

```
(ns experiment.async
  (:require [cljs.core.async :as async])
  (:require-macros
    [cljs.core.async.macros :as async-macros]))

(def channel (async/chan 5))

(defn enqueue-val
  "Enqueue a new value into our channel."
  [v]
  (async-macros/go
    (async/>! channel v)))

(defn retrieve-val
  []
  "Retrieve a new value from our channel and log it."
  (async-macros/go
    (js/console.log (async/<! channel))))

(defn enqueue-and-retrieve
  "Enqueue a value into a channel, and then test that we can retrieve
it."
  [v]
  (enqueue-val v)
  (retrieve-val))
```

Let's make sure our application loads this code by making sure that our main namespace, `experiment.core` (located at `src/experiment/core.cljs`), has a `:require` statement for it:

```
(ns experiment.core
  (:require [experiment.consumers :as consumers]
            [experiment.async]))
```

Great, that should have everything up and running. If you're worried that things might not be linked properly, save one of these files and check the Figwheel page you should have open in your browser (`http://localhost:3449`). When you save the file, Figwheel should be showing us that everything's been compiled. If not, pay attention to any error messages that have been shown and make sure to fix those before proceeding.

 A quick review, since we're starting to write some larger namespaces: the use of Figwheel in a development environment means that every time we save this file, Figwheel should be automatically recompiling our application and pushing it to the browser. This means that if you define a function and call it in the namespace, the function will automatically be called in the browser's context.

In other words, if you have Figwheel running, the only thing you need to do to *run* this code is to save the project file.

Good? Great. Now let's step through what's going on here section by section.

```
(ns experiment.async
  (:require [cljs.core.async :as async])
  (:require-macros
    [cljs.core.async.macros :as async-macros]))
```

First, we have our namespace declaration. Looks straightforward enough, we're importing the ClojureScript version of `core.async` and we're also importing the appropriate macros from a separate namespace with an appropriately named alias:

```
(def channel (async/chan 5))
```

This is how we define a `core.async` message channel. Simple! The 5 in this case is an optional argument that specifies how large we want the channel's buffer to be (that is, how many messages it can hold at one time). In addition to specifying the buffer's size, we can also choose what we want the buffer's strategy to be. For instance, we could use the `dropping-buffer` function to generate a buffer that drops new values when the buffer is full or we could use the `sliding-buffer` function to generate a buffer that drops the oldest value in the queue and retains the latest value being added when the buffer is full.

In general, being explicit about your buffer size and behavior is a good idea. If you don't set an explicit buffer size, the buffer size will be set as . In this case, the channel will not allow anything to be published unless there is a waiting consumer. Note that this does not block the thread; it just means that the publisher will be parked, waiting, until such time as a consumer becomes available.

If you don't set an explicit buffer strategy, `core.async` will use a fixed buffer. This may or may not be ideal for your program; you should think carefully about whether you are better served by one particular buffer strategy versus another.

In addition to specifying the buffer, you can also add a transducer to a channel, an example of which we showed earlier on in this chapter. We'll be taking another look at one of the cool ways transducers and channels work together later on in this chapter as well.

```
(defn enqueue-val
  "Enqueue a new value into our channel."
  [v]
  (async-macros/go
    (async/>! channel v)))
```

This function shows how we can add a value to the channel. We call the `>!` macro to put a value into the channel. One thing that's important to be aware of is that a number of `core.async` functions that interact with channels have to take place inside of a `go` block. The `go` blocks are somewhat magical macros in ClojureScript in that they are essentially asynchronous blocks of execution in which the illusion of blocking operations is supported.

Putting values into a channel within a `go` block is more or less instantaneous and will always succeed unless the channel is full, is of buffer size and has no consumers, or has been closed with the `close!` function. However, when taking a value from a channel, being inside a `go` block means that nothing after the take command (`<!`) will execute until a value can be retrieved from the channel.

This doesn't mean that a `go` block will grind your entire application to a halt if it's blocked on waiting for a message. It just means that the subsequent operations inside of the `go` block won't happen until the take command succeeds. The rest of your program will continue to function using the JavaScript event loop.

Now, let's see how we can take a value off of a channel:

```
(defn retrieve-val
  []
```

```
    "Retrieve a new value from our channel and log it."
    (async-macros/go
      (js/console.log (async/<! channel)))))
```

Again, very straightforward. We see the same usage of the go blocks and the function to take a message from a channel is syntactically very similar to the function for putting things into the channel. Easy enough. Let's put all of this together:

```
(defn enqueue-and-retrieve
    "Enqueue a value into a channel, and then test that we can retrieve
  it."
    [v]
    (enqueue-val v)
    (retrieve-val))
```

Then let's try calling this function at our REPL:

```
cljs.user=> (experiment.async/enqueue-and-retrieve "Hello!")
;; => #object[cljs.core.async.impl.channels.ManyToManyChannel]
```

If we check our JavaScript console, we should see `Hello!` printed there.

Note that go blocks return a channel that will contain one message—the last expression in the go block. This can be helpful for error reporting. This is important to keep in mind because you won't otherwise be able to access the return value of the final expression in the block. If you want the return value of the final expression, you have to take from the channel.

Background listeners

Let's take our original idea and expand on it a bit. It feels contrived and very manual to have to call a function to check whether there's something in our channel. What if we could modify our code so that it was just always listening and it did something whenever a new value was found? Let's rewrite our code to do that. Let's add a new function, listen, as follows:

```
(defn listen
    []
    "Listen to our channel for any events and log them to the console."
    (async-macros/go
      (while true
        (js/console.log (async/<! channel))))))
```

This might seem like it would just loop forever, but remember that within `core.async` project's `go` blocks, functions like `<!` are essentially blocking. So as long as `<!` doesn't find a new value on the channel, `listen` won't continue to loop.

We'll want to add a call to this function to the end of our namespace to get the listener started:

```
(listen)
```

You could call this at the REPL instead if you wanted, though in a production application you'd want to start the listener after you defined it or at an appropriate time rather than through a manual REPL process:

```
cljs.user=> (experiment.async/listen)
;; => #object[cljs.core.async.impl.channels.ManyToManyChannel]
```

Now, in theory, if we were to put a new value into our channel, it would be immediately read and logged by our background listener. Let's give it a shot!

```
cljs.user=> (experiment.async/enqueue-val "Is anybody out there?")
;; => #object[cljs.core.async.impl.channels.ManyToManyChannel]
```

You should be able to check your console and see our string in the console-our background listener is working!

Errors and core.async

One of the great advantages of `core.async`, its separation of concerns, can also be a drawback. Specifically, if we have code that expects to be able to read data from a channel that is generated by some sort of producing function, what happens when errors occur? We could just handle the error within the producing function, but that might be a very different part of the program. We might well want a central pipeline for handling errors.

There are a few different ways we could handle this. One possibility might be to create a separate channel for error messages and to have a listener for that channel that logs and reports errors to an exception tracking service. Let's consider what that might look like.

As an example, let's assume that we want our application to be able to poll the kitten factory to make sure everything's going smoothly.

 What even happens at the kitten factory? Is it a factory that makes kittens, or do kittens run the factory? If they're running the factory, what are they making—balls of yarn? We have trouble imagining this would be a very efficient factory.

Such code might look like the following:

```
(ns experiment.kitten.factory
  "Logic for handling messages from the kitten factory."
  (:require [cljs.core.async :as async]
            [ajax.core :refer [GET]])
  (:require-macros
    [cljs.core.async.macros :as async-macros]))

(def channel (async/chan 5))
(def error-channel (async/chan 5))

(defn enqueue-val
  "Enqueue a new value into our channel."
  [c v]
  (async-macros/go
    (async/>! c v)))

(defn success-fn
  [v]
  (enqueue-val channel v))

(defn error-fn
  [e]
  (enqueue-val error-channel e))

(defn kitten-factory
  []
  (GET "/kitten-factory"
       {:handler success-fn
        :error-handler error-fn}))

(defn listen
  []
  "Listen for the latest message from the kitten factory channels."
  (async-macros/go
    (while true
      (let [[v ch] (async/alts! [channel error-channel])]
        (case ch
          channel
          (do #_(send-success-report-to-cat-hq v))
          error-channel
          (do #_(send-error-report-to-cat-sq v)))))))

(listen)
```

Most of this code should look fairly straightforward to you by now, but one new thing is the use of `alts!`. `alts!` is a function that returns a single bound local variable from any of the provided channels. In this case, it's handy since we can define a single `while` loop for all kitten factory-related behavior and just check to see if the message came in on an error message channel or on the normal message channel.

An alternative pattern that we could embrace, if we wanted, would be one in which we actually passed an error itself into the channel. This error-handling pattern is one that David Nolen has written about previously on his blog at `http://swannodette.github.io/2013/08/31/asynchronous-error-handling/`.

In order for the following example to work, we'd need two additional namespaces:

```
(ns experiment.kitten.helpers)

(defn error?
  [x]
  (instance? js/Error x))

(defn throw-err
  [x]
  (if (error? x)
    (throw x)
    x))
```

And we need another macro file (remember to use `.clj`, not `.cljs`, as the file type!):

```
(ns experiment.kitten.macros)

(defmacro <?
  "Actively throw an exception if something goes wrong when waiting on
a channel message."
  [expr]
  `(experiment.kitten.helpers/throw-err (cljs.core.async/<! ~expr)))
```

Lastly, our factory file class might now look like the following:

```
(ns experiment.kitten.factory
  "Logic for handling messages from the kitten factory."
  (:require [cljs.core.async :as async]
            [ajax.core :refer [GET]]
            [experiment.kitten.helpers])
  (:require-macros
    [cljs.core.async.macros :as async-macros]
    [experiment.macros :as m]))

(def channel (async/chan 5))
```

```
(defn enqueue-val
  "Enqueue a new value into our channel."
  [c v]
  (async-macros/go
    (async/>! c v)))

(defn kitten-factory
  []
  (GET "/kitten-factory"
       {:handler (fn [res] (enqueue-val channel res))
        :error-handler (fn [err] (enqueue-val channel (js/Error.
err)))}))

(defn listen
  []
  "Listen for the latest message from the kitten factory channel.
  If message is an error, throw and catch."
  (async-macros/go
    (while true
      (try
        (let [v (m/<? channel)]
          ;; (send-success-report-to-cat-hq)
          )
        (catch js/Error e
          ;; (send-error-report-to-cat-hq e)
          )))))

(listen)
```

The <? macro we've written in this case is a fairly straightforward macro helper that just checks to see if the value that's been pulled off of the channel is an error and, if it is throws an error. Otherwise we'd just be passing an error around by value and the compiler wouldn't actually throw an error.

This seems fine, but it's a little complicated. Do we really need that extra macro and space? If we recall some of the content we covered earlier in the chapter, we see an opportunity for us to use a transducer here. Let's try rewriting this example to use a transducer instead:

```
(ns experiment.kitten.factory
  "Logic for handling messages from the kitten factory."
  (:require [cljs.core.async :as async]
            [ajax.core :refer [GET]])
  (:require-macros
    [cljs.core.async.macros :as async-macros]))

(defn error?
  [x]
```

```
      (instance? js/Error x))

  (defn throw-err
    [x]
    (if (error? x)
      (throw x)
      x))

  (def channel (async/chan 5 (map throw-err)))

  (defn enqueue-val
    "Enqueue a new value into our channel."
    [c v]
    (async-macros/go
      (async/>! c v)))

  (defn kitten-factory
    []
    (GET "/kitten-factory"
          {:handler (fn [res] (enqueue-val channel res))
           :error-handler (fn [err] (enqueue-val channel (js/Error.
err)))}))

  (defn listen
    []
    "Listen for the latest message from the kitten factory channel."
    (async-macros/go
      (while true
        (try
          (let [v (async/<! channel)]
            (js/console.log "All good cap")
          )
          (catch js/Error e
            ;; (send-error-report-to-cat-hq e)
            )))))

  (listen)
```

Wow! Instead of needing a custom macro, we can just pass the error detection function directly to the channel and have it do the transformation when we pull from the channel. This is a great example of the incredible power we can get by combining transducers and `core.async`.

If you're interested in playing with this example in a more interactive fashion, try modifying the `listen` function to add more explicit logging behavior based on the type of value retrieved from the channel, then see what happens when you try calling `enqueue-val` at the REPL with different value types. What happens when you enqueue an error? What happens when you enqueue a normal value?

Summary

At this point, you should be comfortable with some of ClojureScript's more advanced concepts. You've had a chance to familiarize yourself with ClojureScript's functional code patterns and you've learned how to write macros that are capable of changing the way ClojureScript code itself is evaluated. Lastly, you've had an in-depth introduction to `core.async`—an elegant and powerful tool for writing asynchronous code.

In this next chapter, we'll start to dig into the meat of writing web applications in ClojureScript. You'll learn about how to work with the DOM and CSS, as well as newer HTML5 elements like canvas and media. By the end of it, you'll be able to build a basic web application!

4
Web Applications Basics with ClojureScript

ClojureScript, because of its very essence (Clojure targeting JavaScript through the use of the Google Closure library), has led to various approaches as far as developing on the browser is concerned.

As being a hosted language with powerful JavaScript interoperability primitives, ClojureScript empowers its developers to mirror their JavaScript DOM manipulation and events handling habits in their ClojureScript code, as if they were translating it verbatim.

But one can go one level further in abstraction, and take advantage from the Google Closure library's central place in ClojureScript to write better and more browser-agnostic DOM manipulation and events handling routines.

The DOM can also be accessed through the usage of ad hoc developed ClojureScript libraries, built to abstract away the raw browser's API in an idiomatic Clojure-esque way.

Besides manipulating directly the DOM, the development on the browser can be addressed through client-side templating. As ClojureScript is a language in which data plays a central role, it is no surprise that we can see it fuel interesting client-side templating libraries.

Finally, it is possible to streamline, thanks to some ClojureScript libraries, the CSS assets creation process.

In this chapter we'll see:

- Raw DOM manipulation and events handling
- Interacting with the browser via Google Closure
- Dommy – an idiomatic ClojureScript Library for the DOM

- Client side templating in ClojureScript
- CSS preprocessors in ClojureScript

Raw DOM manipulation and events handling

Thanks to the interoperability with JavaScript, we can translate, mostly word by word, the same very mutable JavaScript logic into ClojureScript programs. You'll find yourself select DOM nodes using their IDs or mutating their properties to change their appearance on the browser for instance. In JavaScript, handling events corresponds to setting callbacks, that is, assigning functions – called **callbacks** – to special properties corresponding to those events (like `onmousemove`, and so on). You can follow the same logic in ClojureScript, setting event handlers by mutating those same DOM nodes event descriptor properties.

You only have to remember that if you want to access a DOM's element property, you would write:

```
(-.property a-js-object)
```

And to mutate these properties properties, you would have to make use of the `set!` function:

```
(set! (-.a-property a-js-object)
```

Although this approach means somehow falling back to raw JavaScript, all of the functional operators and powerful data structures that are specific to ClojureScript remain available for the developers to use. You can still store JavaScript objects in ClojureScript vectors, sets or maps, and apply to such collections `map`, `reduce`, `filter` or whatever functional operator you please. You can even map functions that contain raw JavaScript manipulation operations to `seqs` of JavaScript objects.

Let's see an example of how DOM manipulation and events handling can be programmed in a style heavily inspired by plain JavaScript coding practice.

We'll be using Figwheel to work with our project. Create a new Clojure project:

```
lein new raw-dom
```

Edit the `project.clj` file of your freshly created project so it looks like the following:

```
(defproject raw-dom "0.1.0-SNAPSHOT"
  :dependencies [[org.clojure/clojure "1.8.0"]
                 [org.clojure/clojurescript "1.7.228"]]
  :plugins [[lein-figwheel "0.5.0-6"]]
```

```
  :clean-targets [:target-path "out"]
  :cljsbuild {
    :builds [{:id "dev"
              :source-paths ["src"]
              :figwheel true
              :compiler {:main "raw-dom.core"}
             }]
  })
```

Now create a HTML page, index.html, containing the following code:

```
<html>
  <body>
    <h2>Clicks So Far:</h2>
    <h3 id="clicks">0</h3>
    <button id="reset-btn">Reset count!</button>
    <script type="text/javascript" src="main.js"></script>
  </body>
</html>
```

This HTML page contains some text, and a button. Our intent is to implement a functionality which consists of counting the number of clicks on the page and updating them in the h3 HTML header identified as **clicks** in the DOM. If the user hits the **Reset Count!** button, the clicks count is reset to .

Let's implement this functionality. Create the core.cljs file (present in the src/raw_dom directory in your project folder) containing the following ClojureScript code:

```
(ns raw-dom.core)

(def  cnt-holder (.getElementById js/document "clicks"))
(def  reset-btn (.getElementById js/document "reset-btn"))
(def  cnt (atom 0))

(defn inc-clicks!
  []
  (set! (.-innerHTML cnt-holder) (swap! cnt inc)))

(defn reset-clicks!
  []
  (set! (.-innerHTML cnt-holder) (reset! cnt -1)))

(set! (.-onclick js/document) inc-clicks!)
(set! (.-onclick reset-btn) reset-clicks!)
```

The preceding snippet gets two DOM elements, referenced by their identifiers in the DOM. The first one is a h3 HTML header, identified by "clicks", and the second is a button, identified by "reset-btn".

We then define an atom, cnt, which will act a the clicks counter.

You would have noticed that we also defined two functions, inc-clicks!, which increments the counter value and assigns it to the innerHTML property of the h3 HTML header, and reset-clicks!, which resets the counter value and assigns it to the content of the same HTML header (we reset it at -1 because the click on the button will also be accounted for as a click on the page, yielding an automatic increment after hitting the **"Reset Count!"** button).

We finally assign inc-clicks! to the onclick event handler of the JavaScript document, and assign reset-clicks! to the **"Reset Count!"** button.

Now run your project's live-coding session by issuing the following command:

```
lein figwheel
```

And point your browser to index.html, by opening it from your file manager.

You'll notice that when you click on the page, the number increases, and clicking on the button sets it to 0.

You've seen how we can translate raw JavaScript thinking to ClojureScript. Naturally, every JavaScript developer would at this stage wonder: can I use JQuery? It is totally possible to do so, but going this way with the basic JavaScript interoperability style would lead to very bloated code and would probably make us deviate from our original purpose, of benefiting from a high and expressive development experience on the browser. Besides, JQuery, in order to be properly handled at the Google Closure advanced mode compilation, must be referenced in the externs section of your project.clj file, thus adding some more complexity to your work.

That being said, there is one library that abstracts away jQuery use in a good idiomatic ClojureScript way: Jayq (https://github.com/ibdknox/jayq). As the author of this library states, having a good layer of abstraction over one of the most fundamental libraries of the web is a power addition to our ClojureScript toolbox (at the cost of properly managing the externs declarations, of course!). Let's see it in action in a little example.

First, let's create a new project which we'll call, `jq-project` and add the dependency to jayq in our `project.clj`:

```
(defproject jq-project "0.1.0-SNAPSHOT"
  :dependencies [[org.clojure/clojure "1.8.0"]
                 [org.clojure/clojurescript "1.7.228"]
                 [jayq "2.5.4"]]
  :plugins [[lein-figwheel "0.5.0-6"]]
  :clean-targets [:target-path "out"]
  :cljsbuild {
    :builds [{:id "dev"
              :source-paths ["src"]
              :figwheel true
              :compiler {:main "jq-project.core"}
             }]
  })
```

Next, let's prepare an HTML page that we'll change by using ClojureScript powered jQuery. Be sure to include the jQuery JavaScript dependency in the `index.html` page. Since we're not compiling our ClojureScript with `advanced` mode, there's no need to add the jQuery reference in the `externs` section of the Google Closure compilation options.

Here is what our page, `index.html`, should look like:

```
<html>
  <body>
    <head>
      <script src=
"https://ajax.googleapis.com/ajax/libs/jquery/1.11.3/jquery.min.js"></scrip
t>
    </head>
    <div id="some-div"><a>Some Text</a></div>
    <script type="text/javascript" src="main.js"></script>
  </body>
</html>
```

Now, let's write some ClojureScript code that showcases Jayq's usage. Let's edit our project's `core.cljs` file so that it contains the following code:

```
(ns jq-project.core
  (:use [jayq.core :only [$ css html]]))

(def $some-div ($ :#some-div))

(defn change-the-div!
  []
  (-> $some-div
```

```
(css {:background "cyan"})
(html "changed Inner HTML")))
```

 Note how Jayq bridges the gap between ClojureScript and jQuery: it exposes a dollar ($) function, so jQuery developers feel at home. The library enables us to access all jQuery functionality via this dollar function.

In `core.cljs`, we selected the div by its identifier, and stored it in some variable, `$some-div`. Then, we built a function, `change-the-div!`, which when launched, changes `$some-div`'s CSS and HTML properties. See how the access to the jQuery beloved jQuery dollar flows through the Clojure-esque threading macro!

Now let's launch our project's interactive development session:

```
$ lein figwheel
```

And let's point our browser to `index.html`. It should show a white page on which we can read **Some Text.**

Go back in your Figwheel REPL, and evaluate the buffer showing `core.cljs` using the following command on CIDER (provided you followed instructions about using `inf-clojure` in Chapter 1, *Getting Ready For ClojureScript Development*):

```
M-x RET inf-clojure-eval-buffer
```

You can also evaluate this namespace by typing in (`require jq-project.core`) at the Figwheel REPL.

Now launch `change-the-div!` and see how the `div` color and text changed.

The example shows how we can use ClojureScript to interact with the browser in a "raw" way, manipulating the DOM with JavaScript and sQuery. So, now you might be wondering, if ClojureScript is based on the Google Closure Library, why couldn't we manipulate the DOM nodes using this library? Great question! We'll see this in the following section.

Interacting with the browser using the Google Closure Library

Since ClojureScript is built on top of the Google Closure Library, it is possible for it to import facilities from the library directly. We can use the Google Closure Library to access the DOM, respond to events and manipulate style via respective Google Closure Libraries: `goog.dom`, `goog.events` and `goog.style`. They are all directly available to ClojureScript and require no special configuration to work with the Advanced Compilation mode.

Let's have a look at what working with these libraries looks like in the following project. We'll create a Clojure project and name it `raw-goog`.

```
$ lein new figwheel raw-goog
```

We'll use the `index.html` page we built for the click counting project, only here we'll re-implement the project using the Google Closure Library as follows:

```
<html>
  <body>
    <h2>Clicks So Far:</h2>
    <h3 id="clicks">0</h3>
    <button id="reset-btn">Reset count!</button>
    <script type="text/javascript" src="main.js"></script>
  </body>
</html>
```

Now, let's rewrite the click-counting code using the Google Closure Library:

```
(ns raw-goog.core
  (:require [goog.dom :as dom]
            [goog.events :as events]))

(def cnt-holder (dom/getElement "clicks"))

(def  reset-btn (dom/getElement "reset-btn"))

(def  cnt (atom 0))

(defn inc-clicks!
  []
  (dom/setTextContent cnt-holder (swap! cnt inc)))

(defn reset-clicks!
  []
  (dom/setTextContent cnt-holder (reset! cnt 0)))
```

```
(events/listen cnt-holder "click" inc-clicks!)(events/listen reset-btn
"click" reset-clicks!)
```

Launch your interactive ClojureScript development development using Figwheel:

```
$ lein figwheel
```

Our application now increments the counter by clicking on the shown number. Note the use of the `getElement` method of the `goog.dom` library to select a DOM node, and the use of the method `listen` from the `goog.events` library to attach event handlers to specific DOM elements.

But this approach, apart from targeting the Google Closure Library, is practically no different from using basic JavaScript interoperability style. Can we interact with the Google Closure Library in a more idiomatic way? The answer to this question is the purpose of Domina (`https://github.com/levand/domina`), a library abstracting usage of the Google Closure Library in a Clojure-esque way. Let's take a look at it.

Let's create a new Figwheel Project, `domina-project`, and add the `domina` dependency into the `project.clj` file:

```
(defproject domina-project "0.1.0-SNAPSHOT"
  :dependencies [[org.clojure/clojure "1.8.0"]
                             [org.clojure/clojurescript "1.7.228"]
                             [domina "1.0.3"]]
  :plugins [[lein-figwheel "0.5.0-6"]]
  :clean-targets [:target-path "out"]
  :cljsbuild {
             :builds [{:id "dev"
                           :source-paths ["src"]
                           :figwheel true
                           :compiler {:main "domina-project.core"}
                           }]
             })
```

Let's use a stripped-down HTML page, so we can test adding DOM elements to it and attaching events to them with `domina`. Here's what our `index.html` should look like:

```
<html>
  <body>
    <div id="a-div"></div>
    <script type="text/javascript" src="main.js"></script>
  </body>
</html>
```

Now, let's focus on the ClojureScript code. For this example, we'll attach a hyperlink to Wikipedia and a button to our page's `div` element. We'll also add a click event handler to the button that will emit a greeting message. Here we go:

```
(ns domina-project.core
  (:require [domina :as dom]
            [domina.css :as css]
            [domina.events :as events]))

(def the-div (css/sel "#a-div"))
(def the-href (dom/html-to-dom "<a></a>"))
(def the-btn (dom/html-to-dom "<button></button>"))


(defn add-dom-elts!
  []
  (doto the-href
    (dom/set-text! "Wikipedia")
    (dom/set-attr! :href "http://en.wikipedia.org"))

  (dom/append! the-div the-href)
  (doto the-btn
    (dom/set-text! "Click me!")
    (dom/set-attr! :type "button"))

  (events/listen!
   the-btn :click
   (fn[evt]
     (let [my-name (-> evt events/current-target dom/text)]
       (js/alert (str  "hello world! from : " my-name) ))))

  (dom/append! the-div the-btn))
```

We first select the main `div` using its id, `#a-div` as a CSS selector. Then, we create two empty DOM nodes, one `a` element and one `button`.

In the body of the `add-dom-elts!` function, we set the text of the `a` element to "Wikipedia" and attach an `href` attribute to it so it becomes a hyperlink. We then add our freshly created hyper-link to the main div.

Next, we set the "Click me!" text on the button DOM node, and set its type attribute to `button`. After we attach a click event handler to it – showing a greeting and the caption of the event initiator—we add it to the DOM by appending it to the `#a-div` div.

The careful reader may have noticed how our last code snippet looked idiomatic—in the style of pure ClojureScript functionality. It is hard to tell that this code is actually making calls to the Google Closure Library under the hood.

For this next section, we'll start a Figwheel browser-REPL for our project:

```
$ lein figwheel
```

Point your browser to `index.html`. Once done, load the preceding ClojureScript code (either using your REPL or via your editor), and check back in your browser: you should now see that two new elements have appeared on your web page: a hyperlink to Wikipedia and a button:

So far, we've seen how to interact with the DOM using direct JavaScript interoperability as well as using, Jayq for an abstraction layer over jQuery. We've also seen how to interact with the browser's elements using the Google Closure Library, either through direct calls or via an idiomatic wrapper around it.

The ClojureScript community came up with other alternatives as well. These alternatives seek even better conformance to ClojureScript ideals in terms of functional programming techniques. Dommy, from Prismatic, is one of these libraries. Let's get acquainted with its way of working with the DOM and associated event handling.

Dommy – An idiomatic ClojureScript library for the DOM

Dommy follows a different approach than what we've see so far. For instance, selecting DOM elements is done via macros that expand to native JavaScript-like DOM selection calls.

Dommy's selection facilities model jQuery's in that that is possible to select single or multiple DOM nodes (respectively using the `sel1` or `sel` macros), and to specify a hierarchy of CSS selectors that, when chained, identify an element to be accessed.

Dommy's DOM manipulation routines are also heavily inspired by jQuery but fit ClojureScript's functional programming style by permitting, for instance, chaining transformations, as we'll see in the upcoming example.

Event handling procedures in Dommy pretty much resemble the Google Closure Library's by using the `listen!` (and `unlisten!`) mechanisms, and not attaching callbacks to properties related to events in specific DOM elements.

Let's see a Dommy sample project. Let's first create a new ClojureScript project, which we'll name `dommy-project`. Modify its `project.clj` definition so that it contains the following:

```
(defproject dommy-project "0.1.0-SNAPSHOT"
  :dependencies [[org.clojure/clojure "1.8.0"]
                 [org.clojure/clojurescript "1.7.228"]
                 [prismatic/dommy "1.1.0"]]
  :plugins [[lein-figwheel "0.5.0-6"]]
  :clean-targets [:target-path "out"]
  :cljsbuild {
    :builds [{:id "dev"
              :source-paths ["src"]
              :figwheel true
              :compiler {:main "dommy-project.core"}
             }]
  })
```

Let's prepare an HTML page, `index.html`, in which we'll create a `div` holding two `p` elements:

```
<html>
  <head><link rel="stylesheet" href="style.css"></head>
  <body>
    <div id="a-div">
      <p class="changeme">I should have a border</p>
      <p class="changeme">I should have a border,too</p>
    </div>
    <script type="text/javascript" src="main.js"></script>
  </body>
</html>
```

Let's set the contents of `style.css` as follows:

```css
.changeme {
    background-color: yellow;
}

.border {
    border: 2px solid red;
}
```

In the beginning, when we load the HTML page, the two p elements should have a yellow background and show their respective captions.

The aim of our example is to show how we can select a set of DOM nodes by chaining CSS selectors (which will all be p elements inside a-div) and how to apply a Dommy transformation to them that removes the CSS changeme class and applies the new CSS border class.

After that, we will add a button and append it to a-div and attach a click event handler to it that will show a greeting on a click event. Modify the `core.cljs` file, under the `src/dommy_project` directory of our project, to look like the following:

```clojure
(ns dommy-project.core
  (:require
    [dommy.core :as dommy :refer-macros [sel sel1]]))

(defn set-borders!
  []
  (let [ all-ps (sel [:#a-div :p])]
    (->> all-ps
         (map  #(dommy/remove-class! % :changeme))
         (map  #(dommy/add-class! % :border))
         (map  #(dommy/set-text! % "I now have a border!")))))

(defn add-btn!
  []
  (let [the-div (sel1 :#a-div)
        a-btn (dommy/create-element "button")]
    (dommy/set-text! a-btn "Click me!")
    (dommy/listen! a-btn :click
                   (fn[e] (js/alert "You clicked me!")))
    (-> the-div
        (dommy/append! a-btn))))
```

Launch a Figwheel REPL for the `dommy-project` project:

```
$ lein figwheel
```

Next, point your browser to `index.html` (loading it from your filesystem). You should see the following:

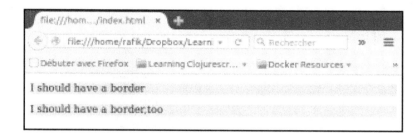

Now, let's load `dommy-project.core` via the Figwheel REPL and call the `set-borders!` function. This function selects all the `p` elements inside `a-div`, then applies a set of transformations using the functional operator `map`: removing each element's initial CSS class, `changeme`, and assigning to them the CSS `border` class and setting a new caption. Note how the threading macro is used, chaining the DOM transformations, with respect to the ClojureScript functional spirit. After you've launched the function, you should see this:

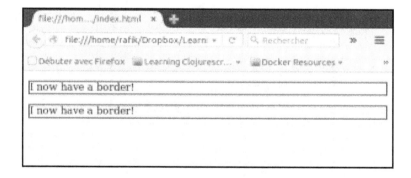

Now let's add a button by calling `add-btn!`. This function creates a "button" DOM node, sets its caption to `Click me!` and assigns a click event handler to it using Dommy's `listen!`. After you've launched this function, you should see:

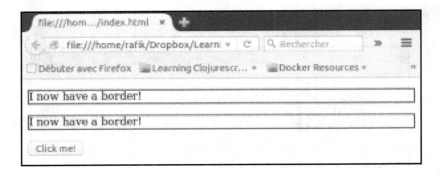

Clicking on this newly created button yields a greeting message, per the function we attached to the click event.

Wow! We've covered quite a range of ways to manipulate the DOM in ClojureScript! We went from the ground up, beginning by interacting with the browser using native JavaScript and then the ClojureScript Library, Jayq. Then, we took advantage of the Google Closure Library that ClojureScript is built upon to issue DOM processing operations, following two approaches: one issuing direct Google Closure Library calls, and one using the help of a ClojureScript wrapper library, Domina. Lastly, we've learned about some idiomatic ClojureScript Libraries that abstract away DOM manipulation and event handling in the browser.

But manipulating the DOM is only one approach to building Web user interfaces. The other one would be to rely on client-side templating tools, where developers can declare their interfaces using ClojureScript data structures without caring about how DOM nodes are created and mutated. Let's take a look at some of our client-side templating possibilities.

Client-side templating in ClojureScript

In Clojure land, there are two big families of HTML templating tools: Hiccup (https://github.com/weavejester/hiccup) and Enlive (https://github.com/cgrand/enlive). Usually used in conjunction with a server framework like Ring (https://github.com/ring-clojure/ring), they are used to programmatically generate the HTML for pages that are eventually served to the web browser. Perhaps unsurprisingly, the ClojureScript community drew inspiration from these two server-side templating philosophies to design libraries offering client-side templating. Let's first take a look at Hipo (`https://github.com/jeluard/hipo/`), the client-side alter-ego of Hiccup. But before we do that, let's discuss Hiccup's syntax.

Hiccup's general idea is as follows: HTML tags are represented as vectors, and any attribute these tags enclose are denoted using maps. For example, let's consider the following snippet of HTML, a `div`, with one CSS class, `a-class`:

```
<div class="a-class">some-text</div>
```

The Hiccup vector corresponding to this HTML would be:

```
[:div {:class "a-class"} "some-text"]
```

It is also possible to chain CSS identifiers and classes in Hiccup to benefit from a more concise syntax. Consider the following example:

```
<div id="a-div" class="class1 class2">
some-text
</div>
```

The Hiccup code generating the previous HTML is:

```
[:div#a-div.class1.class2 "some-text"]
```

This syntax makes it possible to generate user interfaces using ClojureScript sequences. For instance, to generate some menu options in HTML, we can use the following Hiccup snippet:

```
[:ul
  (for [x ["item1" "item2" "item3" "item4"]]
     [:li x])]
```

With this little primer on Hiccup syntax under our belt, let's see how, Hipo can be used to build a web user interface in the following example.

As usual, let's begin by creating a new ClojureScript project, naming it `hipo-project`. In this project's `project.clj` file, be sure to have the following:

```
(defproject hipo-project "0.1.0-SNAPSHOT"
  :dependencies [[org.clojure/clojure "1.7.0"]
                 [org.clojure/clojurescript "1.7.170"]
                 [hipo "0.5.1"]]
  :plugins [[lein-figwheel "0.5.0-2"]]
  :clean-targets [:target-path "out"]
  :cljsbuild {
    :builds [{:id "dev"
```

```
              :source-paths ["src"]
              :figwheel true
              :compiler {:main "hipo-project.core"}
           }]
     })
```

Be aware that Hipo internally uses reader conditionals, so you must set your Clojure
version to be at least 1.7.0 (the version of Clojure in which reader conditionals were
introduced).

Next, let's prepare an `index.html` page containing only one div:

```
<html>
  <body>
    <div id="a-div"></div>
    <script type="text/javascript" src="main.js"></script>
  </body>
</html>
```

Now let's prepare our `core.cljs` file, where we'll use Hipo to initialize our user interface:

```
(ns hipo-project.core
  (:require [hipo.core :as hipo]))

(defn create-menu-v [items]
   [:ul#my-menu
    (for [x items]
      [(:li {:id x} x)])])

(def menu (hipo/create (create-menu-v ["it1" "it2" "it3"])))

(defn add-menu!
  []
  (.appendChild js/document.body menu))

(defn reconcile-new-menu! []
   (hipo/reconciliate! menu (create-menu-v ["new it1" "new it2" "new
it3"])))
```

Next, let's launch a live coding session for our project:

> **$ lein figwheel**

Finally, we'll load our `hipo-project.core` namespaces either via the Figwheel REPL or
our editor.

Let's review what's actually going on in our code. The `create-menu-v` function just
returns a Hiccup vector of a `ul` menu with the identifier `my-menu`.

The `menu` var contains the DOM node generated by our first Hipo generation, yielding a menu of `li` elements with the captions `it1`, `it2` and `it3`.

Ler's now call the `add-menu!` function. You should see:

Hipo has built-in "reconciliation" functions that trigger React-style DOM diffs and renders. For instance, the `reconcile-new-menu!` function uses the `create-menu-v` function to attach a new Hiccup vector to our `menu` var. If we call this function we should see our menu items get replaced with newer versions.

We've looked at one client-side templating library, Hipo, which is inspired by Hiccup's syntax. Now let's take a look at the other big name in Clojure's HTML/CSS templating world, Enlive. In particular, let's study a client-side templating library called **Enfocus** (http s://github.com/ckirkendall/enfocus).

Unlike Hiccup, which only offers templating as a declarative way of generating HTML, Enlive is both a templating and a transformation library. That means that Enlive includes a set of DOM selection facilities, coupled with transformations that can be applied to any DOM element (once selected).

Generally speaking, Enlive syntax specifies a mapping between CSS3 compliant selectors and corresponding transformations. An example is worth a thousand words, so here is a simple HTML page definition.

 Be aware that this is Enlive on Clojure, and we provide the namespace declaration only to illustrate an Enlive example. A fully working ClojureScript example will follow as we get into Enfocus.

```
(require '[net.cgrand.enlive-html :as html])
(html/deftemplate sample-page "page.html"
                [page]
                [:title] (html/content (page :title))
```

```
            [:h1] (html/content (page :title)))
```

When called, our Enlive function, `sample-page`, will return a sequence of strings. Each string in the sequence corresponds to an HTML tag. So in order to get the resulting HTML, we have to concatenate these strings together, like so:

```
(reduce str (sample-page {:title "My Sample Page Title"}))
```

Note that the `html/deftemplate` call triggers a transformation on every DOM element for which we have provided a selector. For instance, here we've set the `html/content` of all elements matching the `[:title]` and `[:h1]` selectors to be `(page :title)`.

Okay, that's enough about how Enlive works. Let's take a look at Enfocus. Let's set up a new ClojureScript project, and name it `enfocus-project`. Make sure to add Enfocus to your project's dependencies, like so:

```
(defproject enfocus-project "0.1.0-SNAPSHOT"
  :dependencies [[org.clojure/clojure "1.8.0"]
                 [org.clojure/clojurescript "1.7.228"]
                 [enfocus "2.1.1"]]
  :plugins [[lein-figwheel "0.5.0-2"]]
  :clean-targets [:target-path "out"]
  :cljsbuild {
    :builds [{:id "dev"
              :source-paths ["src"]
              :figwheel true
              :compiler {:main "enfocus-project.core"}
             }]
   })
```

Now, as you might have guessed, we will prepare an HTML page, `index.html`, in which we will client-side templating with Enfocus:

```
<html>
  <body>
    <div id="a-div" style="border: 3px coral solid;"></div>
    <script type="text/javascript" src="main.js"></script>
  </body>
</html>
```

In our project's `core.cljs` file, we'll prepare a series of functions to showcase Enfocus, capabilities:

```
(ns enfocus-project.core
  (:require [enfocus.core :as ef]
            [enfocus.events :as events]
            [enfocus.effects :as effects])
```

```
     (:require-macros [enfocus.macros :as em]))

(defn gen-button
  [id caption]
  (ef/html [:button {:id id} caption]))

(defn say-hello!
  []
  (ef/at js/document
         ["#a-div"] (ef/content "Hello From Enfocus!")
         ["body"] (ef/append (gen-button "btn1" "Click me!"))
         ["body"] (ef/append (gen-button "btn2" "Resize the div!")))))

(em/defaction activate-button! []
  ["#btn1"] (events/listen :click #(js/alert "I am Clicked!")))

(em/defaction resize-div! [param]
  ["#a-div"] (effects/chain
               (effects/resize param :curheight 500 )
               (effects/resize :curwidth (* 2 param) 500)))

(em/defaction activate-resize! []
  ["#btn2"] (events/listen :click #(resize-div! 200)))
```

Launch your Figwheel browser REPL:

```
$ lein figwheel
```

Now let's walk through what's going on in our file.

First, we have gen-button. This uses the html function from Enfocus to create DOM nodes using Hiccup's syntax. We can use our knowledge of Hiccup to create new DOM elements and use them in our Enfocus templates. (Enlive permits the use of the Hiccup style helper form version 1.1.0).

Next, we'll study say-hello! This function uses the at operator, which allows us to select DOM nodes and apply transformations to them. A transformation is any function accepting DOM nodes and that returns new transformed DOM nodes. Enfocus comes with many transformations built-in; we can get an exhaustive listing of the Enfocus transformations at the project repository on GitHub (https://github.com/ckirkendall/enfocus). In our example, we've used two of them: content, which changes the text content of a selected DOM element, and append, which adds new DOM nodes to the selected node. In this case, our selected DOM nodes are the buttons we created with the gen-button function.

To create event handlers, we'll use what Enfocus calls actions. Actions are modifications that operate live on the DOM. Let's take a look at the `activate-button!` action, defined by the Enfocus `defaction` macro. We select one of the two buttons by its identifier `#btn1`, and apply to it a listener on the click event using the Enfocus `events/listen` method.

If we call this action whenever we click the button labeled "Click me!", we'll get a greeting from our browser.

Lastly, we'll discuss Enfocus: effects. Effects are simply transformations that you can see occurring over given periods of time. In the case of our example, we are going to resize the `#a-div` div by decreasing its width and increasing its height.

We accomplish this effect by changing two effects together, as you can see in the code. First we resize the div's width, then its height. These chained effects are implemented in an action, `resize-div!`. We want to be able to watch the effects on the div, so we've developed another action, `activate-resize!`, which will add a listener to `#btn2`, triggering the double resizing effect whenever we hit this button.

Use the REPL to call `resize-div!` then `activate-resize!`. From now on, if you click on the button labeled `Resize the div!`, you'll see the orange border first shrinking to the left, then expanding downwards. Here is what your page should look like before the effects have been completed:

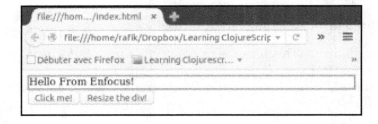

We've now covered quite a few approaches to DOM manipulation and event handling in ClojureScript. You have now a wide range of methodologies to choose from when it comes to building a user interface on the browser with ClojureScript. But as a web applications developer, there is one more family of tools you may want to be able to use in order to gain in productivity: CSS preprocessors. In this next section, we'll take a look at what ClojureScript has to offer with regard to these of tools.

CSS preprocessors in ClojureScript

Broadly speaking, a CSS preprocessor is a language that can help you write CSS. Authoring style sheets in vanilla CSS can be a tedious process, if only because of the lack of variables and control flow structures. Experience has shown that this way of working does not scale well, especially when we add media queries and cross-browser support to the equation.

That's why modern front-end development involves heavy use of CSS preprocessors. Such tools have thrived during the last couple of years, making Less, Sass, Stylus and the like commonplace in web front-end development today.

Generally such tools are server-based, and this is more or less common sense: CSS does not change frequently, so hosting it on the browser might make the client suffer an unnecessary burden.

But recently, as Node.js has gained momentum, the rise of JavaScript preprocessors like Less or Stylus has seen more of this logic reside on the client side. This comes with a few advantages, the biggest being that you no longer need to have your server set up in order to get started since your preprocessor sits in the browser.

Whatever side you may be considering to host your CSS preprocessor, ClojureScript as a platform has a lot to offer. As a language with data manipulation at its heart, it's a perfect fit for hosting an embedded language targeting CSS. Let's see how one ClojureScript library called **Garden** handles this. (`https://github.com/noprompt/garden`)

Garden is a Clojure and ClojureScript library with a Hiccup-like syntax for describing CSS rules. These Hiccup-like data structures are turned into CSS strings using Garden's `css` function. To use an example from Garden's README:

```
user=> (require '[garden.core :refer [css]])
nil
user=> (css [:body {:font-size "16px"}])
"body{font-size:16px}"
```

CSS rules are described by vectors in Garden. The initial non-seq elements of a rule vector are considered to be the selectors of that rule. For instance, let's look at the following vector:

```
[:div :a {:border-style "solid"}]
```

The preceding vector is compiled into the following CSS:

```
"div,a{border-style:solid}"
```

This applies a solid border to all `divs` and `a` elements on the page linking to this CSS.

We can also define hierarchies of selectors by nesting rules vectors. For example, to apply a particular style to all p elements that are children of the `div` with the ID `mydiv` we could write this:

```
[:mydiv [:p {:background-color "yellow"}]]
```

In Garden, accessing parent selectors in a similar manner to Less/Sass is also possible, using the & character:

```
[:mydiv {:border-style "solid"}
        [:&:hover
         {:border-style "dashed"}]]
```

The equivalent CSS would be:

```
"mydiv{border-style:solid}mydiv:hover{boder-style:dashed}"
```

One interesting particularity of Garden's syntax is that in a declaration map, if the value is also a map, the associated key is considered as a prefix to the declaration map's keys. This is particulary useful in situations when you have to assign several prefixed properties, like -moz-border-radius and -moz-box-sizing, as in the following example:

```
[:.box {:-moz {:border-radius "3px"
               :box-sizing "border-box"}}]
```

This translates to:

```
".box{-moz-border-radius:3px;-moz-box-sizing:border-box}"
```

Garden supports media-queries through a special function, at-media. Let's take a look at an example, taken from the Garden project's README:

```
user=> (require '[garden.stylesheet :refer [at-media]])
nil
user=> (css (at-media {:screen true} [:h1 {:font-weight "bold"}]))
"@media screen{h1{font-weight:bold}}"
```

Garden also offers other possibilities which go way beyond its direct capabilities: it is based on ClojureScript data structures, and so we have the power of a real expressive language to generate our CSS, with a bias towards interactive development.

Let's see an example of client-side Garden in action. Create a new project, garden-project, and edit your project.cj to add Garden as a dependency:

```
(defproject garden-project "0.1.0-SNAPSHOT"
  :dependencies [[org.clojure/clojure "1.8.0"]
                 [org.clojure/clojurescript "1.7.228"]
```

```
              [garden "1.3.0"]]
  :plugins [[lein-figwheel "0.5.0-2"]]
  :clean-targets [:target-path "out"]
  :cljsbuild {
    :builds [{:id "dev"
              :source-paths ["src"]
              :figwheel true
              :compiler {:main "garden-project.core"}
             }]
  })
```

As usual, we'll need an HTML page. Prepare an index.html page containing the following code:

```
<html>
  <body>
    <div>
      <p>First paragraph</p>
      <p>Second paragraph</p>
    </div>
      <script type="text/javascript" src="main.js"></script>
  </body>
</html>
```

And, we'll edit our core.cljs file to include the following:

```
(ns garden-project.core
  (:require [garden.core :refer [css]]
            [goog.style]))


(defn modify-css!
  []
  (goog.style/installStyles (css
                              [:div {:border-style "solid"}
                               [:&:hover {:border-style "dashed"}]
                               [:p {:background-color "cyan"}]]))))
```

Lastly, let's launch a Figwheel REPL:

```
$ lein figwheel
```

Point your browser to index.html. You should see a blank page containing two paragraphs.

Our page contains one `div`, which in turn has two child `p` element, displaying some captions. The styling of this page is initially blank. We'll use Garden to generate a style for the `div` and the `p` elements, and we'll activate it using a Google Closure Library facility, `goog.style/installStyles`.

We'll use Garden to first attach a solid border to our `div`, and then to use the parent selector `&` to attach a `hover` attribute adding a dashed order. We'll also specify a style for the `p` elements, a cyan background color.

We can render the Garden vector as CSS with Garden's `css` function, and we'll upload this newly created style-sheet as a whole to the document using Google Closure's `goog.style/installStyles` function.

Here's where we see the magic of the `modify-css!` function. Load your `garden-project.core/modify-css!`. Your page should now look like this:

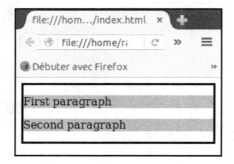

When you hover over the div (which you can recognize thanks to the border), it should change to be bordered with a dashed line.

Fantastic! We now have access to a fully featured CSS pre-processing engine that comes with all of the inherent beauty ClojureScript data structures. With the help of the Google Closure Library, we can also easily upload the resulting CSS to our web pages, empowering us to live-code our CSS!

Summary

In this chapter, we reviewed some of the many possible ways to design user interfaces on the browser with ClojureScript.

First, we've seen how to adopt an approach dictated by ClojureScript's host language, JavaScript, via direct interoperability, as well as via Jayq (a library offering functional access to jQuery).

We've learned how we can use the Google Closure Library, a central piece of the ClojureScript's compiler, either directly or via a layer of abstraction (using Domina).

Then, we saw how to use Dommy, which is a ClojureScript library designed with functional idioms as its main motivation.

Next we delved into client-side templating languages and reviewed two libraries inspired by the two major server-side HTML templating libraries in the Clojure ecosystem: Hipo and Enfocus.

Lastly, we reviewed the place of a CSS preprocessor in front-end web development, and saw how to use Garden, a Clojure/ClojureScript CSS preprocessor, as a means to prototype CSS generation from the comfort of our Figwheel REPL.

All of these approaches remain too close to the browser. Indeed, with these libraries, we still must deal with application state, routing, and data persistence ourselves. We'll address these challenges in the following chapters. We'll start by integrating our single page applications with various data back-ends or authentication providers in the next chapter. In Chapter 6, *Building Richer Web Applications*, we'll introduce the use of more advanced web user interface development approaches like Om, enhancing applications with core.async, and building for the real-time web via the use of WebSockets.

5
Building Single Page Applications

In this chapter, we'll build a simple (**Single Page Application (SPA)**) using Om and React.js. Om is a ClojureScript library that wraps React.js, a library released by Facebook. ClojureScript's power and expressiveness make it an excellent choice for building web applications. In this chapter, we'll cover the following:

- Om and React.js
- Routing using bidi
- HTML5 history and pushState
- Working with the REST APIs using AJAX

Understanding Single Page Appliactions

An SPA is a way of building a web application. In a traditional application, the server returns an HTML response containing the page content. Visiting another page on the application requires an HTTP request to the server, which returns the HTML for the second page and any associated resources, such as the same JavaScript and CSS as the previous page. In an SPA, the page content is generated via JavaScript calling DOM functions directly (for example, `document.createElement`), and links on the page simulate a new page load but don't result in an HTTP request to the server. Many well-known websites, such as Gmail, Facebook, and Twitter are single page applications.

The tradeoffs of SPAs

SPAs have advantages and disadvantages over conventional web applications; we will look at both here.

Advantages:

- Provides richer UI
- Easier to deal with client-side state and data
- Easier to deal with AJAX
- Faster client interactions once the page is loaded

Disadvantages:

- More development work
- Initial page load is usually slower
- Legacy browser support is harder

Let's get into more detail for each advantage and disadvantage, in turn.

Richer UI

React.js (on which Om is based) makes it simple to build a data-driven UI that dynamically changes the contents of the page based on new data. This data can come from anywhere we can imagine: user interactions, AJAX calls, or websockets. In a conventional application, we'd probably use a library such as jQuery to directly manipulate the DOM, but that can get messy and complex as the page gets more complex. Om is data driven with a clear separation between the data used to render the page and the resulting DOM elements, which makes it easier to build large, complex applications.

Easier to deal with client-side data

In a conventional application, when the user clicks on a link to the next page, their state is typically lost. Here, state refers to information that the user has generated, for example, the contents of a shopping cart. Because each new page is a blank slate, that state has to be stored somewhere or it is lost. The user's state can be in a cookie or on the server. In an SPA, the page never actually reloads, so it is trivial to store data in standard JS data structures on the page. Of course, you'll typically want to store the user's shopping cart data somewhere safe, like in a database, but it's possible to store the data on a page in an SPA.

Easier to deal with AJAX

AJAX is somewhat of a synthesis of the previous two advantages. Let's continue with our shopping cart example: the user loads their shopping cart page, which currently contains two items. In a conventional application, the HTML returned from the server contains DOM elements representing each item. The user deletes one item and then clicks on the button to change the quantity on the second. For each action (deleting an item and changing the quantity), there's an AJAX call to the server.

In a conventional application using jQuery, we directly modify the DOM when the AJAX calls are successful. When creating the new item, we need to add content to the page. We have several choices, all suboptimal:

- Reload the page (this is slow, and interrupts the user).
- Make the server return an HTML fragment as part of the AJAX response. Now the shopping cart HTML has to be factored out from the rest of the page render. Furthermore, injecting HTML from AJAX is a potential security hole if any of the data is user-generated.
- Have the client know how to render a new cart item (we have now spread the responsibility of rendering to both client and server).

 Also note that there's a difference between items rendered in the initial page load and items that are redrawn as a result of user interaction.

In an SPA, this story is much simpler. The user visits their shopping cart. The server returns an HTML page that contains a simple link to the SPA JavaScript. Om renders an empty cart and a progress spinner. The browser makes an AJAX call to load the user's data. The AJAX response updates a ClojureScript vector containing the user's items. Om redraws the page. Marking an item as done still makes an AJAX call to the server (for persistence, but this could theoretically be skipped). However, the user code no longer directly modifies the DOM—it's handled by Om for us. Instead, our application modifies the CLJS data for the shopping cart, and Om + React handle the DOM manipulation and redrawing.

The SPA sounds like more work, and in one way it is, but things have also gotten simpler in the Rich Hickey sense of the word.

 To get a better idea about this, refer to Rich Hickey's excellent talk, Simple Made Easy: `http://www.infoq.com/presentations/Simple-Made-Easy`

Responsibility for rendering the page now lies solely on the client side, as opposed to being diffused across client and server. Operations that modify the page have gotten simpler: we just specify how to render items directly from data, and React automatically redraws the "dirty" parts of the page for us, when the data changes. We no longer modify the DOM, we just manipulate data.

Faster client interactions once the page is loaded

Because clicking on a new page in the SPA no longer requires a round trip to the server, page transitions can be immediate. Typically, the SPA will make an additional AJAX request to get data from the server for the new page, but rendering the new page isn't blocked while waiting for an HTTP response from the server. Also, that AJAX request will typically be smaller than requesting the full page HTML. Because the client (browser) is now responsible for rendering the page, it's significantly easier to modify the page in response to, for example, the user clicking on a button. Rendering progress bars, spinners, and opening menus is all immediate.

Like everything else, there are tradeoffs to SPAs. Let's take a look at a few of them.

More development work

SPAs have more moving parts than a conventional application does. The build process is more involved because now you have to compile your CLJS. This downside isn't unique to ClojureScript—it occurs in vanilla JavaScript as well.

Some of the advantages of SPAs come from "taking over" from the standard browser behavior. For example, when clicking on a link to a new page, work must be done to capture the click and prevent the standard browser behavior. But now, the SPA is responsible for controlling the browser's history. Making things like the back button and middle clicks still work as expected takes a little more effort, and provides potential opportunities for bugs.

Legacy browser support is harder

SPA applications rely on modern browser APIs such as the HTML5 history. Some of these APIs are only available in modern browsers. Some browsers (Internet Explorer for instance), tend to lag in support of the APIs necessary to make SPAs work. In some cases, there are workarounds, but it's additional work to properly support legacy browsers. If supporting legacy browsers is a requirement for your app, you may want to reconsider whether an SPA is the best solution.

SPAs in general are possible in older browsers, however, React only supports IE 9 and later, so if you really want an SPA for IE earlier than 9, you'll need to use something other than React to accomplish it.

Understanding Om

Om is a ClojureScript library that wraps Facebook's React.js library. Om was originally developed by David Nolen. At the time of writing, it is the most commonly used ClojureScript library for writing SPAs. There are other perfectly serviceable CLJS libraries that wrap React, but we don't have the space to cover them. Most of the concepts we'll cover transfer over if you're interested in using one of them.

 At the time of writing, there is also Om Next, a kind of Om 2.0. Om Next does not yet have stable official releases, so we will not be covering it. Om Next's main improvements revolve around querying and syncing data between the client and server and efficiently combining data from what would normally be multiple REST API calls. While Om Next's API is different from Om's, the vast majority of the concepts we cover will transfer over.

Understanding React

React is a library developed by Facebook, designed to efficiently render dynamic content on a page using a virtual DOM. React lets us pretend that the entire page is redrawn any time our application's state changes. As a page author, we write functions that take data and return DOM elements. React renders the DOM elements on the page. Importantly, when the data changes, React efficiently diffs the page and re-renders only the parts that have changed. Diffing is essential because re-rendering the entire page is prohibitively expensive on even moderately complex pages. React is an improvement over previous attempts at solving the problem because there's no need to specify data bindings or watchers. We just describe how to render the page and React handles the change detection for us.

The React terminology

React uses several terms that we'll define here.

- **Component**: This is a single JS class implementing the React component interface. The most important function for a component is `render()`, which returns DOM elements based on the application's data. A typical application will have many components, forming a graph of classes to render a page. For example, a todo list might have one component that renders a single todo item, a parent component that renders the list border, and many instances of the single todo item.

 A React component is not the same as an Om component. We'll describe the differences in more detail later.

- **Virtual DOM**: React uses what they refer to as a virtual DOM. Traditional DOM traversal and manipulation is slow, so React uses a hack. When React components return DOM elements, they don't return real browser DOM nodes, but virtual nodes. These virtual nodes are standard JS objects that implement React protocols. For example, the `React.DOM.div` function returns a JavaScript object that, if rendered, will become a real `<div>` element on the page. When our data changes, React creates a new virtual DOM tree and diffs the current tree and the new tree. When differences are found, React inserts, updates, and deletes real DOM nodes corresponding to our virtual nodes, as required.
- **JSX**: This is a templating library for writing HTML in JavaScript. JSX files look identical to JavaScript, but allow us to write the following:

```
var myDivElement = <div className="foo" />
```

rather than

```
var myDivElement = React.createElement('div', {className: 'foo'})
```

 JSX is a separate library from React, but was also written by Facebook. Om projects don't need it, but it's nice to know what it is in case you ever encounter mentions of it in the React documentation, or other third-party JavaScript libraries that use React.

The components of an SPA

Let's write an SPA. Om and React are both small libraries that only deal with rendering; other components of an SPA, such as routing and history, are handled with separate libraries. We'll also need to handle routing, which is the process of simulating different URLs (that is, /foo /bar) and displaying the appropriate one without actually reloading the page. Finally, we'll cover using AJAX to send and load data from a REST API.

Setting up

Let's get started with a simple example—Hello World—and then we'll explore in depth how Om and React work. Let's create a new om-tutorial project. In a terminal, go to a directory that will be good for holding a new project directory and run the following:

```
$ lein new figwheel om-tut -- --om
```

This will create a new directory, om-tut, and generate a bunch of files for you, for a quick Om project.

Next, we'll cd into om-tut/ and run the following:

```
$lein figwheel
```

When you visit http://localhost:3449 in your browser, you should see:

Hello World!

What just happened?

Let's take a brief step-by-step review of how **Hello World!** appeared on our screen. In our om-tut/ directory, open project.clj. We should notice several things, as follows:

- Our project dependencies include [org.clojure/clojurescript] [org.omcljs/om]
- Figwheel and cljsbuild are both plugins
- Cljsbuild defines a ClojureScript build configuration that compiles .cljs files under src/, and outputs them to resources/public/js/compiled

Now, let's take a look at `resources/public/index.html` and note a few more things. `index.html` is a standard HTML file containing the content `Figwheel template` and a link to the compiled JavaScript. When we reload `localhost:3449`, if we quick, we can observe the `Figwheel template` content before `Hello World!` is redrawn on screen.

Finally, let's view `src/om_tut/core.cljs`:

```
(defonce app-state (atom {:text "Hello world!"}))

(om/root
  (fn [cursor owner]
    (reify om/IRender
      (render [_]
        (dom/h1 nil (:text cursor)))))
    app-state
    {:target (. js/document (getElementById "app"))})
```

This is some very dense code that's doing a lot at once, so we'll break it into pieces.

The `app-state` state is, like it sounds, an application state. Om applications have one piece of state, typically an atom holding a map. Our `app-state` contains {`:text "Hello World"`}.

The `om/root` directory defines a render loop. It takes a *component constructor function*, an `app-state`, and a map of configuration. The `:target` key is required and specifies the DOM element that React will "own" and render to. This element must exist in the HTML. Note that our `index.html` file has a `<div id=app>` element. The output of the `om/root` render loop will be placed there.

The first argument to `om/root` is a component constructor function. This is a function of two or three arguments, either `[cursor owner]` or `[cursor owner options]`. The function must return an Om component. An Om component is a JS object that must implement at least the `om/IRender` or `om/IRenderState` protocol, and it may optionally implement any of the other Om protocols.

Most frequently, OM applications use `reify` to create objects that satisfy the protocol, though any of the ClojureScript constructs for implementing a protocol will work. A complete list of Om protocols can be found in the Om documentation at `https://github.com/omcljs/om/wiki/Documentation`. We will review the complete list of Om protocols later in this chapter.

Finally, our OM component implements one method, `render`, from the `om/IRender` protocol. It simply calls `om.dom/h1`. Render, and its sibling, `render-state`, from `om/IRenderState`, must return something renderable: either a string (representing an HTML text node), a virtual DOM element (such as a call to `om.dom/h1`), or another Om component (using `om/build` or `om/build-all`).

The `om.dom` functions all return virtual DOM nodes, and they all have the signature `[class-attrs & children]`. `class-attrs` is a map of strings or keywords to strings, representing HTML attributes for the DOM element. The `children` attribute passed in will become child elements of the new virtual DOM element. Children must be renderable (strings, virtual DOM elements, and OM components, the same as the return value of `render`). In this case, our h1 element contains the contents of (`:text @app-state`), `Hello World`.

Don't worry, that was quite a lot to take in. We'll review each part in more detail throughout this chapter.

So, why did we go through all that work? The key advantage is that our UI is now completely dynamic and data driven. We have a function that returns HTML based on the contents of a ClojureScript variable, `app-state`. We can modify `app-state` using standard ClojureScript function calls, and the UI redraws, without having to specify any bindings, watchers, or on-change hooks. Our UI is also guaranteed to stay in sync with the data, a common mistake that's easy to make using jQuery, for example.

Child components

We'll go through one slightly more involved example to really demonstrate how Om and React are used. Let's extend our om-tut example to the barest beginnings of a To-Do List. Let's modify `app-state` so that it looks like this:

```
(defonce app-state (atom {:text "Hello world!"
                          :todos [{:id 1
                                   :done? true
                                   :text "buy book"}
                                  {:id 2
                                   :done? false
                                   :text "learn CLJS"}]}))
```

Then, before `om/root`, we'll add a new function:

```
(defn todo-item [data owner]
  (reify om/IRender
    (render [this]
```

```
              (dom/span #js {:className (when (:done? data)
                                          "done")}
                  (:text data)))))))

  (defn todo-list [cursor owner]
    (reify om/IRender
      (render [_]
        (dom/div nil
          (dom/h1 nil (:text cursor))
          (om/build-all todo-item (:todos cursor) {:key :id}))))))
```

Next, we'll modify `om/root` so that it looks like this:

```
(om/root
  todo-list
  app-state
  {:target (. js/document (getElementById "app"))})
```

And finally, in `resources/public/css/style.css`, let's add the following:

```
.done {
   text-decoration: line-through;
}
```

When the page reloads, we should see two items. One should have a strikethrough indicating that the list is done.

We've done a few things. First, we've refactored the main render `dom/h1 nil (:text cursor)` into its own Om component. This is just to make the example more idiomatic; we'll almost always have one root component that calls other components.

We've extended `app-state` to now contain a vector of the `:todo` items. Each todo item is a map containing a todo item's text and stating whether it's done or not.

Finally, we've added `dom/div` to render a `<div>` element, and we added a call to `om/build-all`. The `om/build-all` element creates a `todo-item` component for each item in the `(:todos data)` vector. There's also `om/build`, the singular version of build-all.

The `todo-item` function is another Om component constructor function (a function with arity `[cursor owner]` or `[cursor owner options]` and returns an Om component, a JS object that implements `om/IRender`, or `om/IRenderState`). It returns a `<span>` item with the CSS class of either done or nil, when the item is marked done.

React requires : `className` rather than the more familiar `:class`

We use `#js {}` for the attributes map because the map is being passed directly to React code. By default, writing `{}` in ClojureScript creates an instance of one of the immutable maps, `PersistentArrayMap` or `PersistentHashMap`. React doesn't know about immutable maps, so we use `#js` to tell the ClojureScript compiler to create a plain JS object instead.

Items in the Om constructor signature

At this point, you maybe curious as to what the arguments in an Om constructor mean. We'll describe each in the following sections.

Cursors

Cursors are a custom Om datatype; they're used to pass a piece of `app-state` data around, while staying in sync with `app-state` and keeping track of where the data came from. Imagine we want to refer to one of the todo items. Without cursors, we can just add `(get-in @app-state [:todos 1])` and pass that data around. But, cursors have an advantage; they keep track of the path into app-state where the data came from. Consider the following map:

```
{:id 2
 :done? false
 :text "learn CLJS"}
```

At first glance it might not be clear where the data in the `app-state` came from. If the original data gets modified, our copy doesn't change with it. Since cursors do keep track of the original data, a new cursor can be generated with the updated data, and your reference will stay in sync.

A cursor consists of two parts—a reference to its original atom and a path. The path of a cursor is the vector we would use to access nested data with `get-in`, from the root of app-state. In this example, that would be `[:todos 1]` because `(get-in @app-state [:todos 1])` returns this todo item.

Accessing a key of a cursor returns a new cursor with an updated path. Let's walk through an example in detail. When we create `(om/root component app-state)`, Om returns a new cursor with a reference to `app-state`. The cursor is at the top level, so its path is `[]`. Accessing `(:text data)` returns a new cursor with the `[:text]` path. Dereferencing this cursor returns the value `(get-in @app-state [:text])`, `Hello World`.

In `(om/build-all todo-item (:todos data))`, accessing `(:todos data)` creates and returns a new cursor with the `[:todos]` path. The `om/build-all` function maps over each item in todos. Mapping over a cursor returns a sequence of cursors with paths `[:todos 0]`, `[:todos 1]`, and so on.

Cursors allow for reusable components. We can have multiple components with data all coming from disparate locations in `app-state` (for example, each of our todo items is rendered the same way, but they have different paths because `(not= [:todos 0] [:todos 1])`). Cursors also participate in changing `app-state`, which we'll see shortly.

owner

`owner`, passed into an Om constructor function is the DOM element where this component will be rendered. This is the real element, not a virtual element. For example, `(.-class owner)` gets the CSS classes on the element. The `owner` element is necessary when using a component-local state and when doing `interop w/ non-react` libraries.

Opts

`Opts` is just extra data you can pass into a constructor function. Since the function signature for building a component is fixed— `[cursor owner]` or `[cursor owner opts]` —opts is the only place to pass extra arguments. Opts are passed into a component constructor via the `:opts` option in `om/build` and `om/build-all`:

```
(om/build foo cursor {:opts {:bar 42}})
```

In this example, the `foo` component will receive `{:bar 42}` in options. If arguments are passed in, the three-argument version of the function is called, otherwise the two-argument function is called.

Input

Let's make our todo example slightly more useful. Let's modify it so we can mark items as completed:

```
(defn todo-item [cursor owner]
  (reify om/IRender
    (render [this]
      (dom/div
       nil
       (dom/input #js {:type "checkbox"
                       :checked (:done? cursor)
                       :onChange (fn [e]
                                   (om/update! cursor [:done?] (-> e .-
target .-checked)))})
       (dom/span #js {:className (when (:done? cursor)
                                   "done")}
                 (:text cursor)))))))
```

Now, we'll try checking and unchecking the items.

 The strikethrough stays in sync with the checkbox.

We've added a checkbox. It is checked if `(:done? cursor)` is `true`: `onChange` is a React event handler. When the input box changes (because the user clicked on it or JavaScript code modified the checked state, such as `(set! (.-checked elem) true)`), our `onChange` function is called. It takes one argument, the event. We call `om/update!` to set the `:done?` state of our item to the new checked state. Om will trigger a re-render, so the input's checkbox stays synced with the data. React supports the complete list of event handlers you would expect in a normal JavaScript application, such as `onClick`, `onFocus`, and so on. Consult the React documentation for the entire list.

`om/update!` is essentially analogous to atom's `swap!` when used with assoc-in. It takes a cursor, a path, and a new value. Under the covers, it combines the cursor's path and the path passed in and swaps the `app-state` atom. (Om also provides `om/transact!`, which behaves similarly, but uses `update-in` rather than `assoc-in`, that is, it takes a function and applies the function with the current value of the path and any arguments passed in).

The `update!` and `transact!` functions close the circuit on a typical Om application. The primary functions of any Om application are:

- Rendering components using data from app-state
- Calling `om/update!` and `om/transact!` in response to either user input or AJAX

As we can see here, our React component rendered a checkbox that the user can interact with. In response to the user clicking, we can call arbitrary code and update the app-state.

In a production application, our todo example might make an AJAX call to update the todo item stored in the database on a server. A more responsive UI might display a progress spinner when the AJAX call starts and then display the result when the AJAX operation is completed. We'll walk through an example of this later in this chapter.

Now that we've covered a brief example, let's take a deep dive and explain how React and Om work in detail.

Rendering

Rendering is probably the most complex part of this project, so we'll be covering it in some detail. Since Om is built on top of React, we'll cover how React works as well.

The React diffing algorithm

React lets us pretend that our entire app is re-rendered on every modification. This is nice because naively re-rendering the entire page on every change is prohibitively slow. Instead, when modifications happen because the `app-state` has changed, React diffs the changes and only inserts/modifies DOM nodes as necessary.

This is still a challenging problem because comparing and diffing two arbitrary trees is $O(n^3)$ in the best case. React uses several heuristics to get that down to $O(n)$. While most of time the details aren't important, there are a few edge cases that are useful to keep in mind.

When we first call `om/root`, React calls render on the root component, which builds up a tree of virtual DOM elements. There's nothing to diff, so React just inserts the whole tree under `#app`, creating a real DOM element corresponding to each element in our virtual tree. React saves a copy of the virtual tree for diffing later.

When the application state changes, React calls render on the root component (the one passed into `om/root`) and lazily builds up the new virtual DOM tree; we'll refer to this as the new tree.

The algorithm recursively walks down both the current virtual DOM tree and the new tree. There are two item types in the tree: DOM nodes and React components. If two items are DOM nodes of different classes, React will just destroy the old and insert the new. Similarly, React will destroy the old component, and build an instance of the new component.

If the two nodes are both DOM nodes (not components), React will diff their attributes and insert and update attributes as necessary.

If the two nodes are both components of the same React or Om class, React will call `componentWillReceiveProps()` and `componentDidReceiveProps()`, as necessary. The `componentWillReceiveProps()` and `componentDidReceiveProps` functions are React-specific—they aren't exposed to the user of Om. (There is `om.core/IWillReceiveProps`, which sounds the same, but is conceptually different). This process mutates the existing real DOM node until it looks identical to the virtual DOM node.

Because React claims ownership of all DOM nodes in its containing DOM element, we can't simply use traditional DOM manipulation, for example, jQuery, because those changes will be lost on the next render. In our preceding example, that's any DOM element that is a child of `#app`. We can theoretically use jQuery on page elements outside of `#app`. In an SPA, the base HTML (`index.html` from our example) is typically only used to serve links to .js and .css files, and 100% of the visible elements on the page are rendered via the application.

Differences between Om and React

There are a few areas where Om does things differently than React. Let's dig into those in the following sections.

Components

Om components are not strictly React components. Om creates a hidden object that implements React's interface, and that interface delegates to the reified object returned from an Om component constructor. For the most part, this is an implementation detail, and we don't need to worry about it.

State models

React is somewhat less opinionated about its state and where it is stored. Om is strongly opinionated that you should have one consistent source of state—the application state atom. Every component on the page reads and writes to that atom, which provides a consistent view of our application with cursors to provide isolation and reusability, as necessary.

Cursors

Cursors are a new feature unique to Om; they don't exist in React.

Determining the size of a component

As an Om neophyte, you might be wondering what the difference is between building subcomponents and just regular functions that return HTML. Let's look at a hypothetical choice borrowed from our previous todo list example:

```
(defn todo-item [cursor owner]
  (dom/div nil
    (dom/span #js {:className (when (:done? cursor)
                               "done")}
      (:text )))))cursor))))
(defn todo-list  [cursor owner]
  (reify om/IRender
    (render [_]
      (dom/div nil
        (dom/h1 nil (:text cursor))
        (dom/div nil
                  (for [t (:todos cursor)]
                    (todo-item t owner))))))) ```
```

This is a slightly modified version of our previous todo application. Here, `todo-item` is a standard function that happens to return virtual DOM nodes rather than an Om component constructor. It doesn't call `reify`. The todo-list calls the function directly rather than calling `om/build`. So, what's the difference?

The answer is that there's not much of a theoretical difference, though there are several arguments from a software engineering perspective for splitting components. Similar to how your entire program could theoretically be one large function, your entire UI could be one large function that generates HTML. This is technically possible, but not recommended.

We recommend using components and standard software engineering best practices (for example, minimizing the size and complexity of functions, single responsibility principle, and so on) to determine when to split components.

Another good rule of thumb is to split components at the logical divisions in the application state. Components should receive only the part of `app-state` they actually need. This makes them more reusable, and improves clarity about the structure of the application state and reduces coupling between components.

Preferring components is also slightly faster. Components are a short-circuit opportunity in the React diffing algorithm. If two nodes in the tree are components of different classes, React doesn't try to compare the following HTML—it just discards the old node and keeps going. But of course, this is a premature optimization and we won't need to worry about it 99% of the time.

To get the full picture, let's go on to review the rest of the Om API.

Constructing

The `om/build` and `om/build-all` directory have the same signature, `[constructor cursor options]`.

There are several options that can be passed in:

- – `:key`: The key passed in will be used to look up a unique ID in the cursor's data for the component:

```
(om/build todo-item t {:key :id})
```

In our preceding todo example, we passed in `:key :id`. Om will `(get cursor :id)`. In our `todo` application, the item maps contain `{:id 1}` and `{:id 2}`, so the components would have IDs of 1 and 2, respectively. The ID helps the diffing algorithm, so it can identify whether an item has been inserted or modified in the middle of a sequence. For example, if we have two todos with the ID `[1 2]`, and then we insert a third todo in the middle so that `(mapv :ids todos)` returns `[1 3 2]`, React can correctly identify an insert in the middle and leave the last item untouched. Without IDs, React wouldn't be able to tell whether the second item was mutated and a third item inserted at the end, or the third item was inserted in the middle. If React couldn't tell, it would mutate the old 2 to look like 3 (that is, diff the HTML for 2 and replace/modify DOM nodes until the nodes are identical to the output of 3) and then insert a new 2. Our components should nearly always assign `:id`, especially when creating multiple items via `om/build-all`.

The following are the options which can be used along with the function:

- `react-key`: This is the same as `:key`, but it directly passes a value rather than looking up in `:key`. That is, `{:react-key 1}` would use 1 as an ID rather than the result of `(get cursor :id)`.
- `- :fn`: This applies a function f to the cursor's value before invoking the constructor:
- `(om/build todo (first (:todos cursor)) {:fn (fn [todo] (assoc-in todo :done true))})`: This is basically the same as the following:
  - `(om/build todo (assoc (first (:todos cursor)) :done true)`
- `:init-state`: This is the extra initial state for the component. This will be merged with the result of `IInitState` if the component supports it. This is part of the Component Local state, which we will discuss shortly.
- `:state`: This is the same as the `:init-state`; but will also used to modify a component (whereas the `:init-state` will only be used when a component is created). Imagine a component that simply prints its state and is called with `(om/build todo cursor {:init-state 1 :state 2})`; `:init-state` is used when the child component is inserted into the render tree, so this component will display 1. But if a modification to the parent component causes a re-render, 2 will be displayed because the initial state is only taken into account in the initial render, and this is a re-render.
- `:opts`: This is the extra data to be passed to the constructor function. This should be a map. If this option is supplied, the constructor function will be called with arity `[data owner options]` rather than `[data owner]`.

The local state

While Om is opinionated that an application's state should be consistent and stored in a single place, components have access to what is called the component local state, which behaves pretty much the way we expect, given the name. This is the local state, which is only accessible to the component.

There is often confusion as to what the component local state should be used for. David Nolen, author of Om, makes it clear:

"With the exception of transient values (editing flags, dragging flags) or resources (channels, web sockets, and so on), you should put everything into the application state."

For example, if our component creates a go channel to process user input events, the local state is a good place to store that channel. We'll see an example of that later when working with AJAX.

There are several API functions that touch the local state:

```
(defn get-state
  ([owner] ...)
  ([owner korks] ...))
```

[owner] — takes a component owner (the second argument to a component constructor) and returns the map of the local state for this component.

[owner korks] — korks is a common idiom in Om, which stands for key or keys. If korks is singular, that is, :foo, it behaves like get: (om/get-state :foo). If korks is a collection, [:foo :bar], it behaves like get-in: (om/get-state owner [:foo :bar]).

For functions that set state, korks works the same way but uses assoc/assoc-in rather than get/get-in as shown here:

```
(defn set-state!
  ([owner v] ...)
  ([owner korks v] ...))
```

(om.core/set-state! owner v) — sets the entire component local state: (om/set-state! owner {:foo 42}).

(om.core/set-state! owner korks v) — sets a part of the local state: (om/set-state! owner [:foo] 42).

```
(defn update-state!
  ([owner f] ...)
  ([owner korks f] ...))
```

This is the same as set-state!, but this uses update/update-in rather than assoc: (om/update-state! owner :foo inc).

Changing the local state either through `set-state!` or `update-state!` will cause a re-render.

In addition to the `om/IRender` protocol, which defines the method `(render [this])`, there is also the `om/IRenderState`. Instead of `(render [this])`, `IRenderState` exposes `(render-state [this state])`. In the second argument, `state` is the component's local state at the time of the render. In all other ways, `render-state` behaves identically to `render`. A component should implement either `IRender` or `IRenderState`, never both.

Life cycle protocols

In addition to the required `om/IRender` protocol, there are several protocols that notify a component of various lifecycle and state changes:

```
(defprotocol IInitState
  (init-state [this]))
```

If a component uses the local state, `init-state` can be used to supply an initial value. To use this, our component should implement `om/InitState`. The `init-state` will be called on our component when created; it should return a map. As we mentioned earlier, `om/build` can pass `:init-state` in as an option. If that is the case, the data from `:init-state` will be merged with the value returned by `init-state`:

```
(defprotocol IWillMount
  (will-mount [this]))
```

The `will-mount` function is called when a component is going to be inserted into the DOM. This is a good place to set up and create non-DOM resources such as `core.async` channels because it is the earliest point in the lifecycle where we know the component will be mounted. For DOM resources, we use `IDidMount`, which we'll see next:

```
(defprotocol IDidMount
  (did-mount [this]))
```

If our component implements the protocol, `did-mount` will be called after the component is inserted into the DOM. We can get access to the actual DOM node with `(om/get-node owner)`. Since the DOM node exists now, this is a good place to set up code that interacts with the DOM, so let's do that:

```
(defprotocol IWillUnmount
  (will-unmount [this]))
```

The `will-unmount` function will be called when a component is removed from the DOM, for example, after the diffing algorithm removes a component. This should be used to clean up any resources that were created during `will-mount` or `did-mount`.

The next few protocols revolve around when the component changes state:

```
(defprotocol IWillReceiveProps
  (will-receive-props [this next-props]))
```

The `will-receive-props` function is not called on the first render, but it is called just before all subsequent renders. In React, props and state are different concepts. Props are for immutable data that will never change during the lifetime of the component, and state is for data that can change. In Om, there are no props, just the app-state and component local state, so `will-receive-props` is somewhat poorly named.

Use `will-receive-props` to react to state changes with additional state changes. For example, if we have two pieces of data that should stay in sync and a user action has changed one of them, we can use either `om/set-state!` or `om/update!` and `om/transact!`. The `next-props` is a cursor that contains the data that will be passed to the next `render`.

Use (`om/get-props` owner) to get the current state.

```
(defprotocol IWillUpdate
  (will-update [this next-props next-state]))
```

The `will-update` function is not called on the first render, but it is called just before all subsequent renders. The `will-update` function is called after `will-receive-props`.

We cannot set the local state during `will-update`:

```
(defprotocol IDidUpdate
  (did-update [this prev-props prev-state]))
```

This is called after rendering the component. The DOM element is fully rendered when this is called, so it's useful for third-party interop if, for example, the third-party JavaScript needs to mutate in response to your React component re-rendering:

```
(defprotocol IShouldUpdate
  (should-update [this next-props next-state]))
```

The Om API documentation states the following:

> *"You should only implement this if you really know what you're doing. Even then you probably shouldn't."*

IShouldUpdate is used to take control over whether a component should render based on changes to the application or local state. The implementation should return true or false to indicate whether the component should re-render. Note that, by definition, this is used to make a component's data *not stay in sync* with the DOM, so it should be used carefully.

IShouldUpdate is typically used as a performance optimization. Imagine that the user is performing a drag and drop operation, and we're tracking the current cursor position in the local state, *and redrawing the screen is causing performance problems*. We've determined that redrawing is causing performance problems and :pos—the user's current mouse position—isn't used in redrawing the component. So, we'll ignore it when deciding whether to re-render.

An implementation might look like this:

```
(should-update [this next-props next-state]
  (let [curr-state (om/get-state owner)]
    (not= (dissoc curr-state :pos)
          (dissoc next-state :pos))))
```

Here, we are passed the next state. We fetch the current state and return false, declining a re-render if the maps are equal except for :pos. This could result in speedups, assuming that the render would generate a large number of DOM elements to diff. As always, with performance optimizations, measure first and avoid premature optimization.

 Note that Om provides several functions clearly marked EXPERIMENTAL at the time of writing. The om/commit! function is the same as om/transact!, but it does not trigger a re-render. Similarly, there is om/set-state-nr!, which is the same as set-state! but without the re-render. These might be worth investigating if you find yourself facing performance issues.

The entire render timeline looks something like this:

```
WillReceiveProps -> ShouldUpdate -> WillUpdate -> Render -> DidUpdate
```

Using third-party JS

As we mentioned earlier, we can't simply mix React and standard JS libraries and expect the DOM to stay relatively consistent, however there are some situations where mixing the two is a requirement. We'll discuss how to do that now.

Let's say we'd like to insert a map into our application using Leaflet.js (http://leafletjs.com/). Leaflet is a popular open source JS library for displaying OpenStreetMap data.

Leaflet's API expects to be given a JS element to render into, which is a relatively common pattern in JS libraries:

```
(defn leaflet-map [app owner]
  (reify
    om/IInitState
    (init-state [_]
      {:the-map nil})
    om/IDidMount (did-mount [_]
      (let [the-map (js/L.map "map")]
        (om/set-state! owner :the-map the-map)))
    om/IRender (render [this]
      (dom/div {:id "map"} nil)) ```
```

Here, in render, we create an empty div with the ID map. During IDidMount, after the div is rendered into the page, we call Leaflet, (js/L.map "map"), instructing it to render into #map. Then, we save the resulting map in the local state, in case we want to manipulate it (change the viewport, for example).

Why does this work? Our render method is stable; it always produces a #map div. React's diffing algorithm is also stable; it only removes existing nodes when the render output changes or when the components change.

IDidMount is only called once—the first time this component is added to the page. It would only be called again if the component was removed from the page and then re-inserted.

jQuery listeners

There's a gotcha around this technique that's worth reviewing in more detail. Let's say we're using jQuery to set up an event listener on our React elements (which is again, not recommended, but the failure mode is interesting):

```
(defn todo-item [cursor owner]
  (reify
    om/IDidMount
```

```
(did-mount [_]
  (-> (js/$ "span")
  (.on "click" (fn [e]
             (js/console.log "span clicked")))))
om/IRender
(render [_]
  (dom/div nil
  (dom/span #js {:className (when (:done? cursor)
                           "done")} (:text data))))))
```

Note here that jQuery's `on()` function sets up an event listener. Also, note that a new event listener is created every time a todo item is inserted into the page and never cleaned up. If the user creates many todo items, there will be many event listeners, all listening for the same events.

We recommend using React and Om over other DOM manipulation libraries to the fullest extent possible. jQuery shouldn't be necessary in most Om applications, but if you do end up using it (or other libraries that set up resources), make sure that you dispose of resources properly in `om/IWillUnmount`.

AJAX

Let's continue extending our Todo app. Now, we'd like to persist our todo items on the server. To get the job done only takes a simple Clojure REST API—that said, it still will take some work.

If you'd like to avoid all typing and just read along, we've created a Git repo on GitHub at h `ttps://github.com/learningclojurescript/code-examples`. You can just clone the repo and get ready to go.

Dependencies

Let's open the `project.clj` file in our `om-tut` directory and add some entries:

```
:dependencies [[org.clojure/clojurescript "1.7.170"]
              [org.clojure/core.async "0.2.374"
                  :exclusions [org.clojure/tools.reader]
              [sablono "0.3.6"]
              [bidi "2.0.3"]
              [cljs-ajax "0.5.3"]
              [clj-http "2.1.0"]
              [com.cognitect/transit-clj "0.8.259"]
```

```
[org.clojure/clojure "1.7.0"]
[ring "1.4.0"]
[ring/ring-jetty-adapter "1.4.0"]]
```

Here, we've added several entries to the :dependencies vector:

- bidi: This is a library for matching and destructing URLs. We'll use it to associate REST URLs with functions to respond to API requests.
- cljs-ajax: This is a ClojureScript library that is a convenience wrapper around Google Closure's AJAX API. We'll use it on the client side to make requests.
- clj-http: This is a Clojure HTTP library. It's not strictly necessary for this project, but it is useful to debug the API from a Clojure repl.
- com.cognitect/transit-clj: This is a Clojure implementation of transit. Transit is the standard protocol for Clojure API interop. We'll talk more about it later.
- ring: This is a common Clojure library for writing web servers. It's similar to WSGI in Python or Rack in Ruby, if you're familiar with those.
- ring/ring-jetty-adapter: This is just as the name suggests, the ring adapter for the Jetty web server. Ring is fairly agnostic about which web server to use, so we have to specify that we want Jetty. Jetty is a widespread Java web server.

 The ring-jetty-adapter implicitly pulls in a Jetty dependency, so we don't have to specify it.

The server

In om-tut/src/om_tut/, let's create a new file, server.clj.

We'll create a standard NS declaration:

```
(ns om-tut.server
  (:require [bidi.bidi :as bidi]
            [bidi.ring]
            [bidi.schema]
            [schema.core :as s]
            [ring.adapter.jetty :as jetty]
            [cognitect.transit :as transit])
  (:import [java.io ByteArrayInputStream ByteArrayOutputStream]))
```

Transit

Transit is a standardized serialization format developed by Cognitect. Transit is a high-performance, compact, and extensible format for transferring data between applications. If your business requirements don't require another encoding such as JSON, and one or both ends of the communication are Clojure or ClojureScript, Transit is the go-to protocol to use.

We'll define a few utility functions for working with Transit:

```
(defn to-transit [x]
  (let [baos (ByteArrayOutputStream. 4096)
        writer (transit/writer baos :json {})]
    (transit/write writer x)
    (.toString baos)))

(defn from-transit [s]
  (let [bais (ByteArrayInputStream. (.getBytes s "UTF-8"))
        reader (transit/reader bais :json)]
    (transit/read reader)))
```

Ring

Ring is a Clojure library that presents a standard interface between web applications and HTTP servers. Ring defines a data format for an HTTP request and HTTP response. A Ring request is a Clojure map with a set of required and optional keys, such as `:uri`, `:remote-addr` and `:query-string`. A Ring response is another Clojure map with another set of required and optional keys, such as `:status`, `:body`, and `:headers`.

Ring simplifies web application development because our Clojure application just has to write functions that receive a Ring request map and return a Ring response map. Ring isolates us from messy Java code and makes our app more functional. If you're familiar with Rails, Ring roughly corresponds to the "controllers" section of a Rails application. Ring is only used for handling HTTP requests, it doesn't concern itself with database access or generating HTML.

You can review the ring spec on GitHub at `https://github.com/ring-clojure/ring/blob/master/SPEC`.

CORS

Cross Origin Resource Sharing (**CORS**) is an HTTP standard for declaring who is allowed access to an HTTP resource. For security reasons, browsers won't allow AJAX calls to hosts other than the one that served the current page unless the responses contain specific headers:

```
(defn with-cors [resp]
  (-> resp
      (update-in [:headers]
        merge {"Access-Control-Allow-Origin" "*"
               "Access-Control-Allow-Methods" "GET, POST, OPTIONS"
               "Access-Control-Allow-Headers" "Content-Type"
               "Access-Control-Max-Age" "31536000"}))))
```

Since we're using Ring, our server's response is just a simple Clojure map. We will update the `:headers` map in the response to include several more HTTP headers. `"Access-Control-Allow-Origin" "*"` will allow AJAX requests from anywhere. `"Access-Control-Allow-Methods" "GET, POST, OPTIONS"` allows requests to use the `GET` `POST` and `OPTIONS` HTTP methods. We also allow the `Content-Type` header in a request, and the browser can cache the CORS data for up to one year.

We'll make a simple utility function to mark a Ring response as Transit data.

```
(defn transit-response [resp]
{:pre [(map? resp)]} (-> resp
    (update-in [:headers "Content-Type"] #(or %
    "application/transit+json; charset=UTF-8")) (update-in
    [:status] #(or % 200)) (update-in [:body] (fn [body]
    (str (to-transit body)))) (with-cors)))
```

`transit-response` is a utility function that takes a valid Ring response and modifies it to include all of the necessary Transit stuff. We set the `Content-Type` header to Transit if it isn't already present. We set the HTTP status to 200, serialize the body to Transit format, and add CORS headers.

Data

Let's define a simple data structure to hold our todos. For now, it's just an in-memory atom, a map of IDs (integers) to todo maps. We'll also create `ids`, another atom that increments an integer to guarantee that todos get unique IDs. In a production application, this could be a database, but for now we're focused on the client side, so this will do as shown:

```
(defonce todos (atom {}))
(defonce ids (atom 0))
(defn next-id []
  (swap! ids inc))
```

Now, we can get to our REST API handlers:

```
(defn get-todo [{:keys [route-params] :as req}]
  (if-let [t (get @todos (:id route-params))]
    (transit-response {:body t})
    {:status 404}))
```

This is a ring handler because it's a function that takes a ring request (a map) and returns a response. We look in the todos map and either return a todo in the body of the response or return `{:status 404}` to indicate HTTP status of `404`:

```
(defn create-todo [req]
  (let [id (next-id)
        t (slurp (:body req))
        t (from-transit t)
        t (assoc t :id id)]
    (println "create:" t)
  (swap! todos assoc id t)
  (with-cors (transit-response {:body id}))))

(defn list-todos [{:as req}]
  (with-cors (transit-response {:body (vec (vals @todos))})))

(defn options [req]
  (with-cors {:status 200}))
```

We'll define a few more handlers, which should be pretty straightforward:

```
(def routes ["/" {"todos" {:get {"" list-todos}
                           :post {"" create-todo}
                           :options {"" options}
                           ["/" :id] {:get get-todo}}
                  "" {:options options}}])
```

Finally, we'll define some routes. Ring doesn't concern itself with URL dispatching at all. Here, URL dispatching or routing means returning a different result based on the requested URL, that is, /foo vs. /bar. The spec just defines an interface for a handler (a function that takes a request map and returns a response map). For example, the most basic ring handler is probably just the following:

```
(defn foo [req]
  {:status 200
   :body "Hello World"})
```

This function doesn't check the contents of (:uri request), the page that the user visited. Regardless of the page, the browser will display Hello World. Obviously, this is a common use case, but Ring is very focused and allows other libraries to solve the problem in various ways. There are several possible libraries that can be used; we'll use bidi (https://github .com/juxt/bidi).

 The bidi library, one of the dependencies that we added earlier, is a library that performs URL matching and destructuring. bidi is a DSL for defining a mapping from URI strings to data. It's also reversible, meaning that in addition to mapping strings to data, you can map data to URI strings. bidi also supports ClojureScript, so we'll use bidi for client-side routing later in this chapter.

In routes, we define a pure Clojure data structure. This is just vectors and maps organized in a way that bidi expects. Then, we can use this map to match a given URL to a value using bidi/match-route:

```
user> (bidi/match-route om-tut.server/routes "/todos" :request-method :get)
{:handler #object[om_tut.server$list_todos 0x77ca6601
"om_tut.server$list_todos@77ca6601"],
 :request-method :get}
```

We passed our routes data to bidi along with a /todos string, our request-method is :get, and bidi returned a map with a :handler key, mapping to our list-todos function. Note that bidi just concerns itself with the mapping; it's not particularly concerned about what values it maps to. In routes, we put the list-todos function in the value position, but we could have put anything else there, like a keyword such as :todos-list.

If we pass in a route that bidi doesn't recognize, it will return nil:

```
user> (bidi/match-route om-tut.server/routes "/bogus" :request-method :get)
nil
```

nil is not strictly a legal Ring response, but ring will handle it and serve a default 404 response. A production application should handle this nil and return a custom 404 page.

bidi can also handle route parameters. We want to define the route /todos/<id>, where ID is a number. Note the [/:id] section of the route table. This defines id as a route parameter. We can test it at the REPL:

```
user> (bidi/match-route om-tut.server/routes "/todos/42" :request-method
:get)
{:route-params {:id "42"},
 :handler #object[om_tut.server$get_todo 0x4ec64b04
"om_tut.server$get_todo@4ec64b04"],
 :request-method :get}
```

bidi matched the route and specifies that :id is 42 in the :route-params map. Note that the response now contains a :route-params map in addition to :handler and the map contains {:id 42}.

By default, the valid identifier for a parameter is fairly liberal. We can be more precise with a regex:

```
(def routes ["/" {"todos" {:get list-todos
                           :post create-todo
                           :options options
                           ["/" [#"\d+" :id]] {:get get-todo}}
                  "" {:options options}}])
```

Finally, we can define our ring handler, as follows:

```
(defn handler [req]
  (let [resp ((bidi.ring/make-handler routes) req)]
    (println (:request-method req) (:uri req) "->" (:status resp)) resp))
```

bidi.ring/make-handler is a simple utility function that takes a ring request and calls bidi/match-route on the :uri in the request map. It also updates the request map to contain :route-params if appropriate. When there's a matching handler, and it's a function, bidi assumes that the handler is a valid ring handler function and calls it:

```
(defn start-server []
  (jetty/run-jetty #'handler {:port 8080
                              :host "0.0.0.0"
                              :join? false}))
```

Finally, we can start our server. The `ring.adapter.jetty/run-jetty` function takes a ring handler function and some options, starts the server, and uses the handler to respond to all requests.

Okay, we finally have our working server. To start it, you should be able to do the following:

```
$ lein repl
user> (require 'om-tut.server :as server)
user> (def jetty (om-tut.server/start-server))
#'user/jetty
```

You should get no errors.

Note that we'll still want Figwheel running (to dynamically recompile our ClojureScript as we write it), so use a second terminal. For convenience, we'll continue serving the HTML and JavaScript via Figwheel and serve the REST API from a separate process. In production, there are arguments for and against serving the HTML from the same HTTP host as the API server, but ultimately it comes down to your own business requirements. Serving both the API and the .html from the same host is probably easier for smaller shops, but at scale, you'll probably want to separate the two. Also note that we haven't specified any kind of authorization, authentication, or access controls. In a production application, you will definitely want those.

Now, let's move on to the client. Back in `core.cljs`:

```
(ns om-tut.core
  (:require [ajax.core :as ajax]
            [om.core :as om :include-macros true]
            [om.dom :as dom :include-macros true]))
```

We'll modify the `require` statement to include `ajax`:

```
(def api-server "http://localhost:8080")
```

We'll define the location of our REST API host:

```
(defonce app-state (atom {:text "Hello world!" :todos []}))
```

Now, we'll modify `app-state` to not include any `todos` when loading:

```
(defn load-todos [todos]
  (ajax/GET (str api-server "/todos")
            {:handler (fn [response]
                        (om/update! todos response))}))
```

`load-todos` is our first AJAX call. It takes a URI and a map. The most important item in the map, `:handler`, is a function that will be called if the `ajax` call is successful (2xx status code). There are several other options, including `:error-handler`, a function that will be called when the HTTP response is not successful (4xx or 5xx).

AJAX stands for Asynchronous JavaScript And XML. JavaScript is single threaded, which means that only one function can run at a time. There are no threads or futures or agents. Of course, sending an HTTP request from our browser to a server takes real time. Having our function block all JavaScript from executing while waiting for a response would be unreasonable, so all AJAX operates with callbacks. Your AJAX request happens in the background, allowing other JavaScript to run, and then either `:handler` or `:error-handler` will be run once a response comes back.

The `response` argument to the `:handler` function is the body of the response. At the lowest level, an HTTP body is a string. Our `cljs-ajax` library automatically parses Transit data from the body if the `Content-Type` header from the server response is set appropriately (it will also parse a few other content types, including JSON and EDN). We've already set `Content-Type` on the server in the `transit-response` function, so at this point, our data is ready to use.

Our `load-todos` then is pretty simple. It makes an `HTTP GET` request to our API server. We know the server will respond with a list of todos, so we simply take the list of todos and `om/update!` them into the list of todos on the browser side. Note that `load-todos` expects to be passed a cursor and sets the entire content of the cursor, so `load-todos` should be called like `(load-todos (:todos cursor))`, where the cursor is our root cursor.

The `new-todo` function is pretty straightforward:

```
(defn new-todo [todos]
  (let [todo {:text "New Todo" :done? false}]
    (ajax/POST (str api-server "/todos")
               {:params todo
                :handler (fn [resp]
                           (let [todo (assoc todo :id resp)]
                             (om/transact! todos [] (fn [todos]
                                                      (conj todos
todo)))))})))
```

This is mostly similar to `load-todos` with a few tweaks. We're posting now, so we've added a `:params` key to the map. `:params` is extra data that goes with the request. On a `GET`, params are included as query params in the request; when posting, the data is sent as part of the body (as Transit, by default).

The server response from `/todos` is just a single int, the new ID of the todo, so we add that to our in-memory item and then `conj` it onto our todos list. Depending on your API design, it will make sense for the server to respond with an entire newly created todo and just `conj` that on.

Finally, we'll modify the `todo-list` to call `load-todos` when the component is created:

```
(defn todo-list [data owner]
  (reify om/IRender
    (render [_]
      (dom/div nil
        (dom/h1 nil (:text data))
        (om/build-all todo-item (:todos data) {:key :id})
        (dom/button #js {:onClick (fn [e]
                                    (new-todo (:todos data)))}
                    "New")))
    om/IWillMount
    (will-mount [this]
      (load-todos (:todos data)))))
```

In general, we want to begin long operations (such as AJAX calls) as early in the component construction as possible. The will-mount method is the best place for this because it's the earliest protocol method that gets called after React has decided the component will be mounted. Our AJAX calls don't require the actual DOM nodes, so we can use `will-mount` rather than `did-mount`.

Our current example lets the user create new todos and mark them as completed, but there are a few features we haven't yet implemented, such as the following:

- Persisting done-ness to the server
- Changing the name of a todo

We're running out of space in this chapter, but both of those can be completed using the tools we've already demonstrated. A fancy way of changing the todo title might involve the following:

- If the user clicks on the todo text, update its state to `:editing true`
- When rendering a todo, if it is `:editing true`, render a form input box rather than `dom/span`

- When the form input box is inserted into the page, set up a click handler that detects whether the user clicks anywhere outside the input box. If the user does, update the todo state to :editing false and send the updated todo text to the server using an HTTP PUT.

Routing and HTML5 history

So, at this point, our todo application has some interesting features, but it's very bare bones. It's also literally a single page application, but, of course, real applications typically involve multiple pages. Let's extend ours to have multiple pages.

We've already included bidi as a dependency of the application, and we've already used it on the server side. Now, we will use it to do client-side routing. Here, routing refers to the process of determining which page to display, based on the contents of the URL. Let's get started.

First, we'll modify project.clj and add [venantius/accountant "0.1.7"] to the :dependencies vector. Then, let's add [accountant.core :as accountant] to the om-tut.core ns declaration:

```
(ns om-tut.core
  (:require [accountant.core :as accountant]
            [ajax.core :as ajax]
            [bidi.bidi :as bidi]
            [om.core :as om :include-macros true]
            [om.dom :as dom :include-macros true]))
```

Let's create a simple settings page. For now, it won't do anything useful:

```
(defn settings [app owner opts]
  (reify
    om/IRender
    (render [_]
      (dom/div
       nil
       (dom/a #js {:href "/"} "Back")
       (dom/h1 nil "Settings")))))
```

And let's add a link to the settings page from our todo-list component:

```
(defn todo-list [cursor owner]
  (reify om/IRender
    (render [_]
      (dom/div nil
```

```
       (dom/a #js {:href "/settings"} "Settings")
       (dom/h1 nil (:text cursor))
       (om/build-all todo-item (:todos cursor) {:key :id})
       (dom/button #js {:onClick (fn [e]
                                    (new-todo (:todos cursor)))}
                   "New")))
    om/IWillMount
    (will-mount [this]
      (load-todos (:todos cursor)))))


(def routes ["/" {"" todo-list
                  "settings" settings}])
```

We'll also create our routing table. If this looks familiar, it should. This is another bidi table, but remember how we mentioned earlier that a bidi routing table can match anything? On the server side, our table mapped paths to ring handler functions; on the client side, we're mapping paths to Om component constructor functions. Functions in ClojureScript are first class values, and we're taking advantage of that here:

```
(defn nav-handler [cursor path]
  (om/update! cursor [:active-component] (:handler (bidi/match-route routes
path))))

(defn render-component [app owner]
  (reify
    om/IRender
    (render [_]
      (dom/div
       nil
       (if-let [c (:active-component app)]
         (om/build c app {})
         (dom/p nil "no active component"))))))

(defn main []
  (om/root
   render-component
   app-state
   {:target (. js/document (getElementById "app"))})

  (let [cursor (om/root-cursor app-state)]
    (accountant/configure-navigation!
      {:nav-handler (fn [path]
                      (nav-handler cursor path))
       :path-exists? (fn [path]
                       (boolean (bidi/match-route routes path)))})
    (accountant/dispatch-current!)))
```

```
(main)
```

Phew! This is a decent chunk of code. We've refactored our (om/root...) into a main function because the setup is slightly more complex than it used to be. We will use a library called Accountant to abstract some of the HTML5 pushState API away; we'll describe that in more detail soon. Accountant's configuration takes two settings: a nav-handler, which is a function of one argument when navigation occurs (when the user clicks on a link or when JS code triggers a link click), and path-handler, which is a function of one argument that should return true if the user navigates to a URL that the SPA will handle. We'll describe these in more detail, too. The important part for now is nav-handler. When the user clicks on a link, we receive the new path as an argument. We match the route with bidi and then store that route in app-state under :active-component. Our root component (passed into om/root) is no longer a todos-list but a container component that is simply an om/build the :active-component.

Try adding a few todos, marking some of them complete, and then visiting **Settings** and clicking back. Note that the number of todos is preserved, but their :done-ness is not preserved. This is because the todos-list reloads the list of todos from the server during will-mount, but we're not persisting :done to the server yet.

Okay, now let's dig into what's going on here.

pushState

Modern browsers (those that support HTML5) have an API called pushState. The pushState API tells the browser to do two things:

- Set the current URL in the navigation bar *without actually making a request for that URL*
- Update the back button history, so the back button still works as expected

The pushState is key to single page applications because it allows us to decouple the page that is displayed from the URL the user perceives. In our previous example, the user can move from / to /settings and back with no visible page load.

The `pushState` has some quirks though. Let's say you visit `/settings` and then close the browser and reopen it. Actually, you should try it now and see what happens. You'll get a `404` from Figwheel. Why? The reason is that Figwheel serves static files (it serves `index.html` when visiting `/`), and it doesn't have a `settings.html` file on the disk. This means that, in general, your server implementation should be prepared to handle requests from the fake URLs used on the client side. A reasonable implementation might recognize all client-side URLs and serve the SPA HTML. We'll cover more on that topic in the next chapter.

Navigation

Why does Accountant need the `:path-exists?` handler? Let's review the flow of events to answer that. Let's say the user clicks on the settings link. This triggers the `onClick` event for the link. The default click handler for an `<a href>` element is to trigger a `navigate` browser event to send the browser to the new URL. The `accountant` configuration wraps Google Closure's `html5 History` library, which abstracts low-level differences across browsers and generates a synthetic `navigate` event when the user causes the page URL to change (or clicks the back button).

The `accountant` configuration sets up an event listener for the closure's `navigate`. Because we have an SPA, we don't want the browser to send a real HTTP request for `/settings`. The `accountant` configuration uses the `:path-exists?` handler to decide which URLs are handled by the SPA and calls `.preventDefault()` on the navigate event, which causes the browser to cancel the request. Then, during our `:nav-handler`, we match the route using bidi and `update` the active component. Om triggers a re-render as usual and renders the new page.

Why not `.preventDefault()` all navigate events? It's not uncommon to mix URLs handled by the client and server. For example, `http://yourcompany.com/foo` might be handled by the server, but `http://yourcompany.com/bar` might be handled by the client. If the browser is already on the SPA, visiting `/foo` would trigger the `.preventDefault`, and the SPA would attempt to serve the page rather than the server.

Summary

So, that was a whirlwind tour of an SPA in ClojureScript using Om. In this chapter, we covered the tradeoffs of Single Page Applications, what Om and React are, and how they work. We created a simple todo list example to demonstrate the Om API. Finally, we covered client-side routing and HTML5 history.

In the next chapter, we'll cover some more advanced topics around single page applications, including DataScript, ClojureScript modules, and server-side rendering.

6
Building Richer Web Applications

In the last chapter, we saw what **Single Page Applications** (**SPAs**) are and took a deep dive into learning little details about them. SPAs are, as the name suggests, developed to contain a single page. This page is then refreshed and new content is loaded dynamically, based on the users clicks, using AJAX and HTML5.

In this chapter, we'll cover a few advanced techniques for SPAs. We'll cover the following:

- Real-time communication with websockets
- Improving load times with CLJS modules
- Server-side rendering

Real-time communication with websockets

WebSockets are a modern browser feature that make it easier and more efficient to work with real-time streaming data, without the hackiness of long-polling HTTP connections.

For this project, we'll use WebSockets to run a bot from Slack. Who doesn't love chatbots? This example might seem slightly contrived, in that a Clojure bot might be easier to deploy and run, but there are a few legitimate uses for this such as, creating a specialized Slack UI or piping user communication from your website into Slack. Another advantage of using Slack here means we won't have to set up the server side of this real-time chat client.

You'll need to set up a Slack (slack.com) account if you don't have one already, but it's free.

Understanding the websocket protocol

WebSockets are a separate protocol from HTTP; they too happen to run on TCP port 80. WebSockets provide bidirectional messages with lower overhead than HTTP-based hacks, such as long polling or **Bidirectional-streams Over Synchronous HTTP** (**BOSH**). BOSH is basically long polling, standardized to use XMPP (the protocol used by Jabber and Google chat).

WebSockets have lower overhead because they utilize binary streams rather than base64 encoded XML. WebSockets have their own URL schema starting with ws:// or wss:// (the second s stands for secure, similar to http and https). The initial request happens over HTTP; if the server accepts, the TCP socket "converts" to sending WebSocket messages. Messages consist of a small binary header and then binary data.

Let's create a new CLJS project using the now standard:

```
in new figwheel cljsbot
```

In your project.clj, let's add the following to our :dependencies:

```
[cljs-ajax "0.5.3"]
[jarohen/chord "0.7.0"]
```

We saw the cljs-ajax script earlier. Chord is a ClojureScript library for working with WebSockets. We'll walk through how it works later. For now, let's add it as follows:

```
(ns cljsbot.core
  (:require [ajax.core :as ajax]
            [cljs.core.async :as a]
            [chord.client :as chord])
  (:require-macros [cljs.core.async.macros :refer (go)]))
(enable-console-print!)
```

Next, we'll write a Slack API helper function:

```
(def slack-endpoint "https://slack.com/api")
(defn slack-api [{:keys [path request-method token]
                  :or {request-method :get}
                  :as args}]
  (let [method (condp = request-method
                 :get ajax/GET
                 :post ajax/POST
                 (throw (js/Error. "unrecognized :request-
                 method" (get args :request-method))))]
    (method (str slack-endpoint path) (-> args
            (merge {:format :json
```

```
                         :response-format :json
                         :keywordize? true})
       (assoc-in [:params :token] token))
                  :params {:token token})))
```

This is just standard factoring. Every Slack API request requires an API token and send/receive JSON, so we'll just default it:

```
(defn rtm-start
  "Connect to slack. Returns a channel containing the websocket
   channel"
  [{:keys [token] :as args}]
  (let [ret-chan (a/chan)]
    (slack-api {:path "/rtm.start"
                :token token
                :handler (fn [resp]
                           (go
                           (let [url (get resp "url")
                           {:keys [ws-channel error]}
                           (a/<! (chord/ws-ch url
                           {:format :json-kw}))]
       (if-not error
         (do
           (a/put! ret-chan ws-channel)
           (a/close! ret-chan))
           (println "Error:" (pr-str error))))))))})
    ret-chan))
```

Connecting to Slack's **Real Time Messaging (RTM)** API returns a JSON map with a key URL. This is a WebSocket URL. We use `chord/ws-ch` to connect to the websocket URL. `ws-ch` returns a channel that will have one value, a map containing either `:ws-channel` (on success) or `:error` (on failure). `ws-ch` is a wrapper around raw WebSockets, we'll describe how it works later in the chapter.

If we get a `ws-channel`, we put it in `ret-chan` to return to the caller of `rtm-start`.

Slack's RTM API states that it will send events down the channel when events happen. These events will be notifications such as **add new message in the chat room**, **user joined the room**, **new room created**, and so on. Naturally, we'll need something to handle these events:

```
(defn print-all-handler [ws-chan]
  {:pre [ws-chan]}
  (go
    (loop []
      (when-let [e (a/<! ws-chan)]
        (js/console.log "event:" e)
```

```
        (recur)))))
```

Here, we create a simple `go` loop and log every message to the console. In a full-chat client implementation, we'd probably create a multimethod to handle each type of event and update your application state as, for example, a new chat messages arrive.

To send a message to a chat room, Slack requires us to send the channel ID in the message. So we'll need to list the channels:

```
(defn list-channels [token]
  (slack-api {:path "/channels.list"
              :token token
              :handler (fn [resp]
                         (println "channels" resp))}))
```

So, now you can run this, look in the console for the list of channels, identify the channel you'd like to use, and note the ID—we'll be using it later.

Initialization

Now let's cover initializing the WebSocket and sending a message. Let's take a look at the following commands:

```
(defn init-websocket [appstate]
  (go
    (let [ws-chan (a/<! (rtm-start {:token "YOUR-SLACK-API-
KEY"}))]
      (print-all-handler ws-chan)
      (send-message ws-chan {:channel "YOUR-CHAN-ID" :text
      "hello world"})))))
```

Replace `:token` with your Slack API key from the Slack website. To create a personal testing token, visit `https://api.slack.com/tokens`. Using this token will allow the bot to log into the chat room as you. For more serious applications we would create a separate bot user, but for now, this is fine.

Since connecting with the websocket is asynchronous, our `rtm-start` returns a `core.async` channel that will contain one value, the WebSocket, when the connection is complete. *Channels containing channels* is indeed somewhat awkward, but there's not much we can do about it. Be clear in your variable naming, and it will make everything easier.

After connecting, we set up the print-all-handler and call `send-message`. In a full application, this would also be a good place to store the `ws-chan` in, for example, our Om application state.

Sending messages

Now, let's cover sending a message to Slack. Let's take a look at the following commands:

```
(defonce next-message-id (atom 0))
(defn get-next-message-id []
  (swap! next-message-id inc))
(defn send-message
  [ws-chan {:keys [channel text] :as msg}]
  {:pre [channel text]}
  (go
    (a/>! ws-chan (merge msg {:id (get-next-message-id)
                              :type "message"})))))
```

Slack requires our client to send a unique ID for each message. Simple enough; we'll just increment a counter. Sending a message is as simple as putting a message on the `ws-chan`. In the Slack API, a chat message is a JSON map containing the keys `:id`, `:type`, and `:text`. The `chord` parameter converts ClojureScript maps to JSON for us, so we can just put a map in the channel.

And we're done! Loading the page, you should see no errors, and our application should connect to Slack and display the message Hello World. Check your Slack client and you should see a message from yourself.

Now, let's dig into how Chord works to help understand what WebSockets do.

Understanding Chord

The DOM API for WebSockets is callback based. Chord's main job is converting callbacks to `core.async` channels. This doesn't take too much code because one of `core.async` project's design goals was to eliminate **callback hell**.

Let's take a look at the following commands:

```
(defn write-to-ws! [ws ch]
  (go-loop []
    (let [msg (<! ch)]
      (when msg
        (.send ws msg)
        (recur)))))
(defn read-from-ws! [ws ch]
  (set! (.-onmessage ws)
    (fn [ev]
      (let [message (.-data ev)]
        (put! ch {:message message})))))
```

Most of the action happens in these two functions in `chord/channels.cljc`. We elided the `:clj` conditional code to make this easier to see.

Sending is simply a `go-loop`, waiting for messages to arrive in the `core.async` channel. Messages are taken out of the channel, and we call `.send` on the WebSocket.

Reading is slightly more involved. The websocket object has an `.onmessage` property, which we can assign to a function. This function gets called any time a new message arrives on the websocket. Chord takes the message and puts it in the `core.async` channel.

What we see in Chord is a pretty common use of `core.async` channels: turning callbacks (such as `.onmessage`) into channels. This eliminates callback hell, and makes it easier to follow data flow through your program.

Using Datascript

Datascript is an in-memory database for ClojureScript, modeled after Datomic, the commercial Clojure database produced by Cognitect. Why do we need an in-memory database in the browser? We've spent most of the book learning how to create more powerful applications. The `core.async` channels, WebSockets and Om have given us the tools to collect and render large amounts of data. Adding a database to our large, complex SPA provides a useful tool for conveniently organizing and locating our data.

Understanding the Datascript/Datomic data model

Datascript is closely modeled after Datomic due to Datomic's powerful API, and using the same API on client and server eliminates the need for a translation layer. We'll cover Datomic's data model and point out differences between the two.

Datomic is a consistent (CP, in CAP terms), ACID, non-SQL database built around the concept of a datom.

 A datom is a tuple (an ordered list of elements) composed of entity/attribute/value/time, commonly abbreviated as EAVT.

Let's look at a simple example. Say we want to model movies similar to IMDB—it might look like this:

```
{:movie/title "Top Gun"
 :movie/year 1986}
```

In Datomic, this map would be broken into a series of datoms, with each datomrepresenting a single key-value pair, such as [1 :movie/title "Top Gun" 1234] and [1 :movie/year 1986 1234].

Remember EAVT? Here, 1 is the entity ID , :user/name is the attribute, Top Gun is the value, and 1234 is the time or transaction ID that introduced the datom. The database's primary storage is just an ordered sequence of EAVT tuples. An example from the datascript documentation is as follows:

```
[<e-id>    <attribute>      <value>           <tx-id>]
...
[ 167      :person/name     "James Cameron"    102    ]
[ 234      :movie/title     "Die Hard"         102    ]
[ 234      :movie/year      1987               102    ]
[ 235      :movie/title     "Terminator"       102    ]
[ 235      :movie/director  167                102    ]
```

Tuples with the same e-id are facts about the same entity, while tuples with the same transaction ID were introduced in the same transaction. A transaction is just a sequence of datoms to add and/or retract at once, and may contain any number of datoms about one or more entities.

Since all entities are tracked at the key-value level and every datom includes the transaction ID that introduced it, fine-grained tracking of history is possible and easy.

Let's walk through an example. Launch Figwheel:

```
$ lein new figwheel ds
```

Now, we'll add [datascript "0.15.0"] to our :dependencies:

```
(ns ds.core
  (:require [datascript.core :as d]))

(enable-console-print!)

(defn datascript-test []
  (let [schema {:movie/actors {:db/cardinality :db.cardinality/many
                               :db/valueType :db.type/ref}
               :movie/director {:db/valueType :db.type/ref}}
        conn (d/create-conn schema)]
```

```
          (d/transact! conn [{:db/id -1
                              :movie/title "Top Gun"
                              :movie/year 1986}])
       (-> (d/datoms @conn :eavt)
           (seq)
           (first)
           (println))))
    (datascript-test)
```

This should print the following:

```
#datascript/Datom [1 :movie/title Top Gun 536870913 true]
```

Transact takes a sequence of maps or datoms. A map in a transaction is syntactic sugar for a sequence of datoms:

```
(d/transact conn [[:db/add -1 :movie/title "Top Gun"] [:db/add
-1 :movie/year 1986]])
```

A map must have a key `:db/id` for the `e-id`, with the rest of the key-value pairs in the map being converted to datoms. In the transaction, we provide the EAV for a sequence of datoms, and the database will assign the same transaction ID to all of the datoms in the transaction when it is committed. We use negative numbers in the `e-id` position, such as `:db/id -1`, to ask the database to assign a new temporary ID. When the transaction is committed, the database will assign a new, permanent, positive ID for our user. If we wanted to introduce two new entities in the same commit, we'd use two distinct negative numbers:

```
(d/transact conn [[:db/add -1 :person/name "Tom Cruise"] [:db/add -2
:person/name "Anthony Edwards"]])
```

Say we wanted to update an existing entity rather than create a new one. Then, we'd use the permanent `e-id`:

```
(d/transact conn [[:db/add 1 :movie/director 2]])
```

Here, we're setting the movie's director to the person with `e-id 2`.

The permanent ID can be retrieved from the return value of `d/transact` or by querying for it.

A basic query

Datomic and Datascript have an enormously powerful query engine that's based on Datalog. Datalog is similar in concept to Prolog (if you're familiar with that). Datalog is a powerful, composable way to write queries using data rather than strings such as SQL. In this section, we'll review some basic concepts just so we can use it to describe the rest of the system. We'll cover more advanced queries later. Reading the Datomic and Datascript docs may also be informative. They can be found at `http://docs.datomic.com/` and `https://github.com/tonsky/datascript`.

A basic query looks like this:

```
(d/q '[:find ?e :in $ ?name :where [?e :movie/title ?name]]
@conn "Top Gun")

=> #{[1]}
```

Semantically, this looks sort of like a select query from SQL, but the entire expression is ClojureScript literals. Datascript has more powerful queries, as we'll see shortly. We're asking the system to find an entity, `?e` in the database `$` and using a variable `?name`, where the entity has an attribute `:movie/title` whose value is equal to `?name`. We're passing our database and the value `Top Gun` as arguments into the query. This returns `#{[1]}`. The result of a query is a set of vectors. In this example, the vector has one item because we asked for one value in `:find ?e`. If our query asked for multiple values, for example, `:find ?movie ?actor`, the result would be a set of vectors where each vector has two elements.

Query arguments

Note that the preceding query is passed as two arguments, the database (`@conn`) and the string `Top Gun`. These are bound in the query in the `:in` clause in positional order, so the database takes the special value `$`, and `?name` is bound to the value passed in to the function. The database name of `$` is special. Queries can also operate across multiple databases, in which case the databases would use the names `$1`, `$2`, and so on, with names based on the order they're passed into the function. The rest of the arguments to query are positional arguments, similar to function arguments. The `:in` parameter creates new variables and binds them to the values passed in as extra arguments to `d/q`. While it's possible to use literal values in queries, this makes the query less reusable. For example, contrast this:

```
(d/q '[:find ?e :in $ ?name :where [?e :movie/title "Top Gun"]]
@conn)
```

With this:

```
(d/q '[:find ?e :in $ ?name :where [?e :movie/title ?name]]
  @conn "Top Gun")
```

The first is legal, but the second is preferred because it's more reusable. In Datomic, there's also a slight performance improvement because it can cache the parsed query.

Schema

Datascript uses a schema to alter the type of attributes. Unlike Datomic, Datascript does not require specifying the type of every attribute. Datascript attributes can store any value, though we want to explicitly specify two types of attributes, refs and cardinality, which we'll explain in the following sections. Let's take a look at the following commands:

```
(let [schema {:movie/actors {:db/cardinality
                                  :db.cardinality/many
                                  :db/valueType :db.type/ref}
              :movie/director {:db/valueType :db.type/ref}
  conn (d/create-conn schema)]
```

Understanding db.type/ref

Refs are a datatype used for storing references to other entity IDs. Think of them as being similar to foreign keys in SQL, though they're a special datatype rather than just ints. Under the covers, refs are ints as well, but because the foreign key relationship is specified explicitly, they have a few extra features missing from SQL, which we'll see later.

Refs are always automatically indexed.

Cardinality

SQL databases are row oriented and typically can't represent a one-to-many relationship without resorting to join tables. Datomic and Datascript natively support these types of relationships in the database schema. If an attribute is declared with `:db/cardinality` `:db.cardinality/many`, the attribute will store a set of values rather than a single value. Consider the following example:

```
@(d/transact conn [[:db/add 1 :movie/actors 2]
                   [:db/add 1 :movie/actors 3]])
```

Because :movie/actors is declared as :db.cardinality/many, this adds actors 2 and 3 to the *set* of :movie/actors. Also, as :movie/director is not declared as :db.cardinality/many, it defaults to :db.cardinality/one. Therefore, calling :db/add on :movie/director updates the value by replacing any previous director.

Let's insert some data so we can play with some more interesting queries. Remove the previous d/transact parameter, so we only have one source of data now:

```
@(d/transact conn [{:db/id -1
                    :person/name "Tom Cruise"}
                   {:db/id -2
                    :person/name "Anthony Edwards"}
                   {:db/id -3
                    :person/name "Tony Scott"}
                   {:db/id (d/tempid :user)
                    :movie/title "Top Gun"
                    :movie/year 1986
                    :movie/actors [-1 -2]
                    :movie/director -3}
                   {:db/id -4
                    :person/name "Arnold Schwarzenegger"}
                   {:db/id (d/tempid :user)
                    :movie/title "Terminator"
                    :movie/actors -4}
                   {:db/id -5
                    :person/name "Mel Brooks"}
                   {:db/id (d/tempid :user)
                    :movie/title "Spaceballs"
                    :movie/actors -5
                    :movie/director -5}
                   {:db/id -6
                    :person/name "Clint Eastwood"
                    :person/birth-year 1930}
                   {:db/id -7
                    :person/name "Morgan Freeman"}
                   {:db/id -8
                    :person/name "Gene Hackman"}
                   {:db/id -9
                    :person/name "Eli Wallach"}
                   {:db/id (d/tempid :user)
                    :movie/title "The Good, The Bad and The
                      Ugly"
                    :movie/actors [-6 -9]}
```

```
{:db/id (d/tempid :user)
 :movie/title "Unforgiven"
 :movie/actors [-6 -7 -8]
 :movie/director -6}])
```

Here, we use literal negative numbers in some cases, so we can reuse the same ID to refer to the same entity later in the transaction. We use d/tempid in others to idiomatically, "Just generate a new unique ID, I won't be referring to it in this transaction". You can also use (d/tempid) in a let block and refer to that tempid when building the transaction. Consider the following example:

```
(let [ahnold (d/tempid)]
  @(d/transact conn [{:db/id ahnold
    :person/name "Arnold Schwarzenegger"}]))
```

Pull

We've been emphasizing tuples so far because they're core to understanding how Datomic and Datascript represent things. But of course, most of the time, we don't care about tuples—we care about compound things such a person and movie. Datomic and Datascript have a feature called pull, which is used to retrieve some or all of an entity. It's somewhat analogous to the select * from a SQL query, where we specify which part of the row to return. Pull can also be used to load data from related refs, similar to .includes and .preload from Rails' ActiveRecord, if you're familiar with that. Let's take a look at the following commands:

```
(let [clint (d/q '[:find ?e :in $ ?name :where [?e :person/name
 ?name]] @conn "Clint Eastwood")]
    (d/pull @conn '[*] clint))
=> {:db/id 7, :person/birth-year 1930, :person/name Clint
    Eastwood}
```

If we have an e-id, we can pull the current value of one or more attributes. Here, [*] is a **pull-expression**. We can use * to ask for all attributes of the entity or a list of keywords such as [:person/name]. When using d/pull directly, * is a symbol, so we can write either [*] or '[*]; but, quoting the vector is idiomatic. More important, pull expressions can be used in queries:

```
(println "all movies:")
(d/q '[:find (pull ?movie [:movie/title]) :in $ :where
 [?movie :movie/title]] @conn)
```

Without the pull expression, writing `:find ?movie` would return entity IDs. We can wrap `?movie` with (`pull ?movie [:movie/title]`), and instead return attributes from the matching entity. Inside a query, we don't need to quote `*` because the vector passed to `d/q` is already quoted.

Let's say we want to pull the list of actors in *Top Gun*. Typically, you'd use `d/q` for this, but you can also use pull:

```
(let [top-gun (d/q '[:find ?mov . :in $ ?title :where [?mov
:movie/title ?title]] @conn "Top Gun")]
        (d/pull @conn '[* {:movie/actors [:person/name]}] top-gun))
  => {:db/id 4, :movie/actors [{:person/name Tom Cruise} {:person/name
Anthony Edwards}], :movie/director {:db/id 3}, :movie/title Top Gun,
:movie/year 1986}
```

This tells Datascript to pull all attributes on the entity, then also look up the `:movie/actors` references, and pull their names. Pulls can be nested recursively.

Interestingly, we can also use pull to look things up in reverse:

```
(let [clint (d/q '[:find ?e . :in $ ?name :where [?e :person/name
?name]] @conn "Clint Eastwood")]
        (d/pull @conn '[* {:movie/_actors [:movie/title]}] clint))
```

Note the `:movie/_actors` value. Using `_` as the leading character in a pull instructs Datascript to look that value up in reverse, that is, every place `clint` appears in the value of `:movie/actors`. This says, "Pull all attributes of Clint Eastwood and then also pull the title of every movie he acted in".

Finding results

Currently, all queries return a set of vectors, which is sometimes awkward when we know that, for example, a query can only have one result. As we've alluded to, but haven't formalized yet, a query returns one or more variables:

```
(d/q '[:find ?person ?movie :in ...]
```

After `:find`, one or more variables (starting with `?`) are listed. The query returns a set of vectors, where each vector's length matches the number of variables to return.

There are a few ways to customize the results:

```
(d/q '[:find ?p . :in $ ?name :where [?e :person/name ?name]]
  @conn "Arnold Schwarzenegger")
```

We use a `.` after `?p` to specify that we only want the first result:

```
(d/q '[:find [?p ...] :in $ ?title :where [?mov :movie/actors ?
p] [?mov :movie/name ?title]] @conn "Top Gun")
```

We wrap `?p` in a vector ending with `. . .` to specify that we want the collection of values `?p` can take on. This is nicer than having to write, for example, (`map first results`).

We can also compose a pull by returning a collection:

```
(d/q '[:find [(pull ?p [:person/name])...] :in $ ?name :where
[?mov :movie/actors ?p] [?mov :movie/title "Top Gun"]] @conn)
```

Unification

The `:where` clause of a query takes one or more EAVT, and the query returns all values in the database that satisfy the constraints. In Datalog, variables can take on any value unless constrained. Constraints are added to a variable by including it in a `:where` clause. We'll see more of that in a moment.

Let's say we want to find all movies:

```
(d/q '[:find (pull ?movie [:movie/title]) :in $ :where [?movie
:movie/title]] @conn)
```

Note here that our `:where` clause tuple is short; it only includes two values corresponding to E and A. This means that the value is unconstrained and can take any value, therefore it returns all `:movie/title` values in the database. A full `:where` tuple can optionally include all three items (or fewer) in EAV. For example, if we want to see all attributes that take on a specific value, we can use the following:

```
(d/q '[:find ?a :in $ ?tx :where [_ ?a "Top Gun"]] @conn)
```

This finds all attributes that take the value `"Top Gun"`, and it predictably returns `:movie/title`. Note that we used a variable to refer to an attribute, which would be very unusual in SQL. Datalog has no problems with this.

As another example, to find all actors in the database, we would use the following command:

```
(d/q '[:find ?act :in $ :where [_ :movie/actors ?act]] @conn)
```

Here, we use "_" to idiomatically mean that the value can be anything, and we don't care about the result. The `?act` parameter binds to all tuples where `[eid :movie/actor ?act]`, and then our `:find` returns `?act`, so it returns the list of all actors.

Let's use the following to find all movies where the director acts in the movie:

```
(d/q '[:find (pull ?p [:person/name]) :in $ :where [?mov
       :movie/actors ?p]
      [?mov :movie/director ?p]] @conn)
```

Okay, you might have noticed that we've introduced a few tricks here. First, our `:where` clause can have any number of vectors. Second, we can introduce new variables in a query just by referring to them. Since both vectors refer to `?mov`, both vectors must agree to find a result. We've already discussed how `?mov :movie/actors ?p` works, so we can finally get to the heart of unification. With just one clause, `[?mov :movie/actors ?p]`, we can return the set of all acting credits in all movies, that is, `[1 :movie/actor 2] [1 :movie/actor 3]`. But with the second clause, we're imposing a second constraint that the same person appears as actor and director in the same film.

 Unification means that a variable must take the same value in all clauses at the same time.

For example, if we wanted to find all people who have ever acted and directed, we can write the following:

```
(d/q '[:find ?p :in $ :where [?mov1 :movie/actors ?p]
                             [?mov2 :movie/director ?p]] @conn)
```

Predicate expressions

In the previous query about finding directors who act in their own films, since we use two variables, `?mov1` and `?mov2` are now free to take on separate values. However, it's still possible for them to return the same value because there's not yet a constraint that `?mov1 != ?mov2`. If we want to find the set of people who have acted and directed, but in separate movies, that looks like the following:

```
(d/q '[:find (pull ?p [:person/name])
             (pull ?mov1 [:movie/title])
             (pull ?mov2 [:movie/title])
       :in $
       :where
```

```
        [?mov1 :movie/actors ?p]
        [?mov2 :movie/director ?p]
        [(!= ?mov1 ?mov2)]] @conn)
=>([{:person/name Clint Eastwood} {:movie/title The Good,
    The Bad and The Ugly} {:movie/title Unforgiven}])
```

Here, `[(!= ?mov1 ?mov2)]` is an **predicate expression**. This is ClojureScript code that returns true or false if the clause does or does not match. The current list of supported functions is undocumented in Datascript, but Datomic promises that it provides the following:

```
- Two argument comparison predicates !=, <, <=, >, and >=.
- Two-argument mathematical operators +, -, *, and /.
- All of the functions from the clojure.core namespace of
  Clojure, except eval.
```

Indexes

As we mentioned earlier, the database can be imagined as a sequence of datoms. To make queries fast, Datascript maintains several indices, which the query planner uses to optimize queries. These are named `eavt`, `aevt`, and `avet`. As you can imagine, each index is sorted in the order corresponding to e, a, v, and t. For example, when looking up an actor by name, you'd use a `:where` clause that looks like `[?p :person/name ?name]`. We know the attribute and the value (their name), but we need to know the entity ID. Therefore, we traverse the `avet` index, jumping to `:person/name`, and then to the value of their name.

Most of the time, the query planner does a good job. On some occasions, it is necessary to get raw access to the datoms, for speed. You can access the indices directly using `d/datoms`:

```
(d/datoms @conn :eavt)
```

You can also provide a starting point to filter the results:

```
(->> (d/datoms @conn :avet :movie/actors)
     (map identity))
```

This will return a sorted set of datoms that use `:movie/actors`. You can provide up to all three of e, a, and v. The `d/datoms` parameter returns a custom iterator, so we use `(map identity)` to convert back to a sequence.

Differences between Datomic and Datascript

While Datascript is powerful and full featured, it's not 100% compatible with Datomic. The primary difference between them is that Datomic is fully time travelling. It stores every datom ever seen, so you can query for things such as, "Show me all values this attribute has ever taken on, and return the transaction IDs when changed". Because Datascript is intended to be in-memory, and it primarily targets browsers, constant memory use is a desirable feature. Therefore, historical datoms are not preserved.

Why Datascript?

We've now provided a glimpse of some of Datascript's power. It might seem counter-intuitive to put a database in the browser, but it can make managing a large amount of state more tractable. For example, if we writing a game, and there are a large number of entities on screen, Datascript can be used to locate and update entites in response to events such as user input or the next frame of the simulation. It's not necessary in every SPA, but when it's necessary, it's a lifesaver.

In the next few sections, we'll talk about optimizing our SPA for faster load times.

Improving load times

Production SPAs frequently contain upward of 1 MB of JavaScript, which takes time to download and parse, especially for mobile browsers. For internal applications, this might not be a big deal, but for SPAs deployed to the public Internet, speed is important. Users are impatient and will abandon a slow-loading page. Faster websites see increased repeat traffic, higher search engine rankings and higher conversion rates. In the next sections, we'll cover techniques that will reduce the download size of our SPA and improve its load time.

ClojureScript modules

ClojureScript modules are a Google Closure Compiler option for breaking a ClojureScript application into multiple `.js` files. The key insight to modules is that the entirety of your ClojureScript code is not typically required to render every page. For example, many applications have an "inner" and "outer" split, where "outer" consists of things such as marketing and pricing pages, while "inner" consists of the actual application. Even in the "inner" application, there could be pages that use `leaflet.js` to display maps, pages that use a charting library to display charts and graphs, and settings UIs which use neither.

Splitting the application into modules allows us to serve less of JavaScript to the user initially and then lazily load other modules as needed, which results in smaller downloads and faster page loads. In practice, it's not uncommon to see a 30% reduction in page load times.

Preparing for modules

In order to take advantage of modules, we should consider our application and identify the largest libraries that can be factored into a module. Typically, the biggest gains come from splitting third-party libraries into modules because they usually contain more code than our Om components. We probably won't be able to get away with splitting ClojureScript, Om/React, and `core.async` into modules, but it is possible for many other large libraries. Mapping libraries such as Google Maps and Leaflet.js are good candidates, as are graphing, and charting libraries. We want to identify the typical use cases of your users and which pages they visit. Are there a large number of settings for UI? Is the settings page infrequently visited? That could be a potential place to refactor.

ClojureScript modules split at the namespace level, meaning that the contents of a single namespace are all in one module or another. Think about whether it makes sense to split your namespaces into smaller namespaces, if necessary.

We'll walk through an example based on a real-world experience of factoring an application to use modules. In this example, we'll split the application into two modules, "inner" and "outer".

Most libraries are pulled in by Om components, so by splitting the Om components into two modules, we can also pull the dependent charting libraries into a module.

Getting started

This entire example, with Git history, is available at `https://github.com/learningcloj urescript/example-code/chapter-6/cljs-modules`. The code under the **master** tab is the finished version, so if you want to follow along with the code, we recommend viewing the entire commit history and starting from the beginning: `https://github.com/learni ngclojurescript/example-code/chapter-6/cljs-modules/commits/master`.

We'll do the now familiar:

```
$ lein new figwheel cljs-modules
```

And, we'll add the following to our :dependencies:

```
[bidi "2.0.3"]
[org.omcljs/om "0.9.0"]
[venantius/accountant "0.1.7"]
```

We'll create a now-familiar Om app with support for two routes:

```
(ns cljs-modules.core
  (:require [accountant.core :as accountant]
            [bidi.bidi :as bidi]
            [om.core :as om]
            [om.dom :as dom :include-macros true]))

(defonce app-state (atom {}))

(defn outer-component [app owner opts]
  (reify om/IRender
    (render [_]
      (dom/div #js {} nil
               (dom/h1 #js {} "Hello from Outer!")
               (dom/a #js {:href "/app"} "inner")))))

(defn inner-component [app owner opts]
  (reify om/IRender
    (render [_]
      (dom/div #js {} nil
               (dom/h1 #js {} "Hello from Inner!")
               (dom/a #js {:href "/"} "outer")))))

(def routes ["/" {"" outer-component
                  "app" inner-component}])

(defn nav-handler [cursor path]
  (om/update! cursor [:active-component] (:handler (bidi/match-
    route routes path))))
(defn renderer [app owner opts]
  (reify
    om/IRender
    (render [_]
      (dom/div
        nil
        (if-let [c (:active-component app)]
          (om/build c app {})
          (dom/p nil "no active component")))))))
(defn main []
  (om/root
    renderer
```

```
    app-state
    {:target (. js/document (getElementById "app"))})
   (let [cursor (om/root-cursor app-state)]
     (accountant/configure-navigation!
     {:nav-handler (fn [path]
     (nav-handler cursor path))
      :path-exists? (fn [path]
     (boolean (bidi/match-route routes path)))})
     (accountant/dispatch-current!)))

 (main)
```

Now when you run, `lein figwheel` and you should see **"Hello from Outer!"**. Clicking on the link should display **"Hello from Inner!"** with a link back to outer.

Route definition

Initially, `routes` is a bidi table that maps URLs to functions. Each of `outer-component`, `inner-component` is an Om constructor function. We use Accountant's `nav-handler` to set `:active-component` in `app-state` to the actual function, and then Om constructs that component when rendering.

Remember that we mentioned earlier that module splitting is done at the namespace level? Now, we'll need to fix that. We need a solution that allows us to not require `inner` and `outer` directly from the `core` namespace. We'll modify the routing table to store keywords rather than the actual functions:

```
(def routes ["/" {"" :outer/outer
                  "app" :inner/inner}])
```

Here, we're using namespaced keywords to identify which module the handler is located in; the namespace must match the module name. If we had other outer modules, they might be called `:outer/landing` or `:outer/pricing` or `:outer/faq`.

We'll use a multimethod to dispatch from namespaced keywords to Om components. Since inner and outer both need to refer to the multimethod (because they extend it), we can't place that multimethod in main. We'll factor it out into its own namespace called **render**:

```
(ns cljs-modules.render
  (:require [om.core :as om]
            [om.dom :as dom]))

(def routes ["/" {"" :outer/outer
                  "app" :inner/inner}])
(defmulti active-component identity)
```

```
(defmethod active-component :default [_]
  nil)

(defn render [app owner opts]
  (reify
    om/IRender
    (render [_]
      (dom/div nil
               (if-let [c (active-component (:active-component
                 app))]
                 (om/build c app {})
                 (dom/p nil "no active component")))))))
```

Then, we'll refactor inner and outer to separate namespaces:

```
(ns cljs-modules.outer
  (:require [om.core :as om]
            [om.dom :as dom]
            [cljs-modules.render :as render]))

(defn outer-component [app owner opts]
  (reify om/IRender
    (render [_]
      (dom/div #js {} nil
               (dom/h1 #js {} "Hello from Outer!")
               (dom/a #js {:href "/app"} "inner")))))

(defmethod render/active-component :outer/outer [_]
  outer-component)

(ns cljs-modules.inner
  (:require [om.core :as om]
            [om.dom :as dom]
            [cljs-modules.render :as render]))

(defn inner-component [app owner opts]
  (reify om/IRender
    (render [_]
      (dom/div #js {} nil
               (dom/h1 #js {} "Hello from Inner!")
               (dom/a #js {:href "/"} "outer")))))

(defmethod render/active-component :inner/inner [_]
  inner-component)
```

If we had other components that belonged in the inner module, we'd add a `defmethod` method for each, as appropriate.

Okay, now let's return to our `cljs-modules.core`, and add a dependency on render:

```
(ns cljs-modules.core
  (:require [cljs-modules.render :as render]))
```

Now, let's modify our `om/root` to call `render` as the main component:

```
(om/root
  render/render
  app-state
  {:target (. js/document (getElementById "app"))})
```

And, there! We see our `nav-handler` remains the same, but we're now storing keywords in `active-component` rather than functions:

```
(defn nav-handler [cursor path]
  (om/update! cursor [:active-component] (:handler (bidi/match-
    route routes path))))
```

If you reload now, you should have no errors and the page should show "No active component". This is actually a success!

Note that the dependency chain here, `cljs-modules.core`, depends on `cljs-modules.render`. The `cljs-modules.inner` and `cljs-modules.outer` method both depend on `cljs-modules.render`. It's important to understand here that, nothing depends on `cljs-modules.inner` and `cljs-modules.outer`. If they happen to be loaded, extra routes are added to the `render/active-component` multimethod. If they haven't been loaded, our logic all works, but `active-component` will return nil. For now, we haven't loaded inner or outer, so there is no active component.

Right about now, you might be asking, "Got it, but what does this solve?" It allows us to effectively name routes and refer to them *without requiring the code to be loaded*. This is important because earlier when we referred to `outer/outer`, it referred directly to the loaded JavaScript. Now, we can refer to `:inner/inner`, regardless of whether the inner module is loaded or not.

Now that we've split our files, we can specify modules in `project.clj`. Let's start by modifying the `min` cljsbuild:

```
:cljsbuild {:builds
            [...
             {:id "min"
              :source-paths ["src"]
              :compiler {:output-dir
                "resources/public/js/compiled"
              :main cljs-modules.core
```

```
:optimizations :advanced
:modules {:outer {:output-to
    "resources/public/js/compiled/outer.js"
:entries #{"cljs-modules.outer"}}
:inner {:output-to
    "resources/public/js/compiled/inner.js"
:entries #{"cljs-modules.inner"}}}
:pretty-print false}}]]
```

 Modules are only supported under :simple or :advanced optimizations, but for the effort they require, we would reserve them for times we need to use :advanced optimizations.

We added a :modules, key, and we've also added :output-dir. Under advanced compilation with modules, the compiler will create a cljs_base.js file, and then a .js file for each module specified. To make switching between development and :advanced easier, let's also modify the :dev build's :output-to:

```
:compiler {:main cljs-modules.core
            :asset-path "js/compiled/out"
            :output-to
              "resources/public/js/compiled/cljs_base.js"
            :output-dir "resources/public/js/compiled/out"
            :source-map-timestamp true}}
```

Then, we'll modify resources/public/index.html and change the script from cljs_modules.js to cljs_base.js.

We'll kill the running Figwheel and run the following:

```
$ lein do clean, cljsbuild once min
```

Everything should work. Run the following:

```
$ ls -1 resources/public/js/compiled/
```

You should see inner.js, outer.js, cljs_base.js, among other files. The inner.js and outer.js files are present because we asked for them to be created.
The cljs_base.js file always gets created, and it contains all the code that wasn't included in one of the explicitly asked for modules. When using modules, cljs_base.js is placed in the root of :output-dir, and :output-to is ignored. Since cljs_base.js includes things such as the ClojureScript standard library and likely contains OM and core.async, you should always serve it before other modules.

Note that right now, our modules are tiny; when we run this, our `cljs_base.js` is 325kB, and `inner.js` and `outer.js` are just 700 bytes (your values might be different, but they should be similar in magnitude). For this application, that's expected. The majority of the size savings from modules come from excluding large libraries, and right now, our example application just isn't doing that much. In larger production applications, modules can save 30-50% in file size, depending on the size of the application and how amenable the application is to isolating libraries.

Loading modules

So, now we have modules on disk, but they aren't being loaded. Let's fix that.

To serve our modules, we'll have to set up a simple HTTP server. We'll use Clojure and Ring to do that.

We'll need to add Ring to our :dependencies:

```
[ring "1.4.0"]
[ring/ring-jetty-adapter "1.4.0"]
```

Now, we'll create a new file, `src/cljs_modules/server.clj`:

```
(ns cljs-modules.server
  (:require [ring.adapter.jetty :as jetty]
            [ring.middleware.resource :as resource]))

(defn handler [req]
  {:status 200
   :body (slurp "resources/public/index.html")})

(def handler (-> handler
                 (resource/wrap-resource "public")))

(defn main []
  (jetty/run-jetty handler {:port 8080
                            :host "0.0.0.0"
                            :join? false}))
```

In a new terminal, we'll run the following:

```
$ lein repl
```

And then:

```
(require 'cljs-modules.server)
(cljs-modules.server/main)
```

If you kill the Figwheel process and visit http://localhost:8080, the page should load, and you should see **No active component**. Success again! Here, we're using the Ring middleware known as wrap-resource to serve all files contained in resources/public. We serve index.html to all other routes (such as "/" and "/app").

Now, back in ClojureScript, we'll need some helper functions to keep track of which modules are loaded:

```
(ns cljs-modules.modules
  (:require [goog.module :as module]
            [goog.module.ModuleManager :as module-manager]
            [goog.module.ModuleLoader]
            [om.core :as om]))

(def modules? false) ;; true if serving modules

(def modules
  ;; "The map of id/uris pairs for each module."
  #js {"inner" "/js/compiled/inner.js"
       "outer" "/js/compiled/outer.js"})

(def module-info
  ;; "An object that contains a mapping from module id (String)
  ;;    to list of required module ids (Array)."
  #js {"inner" []
       "outer" []})

(def manager (module-manager/getInstance))
(def loader (goog.module.ModuleLoader.))

(.setLoader manager loader)
(.setAllModuleInfo manager module-info)
(.setModuleUris manager modules)

(defn loaded? [id]
  (if-let [module (.getModuleInfo manager id)]
    (.isLoaded module)
    false))

(defn require-module
  [app id]
  (if (not (loaded? id))
```

```
        (do
          (om/update! app [:loading id] true)
          (.execOnLoad manager id (fn []
          (om/update! app [:loaded id] true)
          (om/update! app [:loading id] false))))))

(defn set-loaded!
  "Mark a module as loaded"
  [id]
  (-> goog.module.ModuleManager .getInstance (.setLoaded id)))
```

Mostly we're relying on Closure's module libraries to handle loading. The `(def modules ...)` method is a map of module IDs to the URL where the module can be loaded. The `(def module-info)` method forms a simple dependency graph. If outer depends on another module, it would be specified here. Our modules have no extra dependencies, so the vectors are empty.

When we call `require-module`, `ModuleManager` will make an AJAX request to the server at the path listed in `modules` and then evaluate the JavaScript. We'll use `set-loaded!` at the end of each module. In `cljs-modules.inner` and `cljs-modules.outer`, require the `cljs-modules.modules` namespace, and add it at the very bottom of the file:

```
(modules/set-loaded! "outer")
```

This marks the module as loaded, which is important when we're waiting for the module to load before rendering.

Hang in there. We're almost done! There's just one more step, which is adjusting the render component to deal with modules being loaded at runtime:

```
(ns cljs-modules.render
  (:require [cljs-modules.modules :as modules]
            [om.core :as om]
            [om.dom :as dom])
  (:require-macros [cljs.core.async.macros :refer (go)]))

(def routes ["/" {"" :outer/outer
                  "app" :inner/inner}])

(defmulti active-component identity)

(defmethod active-component :default [_]
  nil)

(defn handler-module [handler]
  (namespace handler))
```

```
(defn require-module! [app module]
  (when modules/modules?
    (modules/require-module app module)))

(defn render [app owner opts]
  (reify
    om/IRender
    (render [_]
      (let [c (get-in @app [:active-component])
            module (handler-module c)
            loaded? (modules/loaded? module)]
        (dom/div nil
                 (if loaded?
                   (let [cfn (active-component c)]
                     (om/build cfn app {:opts opts}))
                   "Loading..."))))
    om/IWillMount
    (will-mount [_]
      (let [c (get-in @app [:active-component])
            module (handler-module c)
            loaded? (modules/loaded? module)]
        (require-module! app module)))
    om/IWillReceiveProps
    (will-receive-props [_ next-props]
      (let [next-component (get-in next-props
        [:active-component])
            next-module (handler-module  next-component)]
        (require-module! app next-module)))))
```

Our render method looks the same, but we're implementing two more protocols now:
IWillMount and IWillReceiveProps. In IWillMount, we determine the current module
and require it. In IWillReceiveProps, we determine the module of the next component
and require it.

Why do we need both? IWillMount is called once when the render component is first
added to the page before either module is loaded. IWillReceiveProps is called when
app-state changes, which could be because :active-component changed. Here, it's
important to note when visiting a new page, the nav-handler runs and possibly
updates :active-component. The render method will either build the correct component
or display **Loading...** if it isn't fully loaded yet. When the module is loaded, modules.cljs
calls om/update! on app-state and sets :loaded true, which will trigger a re-render.

It is possible, and a good idea, to serve one of `inner.js` or `outer.js` in the `intial.html` to optimize load times.

Fixing development mode

You may ask, why do we check the value of `modules/modules`? Remember that modules are only supported in `:simple` and `:advanced` optimizations. When we use Figwheel, with `:optimizations :none`, there will be no modules and every `.js` file is served separately. Let's try setting `modules/modules?` to `false`, running `lein do clean`, `figwheel` and reloading the page. We should see our Figwheel REPL hang at **Loading....**

What's going on? Remember that there's no file that requires `cljs-modules.outer` directly and there are no modules, so `render` will wait indefinitely. Let's fix that.

Let's make a new file, `dev.cljs`:

```
(ns cljs-modules.dev
  (:require [cljs-modules.core]
            [cljs-modules.inner]
            [cljs-modules.outer]))
```

The sole point of this file is to require inner and outer.

In `project.clj`, we modify our `dev` cljsbuild to change `:main` from `cljs-modules.core` to `cljs-modules.dev`:

```
:compiler {:main cljs-modules.dev}
```

Next, restart Figwheel, and you should see "**Hello from Outer!**"

The `modules/modules?` parameter is used to control runtime behavior, and it should correspond to the way the app was compiled, or we'll have trouble. In production, we can set it any number of ways. A common technique is to embed an inline JSON object into the HTML that serves the link to our `app.js`. We can insert any number of configuration variables into the JSON, and use that to customize the app's behavior. For example, in our `index.html` we can see the following code:

```
<script>
  var config = {"modules": true};
</script>
<script src="/js/app.js" />
```

Then, in the `modules.cljs` file, we look for the following code:

```
(def modules? (get (js/config) "modules"))
```

In production, we'll be generating `index.html` directly or using a templating engine such as Enlive to modify `index.html`, so it is easy to make the values of modules match the way they were actually compiled.

And we're finally done! That was a big, complex topic. Modules take some work to set up, but they can result in smaller up-front downloads for your users, which results in faster page loads and increased user satisfaction.

.cljc and server-side rendering

As discussed in many places throughout this book, Clojure and ClojureScript are very similar, but they are distinct languages. Clojure 1.7 released a feature called **Reader Conditionals**, which allows files to be loaded by both Clojure and ClojureScript.

There are a few interesting and powerful uses for reader conditionals as they apply to web applications. First, let's review what reader conditions actually are.

Reader conditionals are a new syntax which was added to Clojure 1.7 and ClojureScript. They create a new file extension, `.cljc`, which stands for Clojure Commmon, and new syntax to support loading `.cljc` files from Clojure, ClojureScript, and any future dialect.

.cljc

Clojure files that end in the `.cljc` extension can be loaded by both Clojure and ClojureScript processes, with a few features and restrictions.

`.cljc` files shouldn't directly reference `host interoperability` forms because those aren't common across dialects. In Clojure, this means `.cljc` should avoid using Java classes, such as `java.lang.Integer`. In ClojureScript, this means avoiding JS forms such as `js/Number`.

However, `.cljc` files can reference `host interoperability` forms through the use of reader conditionals. Think of these as `cond` or `case`, except the branch that is taken depends on whether the compiler loading the file is Clojure or ClojureScript. A clichéd example is as follows:

```
(defn str->int [s]
```

```
#?(:clj  (java.lang.Integer/parseInt s)
   :cljs (js/parseInt s)))
```

This defines a function named `str->int` with different implementations for Clojure and ClojureScript. `#?()` is a new reader macro allowing for conditionally loaded code. In Clojure, the `#?()` form takes the `:clj` branch and `(java.lang.Integer/parseInt s)` is returned. In ClojureScript, the `:cljs` branch is evaluated and `(js/parseInt s)` is returned. In a reader conditional, each branch can only contain a single form, though of course you can use `do` to combine forms.

If a reader conditional doesn't contain a value for the current compiler, no form is read; not `nil`, but nothing:

```
[1 2 #?(:cljs 3)]
```

This expression will return `[1 2 3]` in ClojureScript, but `[1 2]`, not `[1 2 nil]`, in Clojure.

Remember unquote-splicing, such as `~@foo` from macros? There is an analogous construct, `#?@()`, for reader conditionals:

```
(ns foo.bar
  (:require #?@(:clj [[clojure.core.async :as a]
                      [schema.core :as s]]
              :cljs [[cljs.core.async :as a]
                [schema.core :as s]]])))
```

When using `#?@`, the value in the pair must be a sequence, and the reader returns all the forms without the containing parenthesis.

There are a few neat tricks we used in this most recent example. First, we can use reader conditionals in a `:require` form to control which namespaces get loaded. Second, we aliased both `clojure.core.async` and `cljs.core.async` to `a`, which means that this namespace logically uses `core.async`, even though they refer to different namespaces. We'll use this technique later.

Armed with reader conditionals, we can create entire libraries that are crossplatform, which can be used by both Clojure and ClojureScript. We've already seen some of them, such as bidi, which we used for both client-side and server-side routing in Chapter 5, *Building Single Page Applications*.

Schema and input validation

The simplest and most straightforward use of .cljc is to share validation code across the client and server. This has been a problem for web applications for over a decade: the user is submitting data and we want to validate the data on the client side because it leads to better UX, but then we still need to validate the data on the server for security and correctness reasons. This typically leads to duplication of logic because we have to write the validation code in both JavaScript and server side.

We cover how to use Schema, a popular library for addressing this problem, in detail in Chapter 7, *Going Further with ClojureScript*. For now, it's enough to know that Schema has been ported to .cljc and our Schema definitions can be loaded by both Clojure and ClojureScript. This provides a solution to our duplication earlier. We simply load our schemas on both client and server, and call s/validate to check the data using the same validation on the client and server.

Server-side rendering

Let's work through a more involved example that requires reader conditionals. We'll implement server-side rendering for an SPA. Like our previous foray into ClojureScript modules, server-side rendering is also about speed. Users are impatient, and a 1 MB JavaScript download slows down the page load. If we were able to render the page and serve it with the HTML before the 1 MB download, the user could interact with the page sooner.

Previous hacky solutions to this involved using a browser on the server, such as **phantomJS** or Selenium with Chrome to render the SPA in the browser, then grabbing the page source and serving that as a request. It is as hacky and error prone as it sounds.

Now that we have reader conditionals and .cljc, we can move our entire Om application to .cljc and render it server-side. This is powerful and not as difficult as it seems.

First, a warning: While the library we're using (Foam) is very early in development, it is likely that the technique will become mainstream in the ClojureScript community. Foam provided a proof of concept that server-side rendering of ClojureScript applications is possible, but the technique has been copied to several other ClojureScript web application libraries, and Foam or something Foam-like might become merged into Om proper. The exact implementation might change in the future, but the technique will likely remain the same.

Setting up the project

Let's create a new project to demonstrate server-side rendering; we'll name ours `ssr`.

```
$ lein new figwheel ssr
```

Next, we'll modify your `project.clj`, and add a few libraries to our dependencies:

```
[arohner/foam "0.1.7"]
[hiccup "1.0.5"]
[org.omcljs/om "0.9.0"]
[ring "1.4.0"]
[ring/ring-jetty-adapter "1.4.0"]
```

We'll create a basic OM app:

```
(ns ssr.core
  (:require [om.core :as om]
            [om.dom :as dom]))

(defonce app-state (atom {:text "Hello from CLJS"}))

(defn home [app owner opts]
  (reify
    om/IRender
    (render [_]
      (dom/div nil
               (:text app)))))

(defn main []
  (om/root
   home
   app-state
   {:target (. js/document (getElementById "app"))}))

(main)
```

This should all be familiar from `Chapter 5`, *Building Single Page Applications*. As usual, we can boot our Figwheel server with the following:

```
$ lein figwheel
```

Now, you should see "**Hello from CLJS**". Great!

Since this project is about server-side rendering, we'll need a server that can render HTML. Also, because we'll use ClojureScript compiled with :optimizations `:advanced`, which Figwheel doesn't support, we'll need to serve compiled ClojureScript as well. Let's get started on the server by creating `src/ssr/server.clj`:

```
(ns ssr.server
  (:require [foam.core :as foam]
            [foam.dom :as dom]
            [hiccup.core :as html]
            [ring.adapter.jetty :as jetty]
            [ring.middleware.resource :as resource]))

(defn handler [req]
  {:status 200
   :body (slurp "resources/public/index.html")})

(def handler (-> handler
                 (resource/wrap-resource "public")))

(defn main []
  (jetty/run-jetty handler {:port 8080
                            :host "0.0.0.0"
                            :join? false}))
```

We'll start a REPL with `lein repl`, run `main`, and visit `http://localhost:8080` (not `3449`). And, you should see "**Hello from CLJS**".

Now, let's port `core.cljs` to `.cljc`. Rename the file to `core.cljc`, and we'll make a few small edits:

```
(ns ssr.core
  (:require #?@(:clj [[foam.core :as om]
                      [foam.dom :as dom]]
                :cljs [[om.core :as om]
                       [om.dom :as dom]])))
....
(defn main []
  #?(:cljs
      (om/root
        home
        app-state
        {:target (. js/document (getElementById "app"))})))
```

Wait! What's going on here? Om is written in ClojureScript, so we can't load it from Clojure. We're using Foam, a library that provides a "fake" implementation of Om's API written in Clojure. It implements (nearly) all of Om's API, including all protocols. Since `foam.core` provides the same functions as `om.core`, our code continues to compile, as long as we refer to `om/IRender` rather than `om.core/IRender`.

We also modify `main`, to essentially no-op it in Clojure. We've used a reader conditional to essentially say, "Only load this code in ClojureScript". We won't be using `main` from Clojure, so that's fine.

Now, back in `server.clj`, we'll add `[ssr.core :as ssr]` to the `require` statement, and reload the file. It should compile with no errors. This means our Om component is now available from Clojure! Let's put it to good use.

In `server.clj`, add the following:

```
(defn base-html [body]
  (html/html
   [:head
    [:meta {:charset "UTF-8"}]
    [:meta {:name "viewport"
            :content "width=device-width"
            :initial-scale 1}]
    [:link {:href "css/style.css" :rel "stylesheet" :type
      "text/css"}]]
   [:body
    [:div {:id "app"}
     (if body
       body
       [:h2 "Server html response"])]
    [:script {:src "js/compiled/ssr.js"
              :type "text/javascript"}]]))
```

Also, we will modify handler:

```
(defn handler [req]
  {:status 200
   :body (base-html nil)})
```

Rather than slurping the static `index.html`, we've used Hiccup to port it to Clojure, and served that. This makes it easier to insert HTML into the base HTML, which we'll do shortly. Now, we can finally call our Om component. Let's take a look at the following commands:

```
(defn app-state []
  (atom {:text "Hello From Clojure!"}))
```

```
(defn foam-html []
  (let [state (app-state)
        cursor (foam/root-cursor state)
        com (foam/build ssr/home cursor {})]
    (dom/render-to-string com)))

(defn handler [req]
  {:status 200
   :body (base-html (foam-html))})
```

We will define our own Om `app-state` and a function for returning Foam HTML. Then, modify the handler to pass the Foam HTML in as the first argument. In base HTML, comment out `[:script {:src "js/compiled/ssr.js"}]`, just to prove that we're not serving ClojureScript. Reload the namespace and reload the page, and you should see **Hello From Clojure!**

You can and should try uncommenting the script tag and watch what happens. If you're fast, you can observe the HTML containing **Hello From Clojure!** being displayed and then being replaced with **Hello from CLJS** when the ClojureScript loads.

Understanding Foam

What exactly is foam doing here? From `Chapter 5`, *Building Single Page Applications*, we know Om is based on React and that Om functions such as `om.dom/div` are wrappers that turn around and call React functions of the same name, and the React functions return virtual DOM elements.

Foam implements the Om public API, but it doesn't use React. Foam functions such as `foam.dom/div` also return virtual DOM elements, but they're not React elements, they're just Clojure `defrecords` that implement a protocol, `foam.core/-render-to-string`. The `foam.core/build` protocol works analogously to `om.core/build` in that it builds up a tree of Foam components and virtual elements. When we call `foam.dom/render-to-string`, it walks the tree and generates an HTML string. We insert that string into our conventional HTML response and serve it just like any other standard HTML response.

Note that we served our server-side Om component into the `#app` div. If `ssr.js` is served, when Om takes over, React will render the client-generated component into the same `div`, overwriting the server-generated one. That's fine, and it provides a seamless experience. Assuming both client and server use the same values for `app-state`, you won't notice a transition. We intentionally change `:text` in this example so that you can observe the transition.

Also note that we're hard-coding `ssr/home`. In a production application, we'll likely have many components and use `bidi` to handle routing. We could easily choose which component to pass to `foam/build` based on the route that `bidi` matches. And of course, `bidi` works in Clojure and ClojureScript, so we can place the routing table in a `.cljc` file, and make the same decision in both places.

Remember that the page loaded just fine without `ssr.js` being served at all. This allows us to shorten load times even more when the rendered page is 100% static. While Foam appears nearly magical, it doesn't provide React, so while the server HTML can look identical to the client-side version, it can't provide React's interactivity. If the page is dynamic at all, for example using Om/React event handlers to change the page in response to user actions or API calls, we'll still need to serve the ClojureScript version of the page as well.

Summary

And there you have it! In this chapter, we covered a few advanced web application topics. We covered real-time communication using WebSockets and handling large, complex data using Datascript as an in-memory database. Finally, we illustrated two techniques for improving the page load time of these large complex applications.

In the next chapter, we'll cover a few more exciting ClojureScript libraries, such as `core.match`, `core.logic` and `schema`.

7

Going Further with ClojureScript

At this point, you have all the tools you need to build serious, production-ready web applications in ClojureScript. You've learned how the language works, how to write functional and idiomatic code, and how to compose that code into greater web applications using the latest industry best practices. We could call it a day here, but we won't. Instead, in this chapter, we'll take a look at some interesting libraries and subject domains in the ClojureScript ecosystem that are a little further afield from the subject matter we've covered so far.

The subjects we'll be examining in this chapter range from more esoteric core ClojureScript namespaces to third-party libraries such as Prismatic's `schema`. We'll also take a look at two of the more interesting "core" libraries—libraries whose development process, like `core.async`, is managed by Cognitect and the core ClojureScript development team, but that are standalone dependencies. Specifically, we'll be taking a closer look at:

- Pattern matching with `core.match`
- Exploring nested data structures with `clojure.zip`
- Declaratively solving problems with `core.logic`
- Runtime type validation using `schema`

Pattern matching with core.match

The first subject of this chapter is the pattern-matching library, `core.match`. Pattern matching in computer languages is a method by which a given sequence of tokens is checked for the presence of specific markers of a pattern (which is typically either a sequence or a tree of some sort). The technique has a somewhat storied history going all the way back to the SNOBOL language (1962), with the first tree-based, pattern-matching features being introduced in an extension of LISP in 1970.

Pattern matching has a number of different practical uses, from search-and-replace algorithms and other low-level regular expression logic to general tree-based data processing. The particular pattern-matching algorithm used by both Clojure and ClojureScript's implementations in core.match is an implementation of an algorithm described in Luc Maranget's paper, *Compiling Pattern Matching to Good Decision Trees*.

Configuring our project

core.match, like core.async, is not a part of ClojureScript's standard library. As a result, we'll need to add it to our dependencies before we can work with it. Let's create a new project that we can work within:

```
$ lein new figwheel match-demo
```

Next, let's add core.match to our :dependencies key in our project.clj.

core.match has been stable at version 0.3.0-alpha4 since December 2014, so that's the version we'll use. Your :dependencies key should now look something like the following:

```
:dependencies [[org.clojure/clojure "1.7.0"]
               [org.clojure/clojurescript "1.7.170"]
               [org.clojure/core.match "0.3.0-alpha4"]
               [org.clojure/core.async "0.2.374"
                :exclusions [org.clojure/tools.reader]]]
```

Now, as usual, we'll start a Figwheel REPL going so that we can get hot-reloading and we can test our code in action:

```
$ cd match-demo
$ rlwrap lein figwheel
```

> Don't forget to navigate a browser window to http://localhost:3449/ to get the browser REPL to connect.

Getting started with core.match

We'll get started with `core.match` with the most basic example possible—matching directly on literals:

```
cljs.user=> (require '[cljs.core.match :refer-macros [match]])

cljs.user=> (let [v [:a :a :b]]
              (match v
                [_ :a :a] 1
                [:a :b _ ] 2
                [_ _ :a] 3
                [_ _ :b] 4
                :else 5))
;; => 4
```

Here, we've locally bound a small vector, v, and provided various patterns that v could match against, as well as the values we'd like to return for each of the possibilities. The way `core.match` checks to see whether a given pattern matches the provided vector, v, is to check against the individual values in the pattern to see whether they match.

Let's take a look at the first of these possible patterns, `[_ :a :a]`, as an example. In the case of this pattern, the first value is _, which to `core.match` is a wildcard, so this would match against the first value of v. The second value in the pattern is the keyword `:a`, which will also match against v. However, the final value in the pattern is `:a` as well, whereas the final value in v is the keyword `:b`, so this pattern fails to match overall.

If one looks at the patterns provided, it's clear that only the fourth pattern matches (where the first two values are wildcards, and the third value is the keyword `:b`), and so we see the returned value is 4, which is what we expect.

 One thing to be aware of about `core.match` is that the underlying algorithm doesn't attempt to match against patterns by checking each one from top to bottom or from left to right. Rather, the algorithm underlying the `match` macro figures out which column has the highest "score", where a `score` is a measure of the degree to which a column must be tested explicitly.

It then checks to see whether a given pattern matches the provided value by checking against each column in decreasing order based on that column's precomputed score. In the case of our simple example using literal matching, the last column would have the highest score, since we must know the value in that column in order to match it against any of the provided patterns. By contrast, the first column would have the lowest score, since we only need to know the element in that column to match against one of the four patterns.

We've already seen how we can match against anything using wildcards. What wasn't obvious from our earlier example is that wildcards are also local bindings (bindings that can be returned as the response for a matched pattern). In this regard, the choice of a wildcard as _ is just an idiomatic indicator that we don't plan on using the binding later. Let's take a look at an example in which we actually use some bindings:

```
cljs.user=> (match [:x :y]
               [:y a] a
               [b :y] b
               :else nil)
;; => :x
```

Here, we've matched against the second pattern, where the first value we're matching against is bound to the local variable b and then returned.

Although the merits of this may not be immediately obvious, this sort of local binding can be extremely valuable if you need to do recursive matching or otherwise retain a particular value within a matched structure that you may not know in advance.

In addition to wildcards, we can also specify a concrete list of possible alternatives using :or when we know there might only be a finite set of acceptable options and we don't want to have to enumerate all of them on separate lines. For instance:

```
cljs.user=> (let [x ["a" "b" "c"]]
               (match x
                 [(:or "a" "z") "d" "c"] :a1
                 ["x" "b" "c"] :a2
                 [(:or "a" "z") _ (:or "d" "c")] :a3
                 :else nil))
;; => :a3
```

If we had to do this without :or, it would be much longer:

```
cljs.user=> (let [x ["a" "b" "c"]]
               (match x
                 ["a" "d" "c"] :a1
                 ["z" "d" "c"] :a1
                 ["x" "b" "c"] :a2
                 ["a" _ "d"] :a3
                 ["a" _ "c"] :a3
                 ["z" _ "d"] :a3
                 ["z" _ "c"] :a3
                 :else nil))
```

```
;; => :a3
```

Matching collections

Now that we've had a look at what matching literals look like, let's take a closer look at the collection matching syntax. As the syntax of literal matching might suggest, we can easily match directly against vectors as follows:

```
cljs.user=> (let [v [:a :b :c]]
               (match [v]
                 [[:a :c _]] 1
                 [[:b _ :a]] 2
                 [[_ :b :c]] 3
                 :else nil)
;; => 3
```

Similarly, we can pattern match against maps with a similar syntax:

```
cljs.user=> (let [v {:x 1 :y 1}]
               (match [v]
                 [{:x _ :y 2}] 1
                 [{:x 1 :y 1}] 2
                 [{:x 3 :y _ :z 3}] 3
                 :else nil))
;; => 2
```

If you specify a key with a wildcard value as part of a pattern, and the value doesn't have that key, `core.match` will not match against it:

```
cljs.user=> (let [v {:x 1 :y 1}]
               (match [v]
                 [{:x _ :y 2}] 1
                 [{:x 1 :y 1 :z _}] 2
                 :else "no match found"))
;; => "no match found"
```

The converse, however, is not true—if you specify a pattern that includes a subset of the relevant keys (that is to say, a case in which the provided value has more keys than the pattern does), then the pattern will successfully match. For instance:

```
cljs.user=> (let [v {:x 1 :y 1}]
               (match [v]
                 [{:x 1}] true
                 :else false))
;; => true
```

If you want to make sure the pattern and the value have the exact same keys, you can use the :only pattern modifier, as follows:

```
cljs.user=> (let [v {:x 1 :y 1}]
               (match [v]
                      [({:x 1} :only [:x])] true
                      :else false))
;; => false
```

We can also match on nested maps in a manner that might be expected at this point:

```
cljs.user=> (let [v {:x {:y :z}}]
               (match [v]
                      [{:x {:y _}}] true
                      :else nil))
;; => true
```

We've seen cases already where we're matching on vectors, but we can also generalize vector-style matching to any sequence using the special :seq keyword. In the following example, we can test the same matching logic against two different concrete types that are both sequences and get the same matching result:

```
cljs.user=> (let [x [1 2 nil nil nil]]
     (match [x]
       [([1 2] :seq)] :a1
       [([1 2 nil nil nil] :seq)] :a2
       :else nil))
;; =>:a2
cljs.user=> (let [x (list 1 2 nil nil nil)]
               (match [x]
                      [([1 2] :seq)] :a1
                      [([1 2 nil nil nil] :seq)] :a2
                      :else nil))
;; => :a2
```

We can combine rest (variable length) patterns with sequences or vectors in the same way we would with function arguments:

```
cljs.user=> (let [x [1 2 nil nil nil]]
               (match [x]
                      [([1 2] :seq)] :a1
                      [([1 2 & r] :seq)] :a2
                      :else nil))
;; => :a2
```

Guards and function applications

This is where things start to get really cool. In addition to all of the matching against discrete value possibilities and wildcards, we can also leverage ClojureScript's functional nature to match on functional filters, both directly and indirectly.

Guards are one way that we can match on the result of a function—think of them as being analogous to `filter`. We use guards via the `:guard` keyword and structure as follows:

```
cljs.user=> (let [x [1 3]]
              (match x
                [(_ :guard odd?) _] :a1
                [(_ :guard even?) (_ :guard even?)] :a2
                :else nil))
;; => :a1
```

In addition to guards, we can also match directly on the result of applying a particular function using the `:<<` keyword as follows:

```
Cljs.user=> (let [x [1 3]]
              (match x
                [(2 :<< dec) 3] :a1
                [1 (2 :<< dec)] :a2
                :else nil))
;; => :a2
```

Wrapping up

This concludes our section on `core.match`. In the real world, pattern matching has a number of potential applications, such as parsing inputs and writing function dispatch logic (for instance, if you were to write a compiler in ClojureScript, you could use `core.match` to do polym

Exploring nested data structures with clojure.zip

In this section, we'll be taking a closer look at `clojure.zip`orphic function dispatching). In general, pattern matching provides a highly flexible dispatch mechanism for your applications. Exploring nested data structures with clojure.zip In this section, we'll be taking a closer look at clojure.zip, one of the libraries that ships with ClojureScript as part of its standard library. `clojure.zip` provides purely functional generic tree walking and editing, using a technique called a zipper. A zipper is a data structure representing a location in a hierarchical data structure and the path it took to get there. It provides down/up/left/right navigation and localized functional editing, insertion, and removal of nodes.

Zippers are remarkable in that the code involved in interacting with them looks highly imperative, meaning it's much closer to what you might write if you were trying to do something similar in native JavaScript. However, nothing is actually mutated—it's all purely functional code passing immutable values under the hood.

Example – Replacing values in a tree

Let's say we've got the following data structure:

```
(def data
  [:type :state
   :name "California"
   :population 39144000
   :capital [:type :city
             :name "Sacramento"
             :population 500]])
```

If you were writing a program from scratch, you'd probably choose to represent this data as a map, but for the moment let's not worry about that. The observant reader will notice that the population number for Sacramento is way off—in fact, I just made it up off the top of my head. Let's assume that this isn't a hardcoded value. Perhaps you've got a program where you retrieve data from an external source, where the author is me, and I've told you in advance that I stubbed out the value of the Sacramento population with 500.

What to do? Well, you're just going to have to replace it.

There are a number of possible ways of doing this, but clojure.zip gives us a handy way of walking arbitrary tree-like data structures and modifying their values in place. In doing so, we're not actually mutating any of the underlying data; we're continuing to hold onto the entire original structure, while also replacing components of it. When we're done, we can return the new structure with its different elements.

If we just wanted to replace the value 500 with the correct value (about 466,500), we could do the following:

```
cljs.user=> (require '[clojure.zip :as zip]))
;; => nil
cljs.user=> (let [data (zip/vector-zip data)] ;; make a zipper
  (loop [loc data]

    ;; when we reach the end of our search, return the tree
```

```
(if (zip/end? loc)
  (zip/root loc)
  (recur

    ;; depth-first search the tree
    (zip/next
      (if (= (zip/node loc) 500)

        ;; replace the value
        (zip/replace loc 466500)
        loc)))))))
;; => [:type :state :name "California" :population 39144000 :capital [:type
:city :name "Sacramento" :population 466500]]
```

Okay, that's pretty nifty. We're basically searching the entire data structure, and when we find the value 500, we replace it with the correct population. If we wanted to, we could write a more generic replace-all function as follows:

```
(defn replace-val
  "Given a zipper, replace all instances of oldv with newv"
  [d oldv newv]
  (loop [loc d]
    (if (zip/end? loc)
      (zip/root loc)
      (recur
        (zip/next
          (if (= (zip/node loc) oldv)
            (zip/replace loc newv)
            loc))))))
```

Here we're focusing on a piece of data, but what about if we were to think about code as data? Let's try to apply clojure.zip to a situation where we're treating code as data. Remember our macro example in Chapter 3, *Advanced ClojureScript Concepts*, where we were writing a macro to replace the function in the calling position with a different function? Let's try extending that idea—instead of replacing the function in the calling position, let's say we want to replace **all** instances of that function in a given body of code.

Let's say we've got the following body of code:

```
cljs.user=> (+ 1 (* 3 (+ 1 4)) (+ 3 10)))
;; => 29
```

To make things simple, we can replace + in this code with * by declaring the body as a quoted value (which is what the data we'd have available at macro-evaluation time would look like):

```
cljs.user=> (def data2
  '(+ 1 (* 3 (+ 1 4)) (+ 3 10)))
;; => cljs.user/data2

cljs.user=> (replace-val (zip/seq-zip data2) '+ '*)
;; => (* 1 (* 3 (* 1 4)) (* 3 10))

cljs.user=> (* 1 (* 3 (* 1 4)) (* 3 10))
;; => 360
```

Okay. Let's try plugging this back into our macro namespace from Chapter 3, *Advanced ClojureScript Concepts*, to see whether it works:

```
(ns experiment.macros
  (:require [clojure.zip :as zip]))

(defn replace-val
  "Given a zipper, replace all instances of oldv with newv"
  [d oldv newv]
  (loop [loc d]
    (if (zip/end? loc)
      (zip/root loc)
      (recur
       (zip/next
        (if (= (zip/node loc) oldv)
          (zip/replace loc newv)
          loc))))))

(defmacro replace-anything
  "Replace all instances of oldv with newv in body"
  [body oldv newv]
  (replace-val (clojure.zip/seq-zip body) oldv newv))
```

Now let's try calling this on the command line:

```
cljs.user=> (experiment.macros/replace-anything (+ 1 (* 3 (+ 1 4)) (+ 3
10)) + *)
;; => 360
```

Sweet! Just for demo purposes, let's check that it works with our example from Chapter 3, *Advanced ClojureScript Concepts*:

```
cljs.user=> (experiment.macros/replace-anything (+ 1 2) + -)
;; => -1
```

Okay, so maybe that's actually less impressive than the original, but still! This example shows that, in ClojureScript, there are many ways of approaching a given problem.

Example – Removing values from a tree

Let's now take a look at another example—one in which we want to remove a given value from a tree entirely. Our code for this doesn't look too dissimilar from our earlier example where we were replacing a value. We're just searching for a match, and then removing it from the tree.

Let's say we have a nested sequence and we want to remove all occurrences of the term alfalfa from the nested sequence. I really don't like alfalfa. I tried to grow it once and then it grew too fast and there were seeds everywhere, even though I just wanted something light and breezy to put on my sandwich.

 If we weren't worried about having to deal with a nested data structure, filter would suit us fine for this sort of thing, but zippers are great when you know you're dealing with a nested data structure of an unknown form.

This sort of problem could also be generalized to a larger problem of searching for swear words or other inappropriate user input in larger forms on a web application, particularly one with nested sections.

At any rate, let's start with some input data:

```
cljs.user=> (def data (list "sprouts" "beans" "onions" (list "alfalfa"
"parsley") "alfalfa" "leeks"))
;; => #'cljs.user/data
```

And now, let's remove all that icky alfalfa:

```
cljs.user=> (let [data (zip/seq-zip data)]
  (loop [loc data]
    (if (zip/end? loc)
      (zip/root loc)
      (recur
       (zip/next
        (if (= (zip/node loc) "alfalfa")
          (zip/remove loc)
          loc))))))
;; => ("sprouts" "beans" "onions" ("parsley") "leeks")
```

Further possibilities

The examples we've covered so far in this section represent just a small fraction of the ways that `clojure.zip` can help you navigate and transform tree-like data structures. For instance, zippers can be amazing for scraping structured data out of HTML (another tree structure!). In addition to replacing or removing values, you can add new values to specific parts of the tree, generate fast search paths to individual nodes, apply functions to values at different nodes, and more. All of this is available to you as part of the core ClojureScript library, and all of it is purely functional and (perhaps most importantly) extremely fast from a performance standpoint.

Declaratively solving problems with core.logic

`core.logic` is a logic programming library for ClojureScript. It offers Prolog-style relational programming, constraint logic programming, and nominal logic programming for ClojureScript. It is based on a family of languages described by William Byrd as *miniKanren*, as well as subsequent extensions known as *cKanren* and *αKanrenA*.

Logic programming is an unfamiliar knowledge domain for many software engineers, and we expect many of the concepts we'll be covering in this section to be quite different from anything you've encountered before, whether in this book or elsewhere.

We've done our best to make the subject matter approachable, but if you find yourself with questions or are curious to learn more, we recommend taking some time to investigate the project's public wiki, located at `https://github.com/clojure/core.logic/wiki`.

At a high level, a logic program consists of one or more logic expressions, and a solution engine or solver (in this case, `core.logic` is the solver). Inside the library, the provided expressions are input to a logic engine, which returns all assignments to the logic variables that satisfy the constraints in the expressions.

If you're familiar with SQL or other database languages that orient around relational statements, this concept is somewhat similar—we provide a series of statements to an engine, with the desire of retrieving all data that is consistent with the statements provided.

Configuring our project

As we did with `core.match` earlier in this chapter, we're going to need to modify our dependencies a bit to make `core.logic` available at runtime. For simplicity, let's just quickly create a standalone project to work in:

```
$ lein new figwheel logic-demo
```

Next, let's add `core.logic` to our `:dependencies` key in our `project.clj`.

`core.logic` still receives the odd update, but is fairly stable, with the last stable release being `0.8.10` from March 2015. Your `:dependencies` key should now look something like the following:

```
:dependencies [[org.clojure/clojure "1.7.0"]
               [org.clojure/clojurescript "1.7.170"]
               [org.clojure/core.logic "0.8.10"]
               [org.clojure/core.async "0.2.374"
                :exclusions [org.clojure/tools.reader]]]
```

Next, we'll start a Figwheel REPL going so that we can get hot-reloading and we can test our code in action:

```
$ cd logic-demo
$ rlwrap lein figwheel
```

Don't forget to navigate a browser window to `http://localhost:3449/` to get the browser REPL to connect.

Getting started with core.logic

First, let's require the main `core.logic` namespace:

```
cljs.user=> (require '[cljs.core.logic :as l])
;; => nil
```

Now, let's take a look at a simple example using `core.logic`. In this example, we're asking the logic engine to find all possible solutions that are members of the collections `[1 2 3 4]` and `[3 4 5 6]`:

```
cljs.user=> (l/run* [q]
  (l/membero q [1 2 3 4])
```

```
    (l/membero q [3 4 5 6]))
;; => (3 4)
```

Like `core.match`, `core.logic` has a core macro that wraps everything else. Where it was previously `match`, here it is `run*` (there's also `run`, which takes an additional argument specifying a limit on the number of requested solutions).

The function `membero` here seeks to satisfy q such that q is a `member` of the provided collection. In general, `core.logic` functions have a vowel appended to the end, hence `membero` means `member`. Another example is `conde`, which behaves like ClojureScript's built-in `cond`.

Perhaps an even simpler `core.logic` example can be found with the == macro (also known as unify), which seeks to constrain the local variable to the exact set of possible values. Concretely, that looks like the following:

```
cljs.user=> (l/run* [q]
  (l/== q 5))
;; => (5)
```

Note that the returned value is always a lazy sequence, even in the case where there's only one solution. This is because `core.logic` returns a sequence of all possible solutions, whether there are many solutions, one solution, or no solutions at all.

Now, you may be wondering what the use case for unify might be. After all, if all it does is solve for a possible solution in which one value is equal to another, why wouldn't we simply return that value from the start, or in other circumstances just check for equality?

The key insight here is that unify becomes more powerful once we begin using `core.logic` to solve more elaborate problems; in particular, ones in which there are other "unknown" values that we're using the logic engine to solve for. For instance, let's consider the following example:

```
cljs.user=> (l/run* [q]
              (l/fresh [a]
                (l/membero a [:animal :mineral :vegetable])
                (l/membero q [:animal :plant :fungi :bacteria])
                (l/== a q)))
;; => (:animal)
```

We haven't seen the `fresh` macro before, so let's cover that first. The `fresh` macro works sort of like `let` in ordinary ClojureScript, only it doesn't bind a specific value to the variable. Instead, like our solver variable q, it marks an unknown value that the logic engine must solve for.

In this example, then, we've required that a must be a member of the collection including :animal, :mineral, and :vegetable, while q must be a member of the collection including :animal, :plant, :fungi, and :bacteria. Finally, we've required that a must be equal to q. This leaves only one answer, which is :animal.

This example is a little contrived, but let's dig deeper. First, note that the order of the constraints doesn't matter. We could specify that a equals q first and get the same result:

```
cljs.user=> (l/run* [q]
              (l/fresh [a]
                (l/== a q)
                (l/membero a [:animal :mineral :vegetable])
                (l/membero q [:animal :plant :fungi :bacteria])))
;; => (:animal)
```

Next, let's take a look at an example in which a being equal to q means there is more than one possible answer. For this, we'll modify our example from earlier in the chapter and reuse it here:

```
cljs.user=> (l/run* [q]
              (l/fresh [a]
                (l/== a q)
                (l/membero a [1 2 3 4])
                (l/membero q [3 4 5 6])))
;; => (3 4)
```

This example shows the true power of unify. The constraint that a being equal to q doesn't mean that there's only a single possible value, but rather that for all of the possible values of a and q, the only valid solutions are ones where a can also be found in q.

The last of core.logic essential macros is conde. Unsurprisingly, conde behaves very similarly to ClojureScript's conde macro. It checks against various predicates and then returns the corresponding value.

conde is a little bit different, in that both the predicate and the returned value have to be true in order for the value to be returned. Let's look at a fairly simple example:

```
cljs.user=> (l/run* [q]
              (l/conde
                (l/succeed l/succeed)
                (l/succeed l/fail)
                (l/fail l/succeed)))
;; => (_.0)
```

We haven't seen `succeed` or `fail` before now, but they're goals that either always succeed or always fail. When `succeed` is returned, it shows up at the REPL as `_.0`.

Let's break down what's going on here. `conde` evaluates each of the conditions in order, and then returns the ones for which both the predicate and the value are true. Our first condition always succeeds, and so does the value, so we return `succeed` (or `_.0`, as per the previous info box). The second condition is successful, but the value fails, so we don't return that. Our final condition fails, so even though the value would succeed we don't return it either.

Let's take a look at a slightly more advanced example:

```
cljs.user=> (l/run* [q]
               (l/conde
                 ((l/== :apricot q) l/succeed)
                 ((l/== :banana q) l/succeed)))
;; => (:apricot :banana)
```

Here, both predicate conditions evaluate successfully, and so do the values. The values evaluating successfully also retain the constraint of the predicate, which means that even though the values only indicate success, we remain constrained by the limits we created in the predicates. Thus, our final possibilities for the logical engine are those determined by the predicates.

If we wanted to think about this in a purely logical sense, `conde` works like the following:

```
(pred AND val) OR (pred AND val) ...
```

One final example should help illustrate the AND aspect of this logical relationship:

```
cljs.user=> (l/run* [q]
               (l/conde
                 ((l/membero q [:a :b :c]) (l/membero q [:b :c :d]))
                 ((l/== :banana q) l/succeed)))
;; => (:banana :b :c)
```

Here, the logical AND of our two `membero` constraints give us the values of `:b` and `:c`. Combined with `conde` logical OR, we also get `:banana` for the final result of all three.

Advanced core.logic

So far, we've covered the major focus areas of `core.logic`: the main logic engine, `run*`, `membero`, as well as the core *operators* from `miniKanren`, upon which `core.logic` is based: `unify`, `conde`, and `fresh`. In this section, we'll take a look at some higher-level constraints—namely, `conso` and `resto`.

`conso` is, as the name would suggest, a `core.logic` analog to ClojureScript's `cons`. Let's quickly recall the behavior of `cons`:

```
cljs.user=> (cons 0 [1 2])
;; => (0 1 2)
```

`conso` works like `cons`, but accepts an additional argument: the resulting sequence from the operation is also provided as an operation (making its function signature `(conso x r s)`). So, an analog for the previous example using `core.logic` would look something like the following:

```
cljs.user=> (l/run* [q]
              (l/conso 0 [1 2] q))
;; => ((0 1 2))
```

Okay, so that's not particularly impressive by itself. What is impressive is that we can pass in our logic variable to any part of the equation. Observe:

```
cljs.user=> (l/run* [q]
              (l/conso q [1 2] [0 1 2]))
;; => (0)

cljs.user=> (l/run* [q]
              (l/conso 0 q [0 1 2]))
;; => ((1 2))
```

We can even pass our logic variable into a specific index of one of the constraint's arguments:

```
cljs.user=> (l/run* [q]
              (l/conso 0 [1 q] [0 1 2]))
;; => (2)
```

Finally, we have `resto`, which is a complement to `conso`. As with the other functions we've seen in this section, `resto` corresponds to the core ClojureScript function `rest`, which gives us the remaining items in a sequence (and an empty sequence if there are no remaining items). It behaves in a very similar way to `conso`, so rather than show all of the possible examples, we'll jump right to one that should, at this point, be fairly comprehensive:

```
cljs.user=> (l/run* [q]
              (l/resto [1 2 3 4] [2 q 4]))
;; => (3)
```

We've covered `membero` already in some detail in this section, but one thing we haven't covered is that `membero` works just like `conso` and `resto` in terms of being able to substitute the logic variable into the collection in question. For instance:
```
cljs.user=> (l/run* [q]
(l/membero 1 [q 2 3]))
;; => (1)
```

Going even further

This concludes our section on `core.logic`. We'd like to stress that we've only covered the basic building blocks of how `core.logic` works, and that these basic building blocks only give a subtle hint as to how powerful the library truly is. `core.logic` is easily extended to solving more advanced problems, such as writing in-memory databases or dealing with arbitrary and/or runtime inputs.

If you'd like to learn more about `core.logic` and to see just a few of the many possible extensions and use cases for the library, we encourage you to take a look at the list of examples available on the `core.logic` wiki (link: `https://github.com/clojure/core.logic/wiki/Examples`), which include, among other things:

- A classic AI program
- A Sudoku solver
- A type inference machine

Runtime data validation using schema

Like JavaScript, ClojureScript is dynamic; no type declarations are required, and attempting to provide them doesn't really give much meaningful support since ClojureScript's close relationship with the Google Closure compiler ensures your applications will already be fairly optimized when such type-related optimizations are available.

However, there are reasons you might want to have type checking as part of your program that aren't performance oriented. For instance, you might want to do input validation, or you might need to ensure that your functions are correctly passing the right data to each other in a test environment. For essentially all scenarios in which you might want to do runtime data validation, Prismatic's `schema` library is the perfect fit.

At a high level, the `schema` library provides functionality for data validation, function annotation, and coercion. It is an invaluable tool when it comes to making runtime assertions about programs and designing tests that can ensure that your applications behave in the way you expect them to.

For most of the lifetime of the `schema` project, it's been under the careful stewardship of the San Francisco-based company, Prismatic. Prismatic recently changed their business model and more-or-less removed their online presence. In the process, they migrated their prior GitHub organization from "Prismatic" to "plumatic". This means that the source code for `schema` can now be found online at `https://github.com/plum atic/schema`.
Users of the library shouldn't worry, however; the same people who were maintaining the library before are still actively developing it and responding to issues, and the source code remains available on `clojars.org` under the original organization name as `prismatic/schema`.

Configuring our project

`schema` is a third-party library, so we'll need to add it to our dependencies if we want to have it available to the compiler. This probably seems like old hat by now, but let's quickly throw together a new project for us to work within:

```
$ lein new figwheel schema-demo
```

And let's add `schema to our :dependencies key in our `project.clj`. At the time of writing, the most recent version of `schema` is 1.0.4, so we'll use that.

Your `:dependencies` key should now look something like the following:

```
:dependencies [[org.clojure/clojure "1.7.0"]
               [org.clojure/clojurescript "1.7.170"]
               [prismatic/schema "1.0.4"]
               [org.clojure/core.async "0.2.374"
                :exclusions [org.clojure/tools.reader]]]
```

Then we'll start a Figwheel REPL going so that we can get hot-reloading and we can test our code in action:

```
$ cd schema-demo
$ rlwrap lein figwheel
```

A quick introduction to schema

Let's start out with an example. Let's try to validate some high-level demographic information. In particular, let's go back to the data examples we were using when we were looking at `clojure.zip`, and let's try to adapt those examples for use here. Let's assume we've got some data in the following form:

```
cljs.user=> (def data
  {:type :state
   :name "California"
   :population 39144000
   :capital {:type :city
             :name "Sacramento"
             :population 500}})
;; => #'cljs.user/data
```

How might we want to validate this?

A naïve approach using schema would entail defining a corresponding data structure where the keys are the same as our desired data structure, and the values correspond to the data type we'd expect to find there. So, for the example data provided previously, a relevant schema would look like the following:

```
;; import schema.core so that we can use it at the REPL

cljs.user=> (require '[schema.core :as s :include-macros true])
;; => nil

;; note that our defined schema is just a normal map, which makes
;; extending it or defining other variants of it easy

cljs.user=> (def state
```

```
  "A schema to describe a state"
  {:type s/Keyword
   :name s/Str
   :population s/Int
   :capital {:type s/Keyword
             :name s/Str
             :population s/Int}})
;; => #'cljs.user/state
```

Let's see whether this schema works to validate our test data. If the data we pass in is valid, `validate` just returns the data:

```
cljs.user=> (s/validate state data)
;; => {:type :state, :name "California", :population 39144000, :capital
{:type :city, :name "Sacramento", :population 500}}
```

If the data we pass in is invalid, schema throws an error:

```
cljs.user=> (def invalid-data
  {:type :state
   :name "California"
   :population "39144000" ;; we've changed population to a string
   :capital {:type :city
             :name "Sacramento"
             :population 500}})
;; => #'cljs.user/invalid-data

cljs.user=> (s/validate state invalid-data)
;; => #error {:message "Value does not match schema: {:population (not
(cljs$core$integer? "39144000"))}", :data {:type :schema.core/error,
:schema {:type #schema.core.Predicate{:p? #object[cljs$core$keyword_QMARK_
"function cljs$core$keyword_QMARK_(x){
return (x instanceof cljs.core.Keyword);
}"], :pred-name cljs$core$keyword?}, :name #schema.core.Predicate{:p?
#object[cljs$core$string_QMARK_ "function cljs$core$string_QMARK_(x){
return goog.isString(x);
}"], :pred-name cljs$core$string?}, :population #schema.core.Predicate{:p?
#object[cljs$core$integer_QMARK_ "function cljs$core$integer_QMARK_(n){
return (typeof n === 'number') && (!(isNaN(n))) && (!((n === Infinity))) &&
((parseFloat(n) === parseInt(n,(10))));
}"], :pred-name cljs$core$integer?}, :capital {:type
#schema.core.Predicate{:p? #object[cljs$core$keyword_QMARK_ "function
cljs$core$keyword_QMARK_(x){
return (x instanceof cljs.core.Keyword);
}"], :pred-name cljs$core$keyword?}, :name #schema.core.Predicate{:p?
#object[cljs$core$string_QMARK_ "function cljs$core$string_QMARK_(x){
return goog.isString(x);
}"], :pred-name cljs$core$string?}, :population #schema.core.Predicate{:p?
```

```
#object[cljs$core$integer_QMARK_ "function cljs$core$integer_QMARK_(n){
return (typeof n === 'number') && (!(isNaN(n))) && (!((n === Infinity))) &&
((parseFloat(n) === parseInt(n,(10)))));
}"], :pred-name cljs$core$integer?}}}, :value {:type :state, :name
"California", :population "39144000", :capital {:type :city, :name
"Sacramento", :population 500}}, :error {:population (not
(cljs$core$integer? "39144000"))}}}}

;; longer stacktrace follows
```

In addition to schema's `validate` function, there's also a `check` function, which does much the same thing, only without the thrown exception. Instead, `check` returns nil if the validation is successful, and if the validation fails, it returns a value that looks like the non-matching parts of the input data with errors at the leaves describing the failures. We'll be using `check` instead of `validate` for the rest of this chapter, since the error messages in ClojureScript can be rather verbose.

This example, where we define the expected types for values in a map, is a good place for us to start because the odds are good that you'll end up writing something similar to it. That having been said, it'd behoove us to go over `schema`'s capabilities from the ground up, so that you can have a more complete idea of how the library works on a more intuitive level.

One thing to be aware of early on is that `schema` type variables (`s/Keyword`, `s/Int`, `s/Str`, and so on) are actually functions, not references to the types themselves. For instance, the source code of `s/Str` is just `(pred string?)`, where `pred` is a fairly straightforward predicate utility function in `schema.core`.

We can test this ourselves by quickly substituting a sample `schema` function ourselves, modeled in a similar way:

```
cljs.user=> (s/check (s/pred even?) 1)
;; => (not (cljs$core$even? 1))

cljs.user=> (s/check (s/pred even?) 2)
;; => nil
```

From the previous example, we can see that all `schema` is really doing is calling the provided function on the data it's validating. This insight will become even more apparent later on in this chapter, when we start experimenting with schema's non-type-related validation capabilities in greater depth.

The simplest sort of validation we can do is by checking against basic types (numbers, strings, keywords, and so on):

```
cljs.user=> (s/check s/Num 42)
;; => nil
```

Now let's try with a string (obviously not a number!):

```
cljs.user=> (s/check s/Num "42")
(not (instance? #object[Number "function Number() { [native code] }"]
"42"))
```

Against a keyword schema:

```
cljs.user=> (s/check s/Keyword :party)
;; => nil
```

And when that fails:

```
cljs.user=> (s/check s/Keyword 'party)
(not (cljs$core$keyword? party))
```

This sort of low-level validation exists for all of ClojureScript's primitives, with the corresponding `schema` type defined as `s/Str`, `s/Keyword`, `s/Num`, `s/Symbol`, and so on.

Collection schemas

Next, let's see how we can compose these basic `schema` functions into greater validations for collections. We've already seen a pretty clear example about how we can validate the types for values in a map with known keys, so let's take look at some more generic examples:

```
;; We can validate that a vector's elements are numbers

cljs.user=> (s/check [s/Num] [1 2 2 3])
;; => nil
```

Similarly, we can define a generic map where keys must be integers and values must be strings:

```
cljs.user=> (s/check {s/Int s/Str} {1 "first" 2 "second"})
;; => nil

;; We can also define multiple possible key types; for instance
;; here a key can be an integer or the keyword :foo
```

```
cljs.user=> (s/check {s/Int s/Str :foo s/Str} {1 "first" :foo "second"})
;; => nil
```

Because `schema` types are just functions, we can easily compose them with other functions, such as `optional-key`:

```
cljs.user=> (def person
  {:name s/Str
   (s/optional-key :occupation) s/Str})
;; => #'cljs.user/person

cljs.user=> (s/check person {:name "David"})
;; => nil

cljs.user=> (s/check person
                     {:name "David"
                      :occupation "Software Engineer"})
;; => nil
```

If we put all of this together, we can create highly customizable schema to capture whatever we think our data might look like. For instance, we can have a generic `person` schema for which the name must be a string, and the age, when provided, must be an integer:

```
cljs.user=> (def person
  {:name s/Str
   (s/optional-key :age) s/Int
   s/Keyword s/Str})
;; => #'cljs.user/person

;; looking good

cljs.user=> (s/check person
                     {:name "David"
                      :age 29
                      :occupation "Software Engineer"
                      :hobby "Billiards"})
;; => nil

;; looking bad

cljs.user=> (s/check person
                  {:age "29"
                   :occupation "Software Engineer"
                   :hobby "Billiards"
                   :bicycles 1})
;; => {:name missing-required-key, :age (not (cljs$core$integer? "29")),
:bicycles (not (cljs$core$string? 1))}
```

We have similar powers of customization when it comes to defining other collection schemas. For instance, we can define a vector where the first element must be a string, a second optional element can be a keyword, and anything after that must be an integer, as follows:

```
cljs.user=> (def form
  [(s/one s/Str "s")
   (s/optional s/Keyword "k")
   s/Int])
;; => #'cljs.user/form
```

 Note that the syntax we've used here (using `s/one`, `s/optional`, and so on) is a function of our desire to have multiple schema types within our vector. If we just wanted a homogeneously typed vector (one with a single possible type), we'd specify it with, for example `(def form [s/Int])`.

The strings `s` and `k` that follow `s/one` and `s/optional` just name the relevant part of the schema. They don't tell you what the value has to be:

```
cljs.user=> (s/check form ["Event"])
;; => nil

cljs.user=> (s/check form ["Event" :logout])
;; => nil

cljs.user=> (s/check form ["Event" :logout 1])
;; => nil

cljs.user=> (s/check form ["Event" :logout 1 2 3])
;; => nil

cljs.user=> (s/check form ["Event" :logout 1 :banana])
;; => [nil nil nil (not (cljs$core$integer? :banana))]
```

We also have an escape hatch for when we truly don't know what type something might be, in the form of `Any`:

```
cljs.user=> (s/check [s/Any] [1 :oh "really?"])
;; => nil
```

Function schemas

In addition to defining validations for data itself, we can also define validations for functions themselves. These types of validations allow you to specify both the argument types and the return types of your functions.

Let's look at a simple example:

```
cljs.user=> (defn untyped-fn
  "A simple un-typed function"
  [x]
  (inc x))
;; => #'cljs.user/untyped-fn

cljs.user=> (s/defn typed-fn :- s/Int
  "A simple typed function."
  [x :- s/Int]
  (inc x))
;; => #'cljs.user/typed-fn
```

 Note that you don't need to define a schema for every argument or return value; those values without a `schema'` are just treated as having been defined with a schema of `s/Any`.

Let's quickly verify that these both work:

```
cljs.user=> (untyped-fn 5)
;; => 6

cljs.user=> (typed-fn 4)
;; => 5

cljs.user=> (typed-fn "a")
;; => "a1"
```

Hey, wait a second! What's the point of providing type annotations when they don't stop you from passing in the wrong type? Well, what's happening under the hood is that the typed functions in schema are leveraging ClojureScript's underlying abilities to provide type *hints*, which are more for documentation purposes than actual compile-time or runtime validation.

Unlike pure ClojureScript type hints, however, schema-type annotations *can* be used for runtime code validation (particularly handy when writing tests!). To turn on function validation, wrap the relevant piece of code in the `with-fn-validation` macro, as follows:

```
cljs.user=> (s/with-fn-validation (typed-fn 1))
;; => 2

cljs.user=> (s/with-fn-validation (typed-fn "a"))
;; => #error {:message "Input to typed-fn does not match schema: [(named
(not (cljs$core$integer? "a")) x)]", :data {:type :schema.core/error,
:schema [#schema.core.One{:schema #schema.core.Predicate{:p?
#object[cljs$core$integer_QMARK_ "function cljs$core$integer_QMARK_(n){
return (typeof n === 'number') && (!(isNaN(n))) && (!((n === Infinity))) &&
((parseFloat(n) === parseInt(n,(10)))));
}"], :pred-name cljs$core$integer?}, :optional? false, :name x}], :value
["a"], :error [(named (not (cljs$core$integer? "a")) x)]}}
;; longer stacktrace follows
```

If you want global runtime-type validation, you can also just call `set-fn-validation!`. There's a slight performance hit to this, but it's generally worth it, especially when you're working in a development environment:

```
cljs.user=> (s/set-fn-validation! true)
;; => true

cljs.user=> (typed-fn 1)
;; => 2

cljs.user=> (typed-fn "a")
;; returns the same error as before
```

To enable function validation during testing (covered in `Chapter 8`, *Bundling ClojureScript for Production*), you can use the following (from the `schema.test` namespace):

```
(use-fixtures :once schema.test/validate-schemas)
```

Advanced schema validation

So far, all of the examples we've looked at have been fairly straightforward—essentially, just iterations on checking whether or not a provided value was of the appropriate type (or types, in the case of a collection schema). However, `schema` is highly extensible, and has built-in support for much more by way of data validation than pure type checking. We've already seen a few hints of what these features look like for instance, with the `optional` modifying function. Let's take a look at a few more advanced examples.

First, we have `maybe`, which validates whether the provided data matches either the provided `schema` function, or is `nil`:

```
cljs.user=> (s/check (s/maybe s/Int) 5)
;; => nil

cljs.user=> (s/check (s/maybe s/Int) nil)
;; => nil

cljs.user=> (s/check (s/maybe s/Int) "a")
;; => (not (cljs$core$integer? "a"))
```

Next, we have features we might expect to see in a fully featured language spec—explicit equality checking by value, as well as `enum` support:

```
cljs.user=> (s/check (s/eq 5) 5)
;; => nil

cljs.user=> (s/check (s/eq 5) 4)
;; => (not (= 5 4))

cljs.user=> (s/check (s/enum :login :signup :logout) :login)
;; => nil

cljs.user=> (s/check (s/enum :login :signup :logout) :email)
;; => (not (#{:login :signup :logout} :email))
```

We've already seen how schema's `pred` function can be used for simple conditionals, but there's also a proper `conditional` function that mirrors the behavior of `cond` within `schema`:

```
cljs.user=> (def KeywordVectorOrString
              (s/conditional vector? [s/Keyword] :else s/Str))
;; => #'cljs.user/KeywordVectorOrString

cljs.user=> (s/check KeywordVectorOrString "I'm a string!")
;; => nil

cljs.user=> (s/check KeywordVectorOrString [:a :vector :of :keywords])
;; => nil

cljs.user=> (s/check KeywordVectorOrString ["This isn't okay, dude."])
;; => [(not (cljs$core$keyword? a-string))]
```

There's a convenience function, `if`, for when there are only two possibilities:

```
cljs.user=> (def KeywordVectorOrString (s/if vector? [s/Keyword] s/Str))
;; => #'cljs.user/KeywordVectorOrString
```

We can define recursive schema as follows:

```
(def Tree {:value s/Int :children [(s/recursive #'Tree)]})
;; => #'cljs.user/Tree

cljs.user=> (s/validate Tree {:value 0, :children [{:value 1, :children
[]}]})
;; => {:value 0, :children [{:value 1, :children []}]}
```

In closing this section, we hope you see how schema's functional programming core allows for practically infinite flexibility when it comes to data validation. Use it to validate types, check for specific values, or provide your own custom validation logic to ensure that the data you're validating is of the expected shape and content for your application.

Schema coercion

So far, our focus has been on validating that a given piece of data satisfied a given schema, but `schema` also supports coercing data into a target schema. The process of coercion is very similar to that of validation under the hood, but involves an initial transformation that is applied to the data before attempting to validate that the data now meets the final schema.

The canonical example here is also the most likely one you'll run into, which is for coercing parsed JSON to a domain-specific schema with different data types (for instance, when one prefers certain values to be ClojureScript keywords instead of strings).

Let's say, for instance, that we have a blog application where users can post comments. Their posted comments include preferences to share their comments with associated social media accounts. The schema for a posted comment might look like the following:

```
cljs.user=>(def CommentSchema
  {:post-id s/Int
   :text s/Str
   :share-services [(s/enum :twitter :facebook :google)]})
;; => #'cljs.user/CommentSchema
```

An actual comment, though, would come in as a JSON object. This means the keys would be strings, not keywords, and the values in the array for :share-services would be strings as well. So a comment would probably look something like this, at the moment it came off the wire:

```
#js {"post-id" 583
     "text" "You're right, ClojureScript *is* awesome!"
     "share-services" ["twitter" "facebook"]}
```

In your application, you'd first translate this JSON object to a ClojureScript map, and in the process cast the string keys to keywords (unless you had some particular reason for keeping them as strings), giving you the following, which we'll store in the post-comment var for easy demonstration purposes:

```
cljs.user=> (def post-comment
              {:post-id 583
               :text "You're right, ClojureScript *is* awesome!"
               :share-services ["twitter" "facebook"]})
;; => #'cljs.user/post-comment
```

So far, the process of converting JSON to our target data format has been fairly straightforward, but here's where things break down. Ordinarily, if we wanted to handle the strings in the :share-services vector (formerly array), we'd have to write a custom function to do so. That function wouldn't be terrible to write, and it'd probably look something like this:

```
(s/defn parse-comment :- CommentSchema
  "Given a comment map, coerce it's share-services to keywords"
  [c]
  (update-in c [:share-services] (partial mapv keyword)))
```

The problem is that, as our application grows, so (generally speaking) do the number of different data types it's likely to handle. Over time, we'd find ourselves having to write similar logic for every possible data type. schema coercion functionality lets us do this in a way that is simple, straightforward, and repeatable.

First, we define a schema coercer for our target schema as follows:

```
;; import schema's coercion namespace

cljs.user=> (require '[schema.coerce :as coerce])
;; => nil

cljs.user=> (def comment-coercer (coerce/coercer CommentSchema coerce/json-
coercion-matcher))
;; => #'cljs.user/comment-coercer
```

`comment-coercer` here is our new coercion function. All we have to do now is to call it on our target data and it'll do the coercion for us:

```
cljs.user=> (comment-coercer post-comment)
;; => {:post-id 583,
        :text "You're right, ClojureScript *is* awesome!",
        :share-services [:twitter :facebook]}
```

Although schema's built-in JSON coercer is by far the most commonly used coercion engine for most ClojureScript applications, it's not inconceivable that you might want to write your own custom coercer (either for handling non-JSON data or for coercing JSON data to types that aren't built-in to `schema`).

 If you're interested in learning more about writing custom schema coercions, you can find a detailed tutorial on how to do so on the `schema` project's wiki, here: `https://github.com/plumatic/schema/wiki/Writing-Custom-Transformations`.

Summary

Congratulations! You now have a working knowledge of some of ClojureScript's more interesting libraries, as well as a good idea of how to take that knowledge and apply it to your particular applications. You've learned how to use `core.match` and `core.logic` to write code that programmatically matches patterns or other logical constraints. With `clojure.zip`, you now know how to rapidly traverse and modify ClojureScript data structures in a way that feels mutable, but has all the safety of immutability. Lastly, you learned how to use `schema` to do runtime data validation.

In the next and final chapter of this book, we'll learn about how to write portable code that'll work for both Clojure and ClojureScript, how to use `cljs.test` to write tests for your code, and how to work with some of the ClojureScript compiler's more advanced compilation options. We'll also show you how to deploy dual Clojure-ClojureScript applications in Docker containers. By the time you're done, you should know everything you need to know in order to be ready to ship your applications to a production environment.

8
Bundling ClojureScript for Production

We've almost come to the end of our journey together in learning ClojureScript. In this final chapter, we'll cover subjects relevant to readers interested in shipping their applications to production environments. In particular, we'll focus on the details of testing, configuration, and deployment as they pertain to ClojureScript applications. This chapter's major areas of focus are the following:

- Testing your application with `cljs.test`
- Advanced ClojureScript compilation options
- Deploying Clojure and ClojureScript applications in a Docker container

Testing your application with cljs.test

In this section, we'll take a look at how to configure your ClojureScript application or library for testing. As usual, we'll start by creating a new project for us to play around with:

```
$ lein new figwheel testing
```

Unlike previous examples where we spent most of our time in the `src` directory, we'll play around in a `test` directory this time. Most JVM Clojure projects will have one already, but since the default Figwheel template doesn't include one, let's make one first (following the same convention used with source directories, that is, instead of `src/$PROJECT_NAME`, we'll create `test/$PROJECT_NAME`):

```
$ mkdir -p test/testing
```

We'll now want to make sure that Figwheel knows to watch the `test` directory for file modifications. To do that, we will edit the `dev` build in our `project.clj` project's `:cljsbuild` map so that its `:source-paths` vector includes both `src` and `test`. Your new `dev` build configuration should look like this:

```
{:id "dev"
 :source-paths ["src" "test"]

 ;; If no code is to be run, set :figwheel true for continued automagical
reloading
 :figwheel {:on-jsload "testing.core/on-js-reload"}

 :compiler {:main testing.core
            :asset-path "js/compiled/out"
            :output-to "resources/public/js/compiled/testing.js"
            :output-dir "resources/public/js/compiled/out"
            :source-map-timestamp true}}
```

Next, we'll get the ol' Figwheel REPL going so that we can have our ever familiar hot reloading:

```
$ cd testing
$ rlwrap lein figwheel
```

Don't forget to navigate your browser window to `http://localhost:3449/` to get the browser REPL to connect.

Now, let's create a new file in the `test/testing` directory, `core_test.cljs`.

By convention, most libraries and applications in Clojure and ClojureScript have test files that correspond to source files with the suffix _test. In this project, that means `test/testing/core_test.cljs` is intended to contain the tests for `src/testing/core.cljs`.

Let's get started by just running tests on a single file. Inside `core_test.cljs`, let's add the following code:

```
(ns testing.core-test
  (:require [cljs.test :refer-macros [deftest is]]))

(deftest i-should-fail
  (is (= 1 0)))

(deftest i-should-succeed
```

```
    (is (= 1 1))))
```

This code first requires two of the most important `cljs.test` macros, and then gives us two simple examples of what a failed test and a successful test should look like.

At this point, we can run our tests from the Figwheel REPL:

```
cljs.user=> (require 'testing.core-test)
;; => nil

cljs.user=> (cljs.test/run-tests 'testing.core-test)

Testing testing.core-test

FAIL in (i-should-fail) (cljs/test.js?zx=icyx7aqatbda:430:14)
expected: (= 1 0)
  actual: (not (= 1 0))

Ran 2 tests containing 2 assertions.
1 failures, 0 errors.
;; => nil
```

Great. So, at this point, what we've got is tolerable but it's not really practical in terms of being able to test a larger application. We don't want to have to test our application in the REPL and pass in our test namespaces one by one.

The current idiomatic solution for this in ClojureScript is to write a separate test runner that is responsible for any important setup and running all of your tests. Let's take a look at what this looks like.

Let's start by creating another test namespace. Let's call this one `app_test.cljs`, and we'll put the following in there:

```
(ns testing.app-test
  (:require [cljs.test :refer-macros [deftest is]]))

(deftest another-successful-test
  (is (= 4 (count "test"))))
```

We're not doing anything remarkable here; it's just another test namespace with a single test that should pass by itself. Let's quickly make sure that this is exactly the case at the REPL:

```
cljs.user=> (require 'testing.app-test)
nil
cljs.user=> (cljs.test/run-tests 'testing.app-test)

Testing testing.app-test
```

```
Ran 1 tests containing 1 assertions.
0 failures, 0 errors.
;; => nil
```

Perfect. Now, let's write a test runner. Let's open a new file that we'll call, simply enough, test_runner.cljs, and let's include the following:

```
(ns testing.test-runner
  (:require [cljs.test :refer-macros [run-tests]]
            [testing.app-test]
            [testing.core-test]))

;; This isn't strictly necessary, but is a good idea depending
;; upon your application's ultimate runtime engine.
(enable-console-print!)

(defn run-all-tests
  []
  (run-tests 'testing.app-test
             'testing.core-test))
```

Again, nothing surprising. We're just making a single function for us that runs all of our tests. This is handy for us at the REPL:

```
cljs.user=> (require 'testing.test-runner)
;; => nil

cljs.user=> (testing.test-runner/run-all-tests)

Testing testing.app-test

Testing testing.core-test

FAIL in (i-should-fail) (cljs/test.js?zx=icyx7aqatbda:430:14)
expected: (= 1 0)
  actual: (not (= 1 0))

Ran 3 tests containing 3 assertions.
1 failures, 0 errors.
;; => nil
```

Ultimately, however, we want something we can run at the command line so that we can use it in a continuous integration environment. There are a number of ways we can go about configuring this directly, but if we're clever, we can let someone else do the heavy lifting for us. Enter doo, the handy ClojureScript testing plugin for Leiningen.

Using doo for easier testing configuration

doo is a library and Leiningen plugin for running the cljs.test in many different JavaScript environments. It makes it easy to test your ClojureScript regardless of whether you're writing for the browser or for the server, and it also includes file watching capabilities like Figwheel so that you can automatically rerun tests on file changes. The doo project page can be found at https://github.com/bensu/doo.

To configure our project to use doo, first we need to add it to the list of plugins in our project.clj file. Modify the :plugins key so that it looks like the following:

```
:plugins [[lein-figwheel "0.5.2"]
          [lein-doo "0.1.6"]
          [lein-cljsbuild "1.1.3" :exclusions [[org.clojure/clojure]]]]
```

Next, we will add a new Cljsbuild build configuration for our test runner. Add the following build map after the dev build map we've been working with up until now:

```
{:id "test"
 :source-paths ["src" "test"]
 :compiler {:main testing.test-runner
            :output-to "resources/public/js/compiled/testing_test.js"
            :optimizations :none}}
```

This configuration tells Cljsbuild to use both our src and test directories, just like our dev profile. However, it adds some different configuration elements to the compiler options.

To start with, we're not using testing.core as our main namespace anymore—instead, we'll use our test runner's namespace, testing.test-runner. We will also change the output JavaScript file to a different location from our compiled application code. Lastly, we will make sure that we pass :optimizations :none in so that the compiler runs quickly and doesn't have to do any magic to look things up.

Note that our currently running Figwheel process won't know about the fact that we've added lein-doo to our list of plugins or that we've added a new build configuration. In order to get Figwheel to play nicely with doo, you should add doo as a dependency to your project on top of having lein-doo as a plugin. Once you've done that, exit the Figwheel process and restart it after you've saved the changes to project.clj.

Lastly, we need to modify our test runner namespace so that it's compatible with doo. To do this, open `test_runner.cljs` and change it to the following:

```
(ns testing.test-runner
  (:require [doo.runner :refer-macros [doo-tests]]
            [testing.app-test]
            [testing.core-test]))

;; This isn't strictly necessary, but is a good idea depending
;; upon your application's ultimate runtime engine.
(enable-console-print!)

(doo-tests 'testing.app-test
           'testing.core-test)
```

This shouldn't look too different from our original test runner—we're just importing from `doo.runner` rather than `cljs.test` and using `doo-tests` instead of a custom runner function. The `-testsdoo-tests` function works very similarly to `cljs.test/run-tests`, but it places hooks around the tests to know when to start them and finish them. We're also putting this at the top-level of our namespace rather than wrapping it in a particular function.

The last thing we're going to need to do is to install a JavaScript runtime that we can use to execute our tests with. Up until now, we've been using the browser via Figwheel, but ideally we want to be able to run our tests in a headless environment as well. For this purpose, we recommend installing **PhantomJS** (though other execution environments are also fine).

If you're on OS X and have Homebrew installed (http://www.brew.sh), installing PhantomJS is as simple as typing `brew install phantomjs`. If you're not on OS X or don't have Homebrew, you can find instructions on how to install PhantomJS on the project's website at `http://phantomjs.org/`. The key thing is that the following should work:

```
$ phantomjs -v
2.0.0
```

Once you've got PhantomJS installed, you can now invoke your test runner from the command line with the following:

```
$ lein doo phantom test once

;; =================================================================

;; Testing with Phantom:
```

```
Testing testing.app-test
Testing testing.core-test

FAIL in (i-should-fail) (:)
expected: (= 1 0)
  actual: (not (= 1 0))

Ran 3 tests containing 3 assertions.
1 failures, 0 errors.
Subprocess failed
```

Let's break this command apart a bit. The first part, `lein  doo`, just tells Leiningen to invoke the `doo` plugin. Next, we have `phantom`, which tells `doo` to use PhantomJS as its running environment.

Doo supports a number of other environments, including Chrome, Firefox, Internet Explorer, Safari, Opera, SlimerJS, NodeJS, Rhino, and Nashorn. Be aware that if you're interested in running `doo` on one of these other environments, you may have to configure and install additional software. For instance, if you want to run tests on Chrome, you'll need to install Karma as well as the appropriate Karma `npm` modules to enable Chrome interaction.

Next, we have `test`, which refers to the `Cljsbuild` build ID that we set up earlier. Lastly, we have `once`, which tells `doo` to just run tests and not to set up a filesystem watcher. If, instead, we wanted `doo` to watch the filesystem and rerun tests on any changes, we would just use `lein doo phantom test`.

Testing fixtures

The `cljs.test` function has support for adding fixtures to your tests that will run before and after your tests. Test fixtures are useful for establishing an isolated state between tests—for instance, you could use tests to set up a specific database state before each test and to tear it down afterwards. You can add them to your ClojureScript tests by declaring them with the "use-fixtures" macro within the testing namespace you want fixtures applied to.

Let's see what this looks like in practice by changing one of our existing tests and adding some fixtures to it. Modify the `app_test.cljs` file to the following:

```
(ns testing.app-test
  (:require [cljs.test :refer-macros [deftest is use-fixtures]]))
```

```
;; Run these fixtures for each test.

;; We could also use :once instead of :each in order to run
;; fixtures once for the entire namespace instead of once for
;; each individual test.
(use-fixtures
  :each
  {:before (fn [] (println "Setting up tests..."))
   :after (fn [] (println "Tearing down tests..."))})

(deftest another-successful-test
  ;; Give us an idea of when this test actually executes.
  (println "Running a test...")
  (is (= 4 (count "test"))))
```

Here, we added a call to `use-fixtures` that prints to the console before and after running the test, and we added a `println` call to the test itself so that we know when it executes. Now when we run this test, we get the following:

```
$ lein doo phantom test once

;; ================================================================

;; Testing with Phantom:


Testing testing.app-test
Setting up tests...
Running a test...
Tearing down tests...

Testing testing.core-test

FAIL in (i-should-fail) (:)
expected: (= 1 0)
  actual: (not (= 1 0))

Ran 3 tests containing 3 assertions.
1 failures, 0 errors.
Subprocess failed
```

Note that our fixtures get called in the order we expect them. You should feel free, at this point, to remove the failing test in `core_test.cljs`, but we'll assume that you've left it in for the rest of this chapter.

Asynchronous testing

Due to the fact that client-side code is frequently asynchronous and JavaScript is single-threaded, we need to have a way to support asynchronous tests. To do this, we can use the `async` macro from `cljs.test`. Let's take a look at an example using an asynchronous HTTP GET request.

First, let's modify our `project.clj` file to add `cljs-ajax` to our dependencies. Your `dependencies` project key should now look similar to this:

```
:dependencies [[org.clojure/clojure "1.8.0"]
               [org.clojure/clojurescript "1.7.228"]
               [cljs-ajax "0.5.4"]
               [org.clojure/core.async "0.2.374"
                :exclusions [org.clojure/tools.reader]]]
```

Next, let's create a new file in our `test.testing` directory, `async_test.cljs`. Inside it, we will add the following code:

```
(ns testing.async-test
  (:require [ajax.core :refer [GET]]
            [cljs.test :refer-macros [deftest is async]]))

(deftest test-async
  (GET "http://www.google.com"
       ;; will always fail from PhantomJS because
       ;; `Access-Control-Allow-Origin` won't allow
       ;; our headless browser to make requests to Google.
       {:error-handler
        (fn [res]
          (is (= (:status-text res) "Request failed."))
          (println "Test finished!"))}))
```

 Note that at the moment, we're *not* using `async` in our test.

Let's try running this test with `doo` (don't forget that you have to add `testing.async-test` to `test_runner.cljs`!):

```
$ lein doo phantom test once
...
Testing testing.async-test
...
Ran 4 tests containing 3 assertions.
```

```
1 failures, 0 errors.
Subprocess failed
```

Now, our test here passes, but note that the `println` async code never fires and our additional assertion doesn't get called (looking back at our previous examples, since we've added a new `is` assertion, we should expect to see four assertions in the summary)! If we actually want our test to appropriately validate the error-handler callback within the context of the test, we need to wrap it in an `async` block. Doing so gives us a test that looks like the following:

```
(deftest test-async
  (async done
    (GET "http://www.google.com"
         ;; will always fail from PhantomJS because
         ;; `Access-Control-Allow-Origin` won't allow
         ;; our headless browser to make requests to Google.
         {:error-handler
          (fn [res]
            (is (= (:status-text res) "Request failed."))
            (println "Test finished!")
            (done))}))))
```

Now, let's try to run our tests again:

```
$ lein doo phantom test once
...
Testing testing.async-test
Test finished!
...
Ran 4 tests containing 4 assertions.
1 failures, 0 errors.
Subprocess failed
```

Awesome! Note that this time we both see the printed statement from our callback and we can see that `cljs.test` properly ran all four of our assertions.

Asynchronous fixtures

One final "gotcha" on testing—the fixtures we talked about earlier in this chapter do not handle asynchronous code automatically. This means that if you have a `:before` fixture that executes asynchronous logic, your test could begin running before your fixture has completed! In order to get around this, all you need to do is to wrap your `:before` fixture in an `async` block, just like with asynchronous tests. For instance:

```
(use-fixtures :once
```

```
{:before
 #(async done
     ...
     (done))
 :after
 #(do ...)})
```

This concludes our section on `cljs.test`. Testing, whether in ClojureScript or any other language, is a critical software engineering best practice to ensure that your application behaves the way you expect it to and to protect you and your fellow developers from accidentally introducing bugs into your application. With `cljs.test` and `doo`, you have the power and flexibility to test your ClojureScript application with multiple browsers and JavaScript environments, and to integrate your tests into a larger continuous testing framework.

Advanced ClojureScript compilation options

In this section, we'll cover more advanced ClojureScript compilation options with an eye to helping you bundle your application for production. Compiling ClojureScript applications for production can involve a significant degree of configuration, and we recommend that you begin thinking about how you're going to compile your application sooner rather than later.

 While we've done our best to cover what we consider the most important aspects of compiler configuration, an up-to-date and exhaustive list of ClojureScript compiler options can also be found online on the ClojureScript project's wiki page at `https://github.com/clojure/clojurescript/wiki/Compiler-Options`.

While we generally believe that premature optimization is the root of many a wasted hour, in this case, it's a better idea to make sure that things are working early and often. This will help you ensure that your compilation configuration is giving you builds that behave the way you expect them to in a production-like environment.

 We've already covered certain aspects of advanced ClojureScript compilation at other points in the book, and our editor has politely asked us not to repeat ourselves. With that in mind, we recommend that you refer to the *The Google Closure Compiler and Using External JavaScript Libraries* section from `Chapter 2`, *ClojureScript Language Fundamentals*, as you work on getting your application's compiler configuration geared for production.

Compilation optimization levels

The Google Closure Compiler supports three different levels of optimizations, and the ClojureScript compiler adds another (or, more precisely, it adds an option to not use the Google Closure Compiler at all). This means that when it comes to compiling a ClojureScript project, we have four different optimization levels for our compiler:

- `:none`
- `:whitespace`
- `:simple`
- `:advanced`

The default ClojureScript Compiler optimization level is `:none`. As the name suggests, when using this setting, the compiler simply concatenates all of the compiled JavaScript into a single file and calls it a day.

The next level on the compiler optimization scale is `:whitespace`, which simply removes all comments from the compiled code as well as line breaks, unnecessary spaces, extraneous punctuation (such as parentheses and semicolons), and other whitespace. Functionally, the output JavaScript is identical to the source JavaScript.

This provides more compression than `:none` but less than `:simple` or `:advanced`.

Next, we have `:simple`, which performs the same optimizations as `:whitespace` but also performs optimizations within expressions and functions, including renaming local variables and function parameters to shorter names. This makes the final output code considerably smaller. Because `:simple` only renames symbols that are local to functions, it does not interfere with any calls to and from compiled JavaScript and other JavaScript. Compilation with `:simple` optimizations preserves functionality on the condition that the codebase doesn't access local variables using string names (that is, by using `eval()` or calling `toString()` on functions). Projects using the Google Closure Compiler directly (that is, not using the ClojureScript Compiler) will have this as the default compilation setting.

The final optimization level is :advanced. This performs the same optimizations as :simple, but adds a number of more aggressive code transformations to achieve a much higher level of compression. As it has been discussed at some length in Chapter 2, *ClojureScript Language Fundamentals*, :advanced optimization makes a number of assumptions about the structure of your code—code that doesn't meet those assumptions will not fail during the compilation phase, but it will behave unexpectedly at runtime.

Getting your project structured to work with the :advanced compilation may seem like a hassle and a lot of work, but code compiled using the :advanced configuration flag is guaranteed to have a much smaller payload (meaning faster load times for your site visitors)! The Google Closure Compiler achieves this by engaging in more aggressive renaming, dead code removal, and global inlining.

 Be aware that :advanced compilation will take considerably longer than other optimization modes, which is why it's not ideal for development.

Generating modules

Recent releases of ClojureScript have added support for emitting Google Closure modules. Modules support splitting a given optimized build into multiple different files. If you provide :modules as a key in your compilation configuration options map, it'll replace the single file path normally given to the :output-to option (that is, :output-to is ignored since it implies only generating a single file, not multiple modules).

 While our coverage of ClojureScript modules in this section will focus on configuration details, Chapter 6, *Building Richer Web Applications*, includes a detailed example of how to actually structure ClojureScript modules in a "real-world" application.

When configuring modules, each generated module needs a name, its own :output-to path, a set of namespaces to be added (under the :entries key), and :depends-on, which is the set of modules upon which the specific module depends. Closure modules are only supported when using :simple or :advanced optimization. An example module configuration might look like the following:

```
{:optimizations :advanced
 :source-map true
 :output-dir "resources/public/js"
 :modules {
   :common
```

```
    {:output-to "resources/public/js/common.js"
     :entries #{"foo.common"}}
  :landing
    {:output-to "resources/public/js/landing.js"
     :entries #{"foo.landing"}
     :depends-on #{:common}}
  :mobile
    {:output-to "resources/public/js/mobile.js"
     :entries #{"foo.mobile" "foo.mobile.util"}
     :depends-on #{:common}}}}
```

In this example, the :landing and :mobile modules both depend on the :common module.

When using modules, any namespace in your source paths that isn't specified in a specific module will be added to a default module, :cljs-base. This module will be written out to the specified :output-dir as cljs_base.js. If you want it to go into a differently named file, just create an additional module for it in which you only specify :output-to, for instance:

```
{:optimizations :advanced
 :source-map true
 :output-dir "resources/public/js"
 :modules {
   :common
     {:output-to "resources/public/js/common.js"
      :entries #{"foo.common"}}
   :landing
     {:output-to "resources/public/js/landing.js"
      :entries #{"foo.landing"}
      :depends-on #{:common}}
   :cljs-base
     {:output-to "resources/public/js/base.js"}}}
```

In this example, we altered our configuration so that :cljs-base is compiled to base.js rather than cljs_base.js.

Targeting a Node.js runtime

Although the focus of this book is primarily on single-page applications, most of the subjects covered in this book will also work on a Node.js runtime. To compile your application for Node.js, add :target :nodejs to your compilation map (by default, the ClojureScript Compiler assumes that you are targeting the browser).

By default, if you choose to target Node.js, the compiler will emit a shebang as the first line of the compiled source to make it an executable. If you're writing a Node.js module rather than an executable application, you should also add `:hashbang false` to your project's compilation options.

 Additional details and examples on running your ClojureScript application on Node.js can be found on the ClojureScript wiki at https://github.com/clojure/clojurescript/wiki/Quick-Start#running-clojurescript-on-nodejs.

General configuration recommendations

We recommend configuring your projects to have at least two compilation profiles—one for development using `:none` and another for deployment using `:advanced`. You may, optionally, find it valuable to have an additional profile for testing, but we encourage you to keep configuration changes limited to things like the inclusion of test file source paths.

You should try to make sure that you get a functioning `:advanced` configuration early and to keep a special eye on it when changing compilation settings or adding foreign dependencies, particularly those using native JavaScript (that is, non-ClojureScript dependencies).

Where possible, we recommend using dependencies downloaded from CLJSJS. Failing that, we encourage you to use widely supported and used externs configurations. In general, having to configure and maintain your own custom configuration for a third-party library is much more work than relying on the open source community for support.

Deploying Clojure and ClojureScript applications in a Docker container

In this final section, we'll cover deploying our client and server application code in a single Docker container. Containers are a technology that you can use to wrap up a piece of software in a complete filesystem that includes everything it needs to run: application code, a runtime, system tools, system libraries, and so on—anything you might otherwise install on a server. Using container technology provides a way of guaranteeing that your application will always run the same regardless of the underlying environment it is running in.

Today, many cloud infrastructure providers offer products and services that have direct support for Docker. For instance, if you're using Amazon Web Service's **Elastic Beanstalk** to host, deploy, and scale your application, you can deploy a container directly by telling the Elastic Beanstalk API to deploy a specific container ID from a given Docker registry and it'll know what to do.

Installing Docker

To install Docker, you have a few different options depending on what operating system you're running. If you're running Linux, you basically just have to `curl` a script from the Docker website. If you're running OS X or Windows, we recommend installing **Docker Toolbox** from the Docker website and following their instructions.

The process of getting Docker installed and configured for every possible architecture is beyond the scope of this book; however, you should be able to find instructions on how to get Docker installed and configured for your system architecture online on Docker's documentation portal located at `https://docs.docker.com/`.

Although Docker's installation and configuration process is still fairly manual for OS X, there's currently an active beta for a better native Docker experience that'll allow you to get up and running even faster. Since you're likely reading this in the future, there's a good chance this is an option for you!

In short, in order to get Docker working, you'll need the following:

- A Docker server running on your machine. If you're on OS X or Windows, this will need to run on a virtual machine, which you can either set up with Docker's Kitematic UI application, using the terminal or an application like Virtualbox.
- The latest version of the Docker client installed. As of the time of writing this, that would be version 1.11.0.

The preceding requirements are what are strictly necessary in order to get Docker working on your machine. In addition to the preceding explanation, and especially if you're on OS X or Windows, we recommend installing Docker Machine. Docker Machine includes, among other things, the ability to easily check to see if the Docker server VM is up and running (using `docker-machine status`) and also the ability to quickly set the appropriate environment variables to connect to said server.

In general, if you're on OS X, we recommend adding the following line to your ~/.bash_profile or other shell initialization file:

eval "$(docker-machine env default)"

This command sets all of the appropriate environment variables in your shell to let your Docker client know how to access the server. If you execute it by itself (that is, outside of the evaluation context), you should see something like the following:

export DOCKER_TLS_VERIFY="1"
export DOCKER_HOST="tcp://192.168.99.100:2376"
export DOCKER_CERT_PATH=
  "/Users/ursa/.docker/machine/machines/default"
export DOCKER_MACHINE_NAME="default"
 # Run this command to configure your shell:
 # eval $(docker-machine env default)

Once you've got Docker set up and configured properly, you should be able to test out that it works by successfully executing `docker run hello-world`:

```
$ docker run hello-world
Hello from Docker.
This message shows that your installation appears to be working
correctly.
To generate this message, Docker took the following steps:

 1. The Docker client contacted the Docker daemon.
 2. The Docker daemon pulled the "hello-world" image from the
    Docker Hub.
 3. The Docker daemon created a new container from that image
    which runs the executable that produces the output you are
    currently reading.
 4. The Docker daemon streamed that output to the Docker
    client, which sent it to your terminal.

To try something more ambitious, you can run an Ubuntu
container with:

$ docker run -it ubuntu bash

Share images, automate workflows, and more with a free Docker
Hub account:
https://hub.docker.com

For more examples and ideas, visit:
https://docs.docker.com/userguide/
```

Compiling an Uberjar

By now, you should have at least a passing awareness of JAR files—the standard mechanism for distributing Java source code (as well as Clojure and precompiled ClojureScript code). An **Uberjar** differs from a jar file in that it includes all of a project's dependencies as well.

This means that while a normal JAR file might include a manifest of which dependencies would need to be downloaded prior to initializing an executable, a comparable Uberjar would have all of the requisite dependencies already included. Uberjars, therefore, represent an excellent way of bundling together all of the application code necessary to run something into a single file.

Leiningen makes it incredibly easy for us to create Uberjars for our projects—all we have to do is run `lein uberjar`. To see how this works, let's first create a sample Clojure/ClojureScript project. If you like, you can reuse the project from `Chapter 5`, *Building Single Page Applications*; otherwise, we can just use a basic Chestnut application. We'll assume that you're creating a new Chestnut application for the purposes of this section.

 Chestnut is a Leiningen template for a Figwheel-enabled Clojure/ClojureScript application based on Om or Reagent. Although converting existing projects to Chestnut's structure isn't usually worth it, Chestnut provides a decent way to get a quick Clojure/ClojureScript project up and running. The project page for Chestnut can be found at `https://github.com/plexus/chestnut`.

First, let's create a new project using the Chestnut template:

```
$ lein new chestnut docker
Generating fresh Chestnut project.
README.md contains instructions to get you started.
$ cd docker/
```

By default, Chestnut's web server will start silently. We'd like to know when the server is done booting, so let's edit the `-main` method in `src/clj/docker/server.clj` to include a quick `println` call once the server's done booting:

```
(defn -main [& [port]]
  (let [port (Integer. (or port (env :port) 10555))]
    (run-jetty http-handler {:port port :join? false})
    (println "Server started!")))
```

Now, let's compile our ClojureScript and start the web server:

```
$ lein cljsbuild once app
Compiling ClojureScript...
Compiling "resources/public/js/compiled/docker.js" from ["src/cljs"]...
Successfully compiled "resources/public/js/compiled/docker.js" in 3.987
seconds.
$ lein run
Server started!
```

Once you see the **Server started!** message, you should be able to navigate your web browser to http://localhost:10555 and see the following:

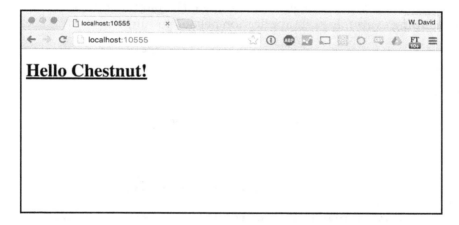

It's not particularly impressive, but what matters here is that we've got a functioning backend web server and some compiled ClojureScript that's rendering an h1 element using React. On the backend, our web server is configured to invoke the -main method that's defined in the Clojure file located at src/clj/docker/server.clj to run. And on the frontend, we configured our ClojureScript to launch from src/cljs/docker/core.cljs. This configuration is set in our project.clj file with the following configuration that Chestnut will have set up for us by default:

```
:main docker.server
```

Now, if we wanted we could attempt to just bundle this up as a Clojure application in a Docker container to run using the same lein run command we just invoked; it's possible to configure Docker to run using Leiningen without too much difficulty. But doing so would mean our application would be a bit slower to start-up since it'd have to deal with Leiningen's startup time as well.

Leiningen starts its own JVM and then uses that to initialize your application. By default, Leiningen's JVM will stay active until the task it's been told to run is complete (which, if you're starting a Clojure web server, could be a long time). You can tell Leiningen to terminate itself using `lein trampoline` command once your application is launched, but even then you have to wait for Leiningen to finish initializing and loading your application first.

In a production environment, it's not unreasonable for us to want our application to load quickly without having to worry about Leiningen's startup time.

It's also one extra dependency we'd have to include in our final container, making the file size a bit larger as well. What if we just built a single Uberjar that didn't contain Leiningen, while still including everything our application needed to run?

It turns out this is relatively straightforward to do. First, let's get rid of any existing compiled ClojureScript or other assets:

```
$ lein clean
```

Next, let's run `lein uberjar` to compile an Uberjar for ourselves:

```
$ lein uberjar
Compiling docker.server
Compiling ClojureScript...
Compiling "resources/public/js/compiled/docker.js" from
  ["src/cljs"]...
Successfully compiled "resources/public/js/compiled/docker.js"
  in 24.857 seconds.
Created /Users/ursa/Code/example-code/chapter-
/docker/target/docker-0.1.0-SNAPSHOT.jar
Created /Users/ursa/Code/example-code/chapter-
/docker/target/docker.jar
```

There are a few things to take note of here. First, note that we've created two separate JAR files. In this case, the former of these two JAR files, `docker-0.1.0-SNAPSHOT.jar`, is not an Uberjar; it just gets generated at the same time. The latter, however, is an Uberjar. Typically, the Uberjar would be named `docker-0.1.0-SNAPSHOT-standalone.jar` (more generally `$PROJECT_NAME-$PROJECT_VERSION-standalone.jar`), but in this case, the Chestnut template sets the `:uberjar-name` configuration flag in the `project.clj` file to just use the name of the project, and so we end up with an Uberjar named `docker.jar`.

The other thing that's worth noting here is that our ClojureScript compiled with `:advanced` optimizations took considerably longer to compile than it did when we were just executing `lein cljsbuild once app`—almost 10 times as long, in fact! We encourage you to take a look at what's different between the `app` build's compilation settings and the `uberjar` build's compilation settings in the `project.clj` file to see what else has been changed here as well.

Now that we have our Uberjar built, let's try running it to see if it works:

```
$ java -jar target/docker.jar
Server started!
```

If you get an **Address already in use** exception, then the server we started earlier in this chapter is still running. Since two web processes can't share a port, you need to kill that server and re-start this one to get it to work.

We should now be able to navigate our browser to `http://localhost:10555` and see the familiar **Hello Chestnut!** page. This means that our Uberjar has compiled all of our JavaScript and is successfully serving it from the bundled Clojure server.

Building a Docker container for our app

In order to build a Docker container for our Chestnut application, we're going to need to put together a Dockerfile. A Dockerfile can be thought of as a recipe for building a container image. Dockerfiles are composed by taking a base operating system layer and then layering on additional modifications to the file system that are then encoded into the file system. Because Dockerfiles support repeated layering, we can even take an existing Dockerfile and then layer additional modifications on top of that, which is exactly what we're going to do!

In this section, we're largely going to use the terms "container" and "image" interchangeably, but this obscures the fact that the two are fundamentally different.

A Docker image is an ordered collection of root filesystem changes, as well as some metadata (including execution parameters for use within a container runtime). Images are immutable—if you make a change to an image, Docker will store the post-change state as an entirely new image. By contrast, a Docker container is an active (or, if its execution has concluded or been stopped, inactive) stateful instantiation of an image. Containers are generated from images, but once running can be mutated in any number of possible ways. Consequently, you have no guarantee that two containers that were started from the same image are in the same state.

A somewhat helpful analogy can be to the world of object-oriented programming; if a Docker image is a class, then a Docker container would be an instance of that class.

For our Dockerfile, we're going to use as a base image the `java:8` image from the official repository on Docker Hub, the public Docker registry. Details on the Java repository can be found on the repository's website on the Docker Hub: `https://hub.docker.com/_/java /`.

Not all repositories on Docker Hub are official; in fact, most belong to normal, everyday contributors hacking on open source projects and systems. Official repositories, by contrast, are a curated set of repositories promoted because they provide essential base repositories (either for an OS or a runtime such as Java), exemplify Dockerfile best practices, have good security hygiene, or provide a channel for software vendors to distribute the latest supported versions of their products.

We strongly recommend that you stick to official repositories when getting started with Docker. You can learn more about official repositories on Docker's website at `https://docs.docker.com/docker-hub/offic ial_repos/`.

We will now add some additional metadata and instructions that will take our Uberjar, add it to the Docker filesystem, and then tell Docker how to run our JAR.

Save the following to a file named `Dockerfile` in the root of your project:

```
FROM java:8
# Feel free to put your name here!
MAINTAINER W. David Jarvis <yournamehere@gmail.com>
ADD target/docker.jar /srv/app.jar
WORKDIR /srv
CMD ["java", "-jar", "/srv/app.jar"]
```

Let's walk through what each of these lines does.

The `MAINTAINER` parameter just adds a bit of friendly metadata about the author to the Docker image that we're building. Feel free to add your name here or leave this line out entirely.

The `ADD` parameter tells Docker to copy a file from our computer's filesystem into the container's filesystem at a specific location. Here, we've told it to take our compiled Uberjar and to store it in the container's filesystem at `/srv/app.jar`.

The `WORKDIR` parameter sets the working directory for any `RUN`, `CMD`, `ENTRYPOINT`, `COPY`, or `ADD` instructions that come afterward. In this case, we're just setting `/srv` as our working directory.

Lastly, the `CMD` instruction tells Docker what executable and arguments to run when we try to start a running container off of this image.

 It's possible to pass a different execution command at runtime to Docker, but in practice, it's best to encode the default run command in the Dockerfile for the convenience of the end user or server.

There can only be one `CMD` instruction in a Dockerfile.

Now that we have our Dockerfile defined, we can use Docker to build a Docker image for our application. Once we're done with that, we'll be able to run it as a container. Run the following command to build our Docker image (your output may differ slightly):

```
$ docker build -t dockerapp.
Sending build context to Docker daemon 34.41 MB
Step 1 : FROM java:8
8: Pulling from library/java
efd26ecc9548: Pull complete
a3ed95caeb02: Pull complete
d1784d73276e: Pull complete
72e581645fc3: Pull complete
1e6509b4af69: Pull complete
cb657b848e5b: Pull complete
a61be2f3cb34: Pull complete
c7e88b44d657: Pull complete
c7335ca7647e: Pull complete
Digest:
  sha256:11ba9d7a2927ae52203aa1a7065fdef70c626a5f780952eb0229
  6a103ed1e0d1
Status: Downloaded newer image for java:8
 ---> 081ce13c85db
Step 2 : MAINTAINER W. David Jarvis <yournamehere@gmail.com>
 ---> Running in cfc28de2d657
 ---> e237c1744882
Removing intermediate container cfc28de2d657
Step 3 : ADD target/docker.jar /srv/app.jar
 ---> 8e6dee0c150a
Removing intermediate container b3ebb00358c1
Step 4 : WORKDIR /srv
 ---> Running in 46e66d7eadc3
 ---> de4f9fab91cf
```

```
Removing intermediate container 46e66d7eadc3
Step 5 : CMD java -jar /srv/app.jar
 ---> Running in f1175d8feea8
 ---> 92693b384187
Removing intermediate container f1175d8feea8
Successfully built 92693b384187
```

What this command does is build an image with the `dockerapp` tag using the Dockerfile found in this directory (hence the ". "). A tag is a handy piece of searchable metadata that is applied to a Docker image so that we can ask Docker to run images with human-readable names. There are a few different conventions around tag naming—in general, you'll probably want to use tags that are of the form `$repository/$image_name:$version`, but for this example, we're sticking with a simple tag.

Next, we'll run our Docker image as a container:

```
$ docker run dockerapp # note that we're passing our image tag here
Server started!
```

Now, let's navigate our browser to `http://localhost:10555` and ... hey! What happened? How come we can't see our application?

The answer is a little complicated, but basically we have either one or two problems. First, we need to tell the Docker server how to map ports from the container we're running to the host machine. Additionally, if we're using OS X or Windows, we need to figure out how to access that host machine (since our Docker host will be running inside of a VM and not on our actual machine as a daemon).

We can resolve the first problem by just passing an extra argument to our invocation of Docker that tells it how to map container ports to host ports, as follows:

```
$ docker run -p 10555:10555 dockerapp
Server started!
```

If you're on Linux, you should now be able to access the app at `http://localhost:10555`. If you're on OS X or Windows, however, you'll need to use `docker-machine` to figure out what IP your VM is available at and then access the app of that URL:

```
$ docker-machine ip
192.168.99.100
```

Now that we know our VM's IP address is `192.168.99.100`, we should now be able to access our application at `http://192.168.99.100:10555`. Perfect!

We've now covered everything you need to know in order to build, test, and run Docker containers locally, but there's a lot more to Docker that's beyond the scope of this book. If you're looking to deploy Docker in a production environment, your next steps would be optionally setting up a private image registry (so as to not expose your source code to anyone outside your company), configuring your continuous deployment system able to push those images to a remote repository, and finally configuring your deployment system to tell whatever hardware or infrastructure you're deploying onto to pull and run the latest image from your Docker repository as part of a successful deployment.

Summary

You now have many of the tools necessary to configure and deploy your ClojureScript application to a production environment, including how to write tests for your application, how to configure more advanced compilation options, and how to build Docker containers for Clojure/ClojureScript applications. Ultimately, the specific test and deployment needs of your application are going to be particular to your application and infrastructure, but the lessons learned in this chapter should prove helpful as a general guide that isn't too dependent on the idiosyncratic requirements you ultimately face.

The end of this chapter also brings us to the conclusion of our journey together in learning ClojureScript. At this point, you have all the tools necessary to write advanced ClojureScript applications as well as an understanding of how to take those applications and prepare them for real-world conditions. We hope you've enjoyed reading this book, and we look forward to see your ClojureScript code live on the World Wide Web!

Index

www.ingramcontent.com/pod-product-compliance
Lightning Source LLC
Chambersburg PA
CBHW080928060326
40690CB00042B/3219